I0004571

Computers for Klutzes®

. .

Basics, Email, & Internet

A familiarization course for older adults

Charles Clark Richmond

Edition 1

Monadnock Mountainside Publications

Bloomington, IN  Milton Keynes, UK

authorHOUSE®

AuthorHouse™
1663 Liberty Drive, Suite 200
Bloomington, IN 47403
www.authorhouse.com
Phone: 1-800-839-8640

AuthorHouse™ UK Ltd.
500 Avebury Boulevard
Central Milton Keynes, MK9 2BE
www.authorhouse.co.uk
Phone: 08001974150

Published by Monadnock Mountainside Publications
8 Colonial Square
Peterborough, NH, U. S. A. 03458

First published by AuthorHouse 8/4/2006

ISBN: 1-4208-2713-8 (sc)

Library of Congress Control Number: 2005901457

Printed in the United States of America
Bloomington, Indiana

This book is printed on acid-free paper.

Publisher's Cataloging-in-Publication Data:

1. Computers for beginners
2. 1st Computer book
3. Computer Education for Seniors
4. Computer Instruction for older adults
5. Technical Education for Older Adults
6. Technical Training for Older Adults

I dedicate this book to all those,
who like me, have been thrust aside and
adjudged by others to be ***untrainable***.

This label has hurt many. We have been
caught in corporate "downsizing,"
judged to be untrainable and denied
the chance to learn new techniques, or
when we reach certain age levels
we are **known** to be unable to learn!

BUT...
We can and do learn
if we are given the information
in an understandable way!
That is what I try to do in this book ... make it easy to understand!

Charles Clark Richmond, Ed. D.

About the Author

Doctor of Education, University of Massachusetts, Amherst. Instructional Technology.

Co-author of "The Technical Writer's Guide" (1958). The Coca-Cola Company, Atlanta Georgia. A book explaining how to present information on the repair and maintenance of automatic vending equipment.

Author of "Multiple Choice Programming Technique" (1983). An object-oriented, relational database system for microcomputers.

Author of magazine articles dealing with microcomputer capabilities.

contents

Welcome Klutzes!

This book is written for those of us who were not brought up on computers and for those of us who never took computers in school. We speak a language different from the language of the television ads today. We came before "keyboarding", "uploading", "online trading", and the like.

We Klutzes are some of the smartest people in the world but we have problems with these "people friendly" machines and the special language that is used to explain them. We have trouble being classed as a "**user**" because that used to be a person who benefited by taking advantage of someone else's desire to be fair. The only mail we knew was that which was delivered by the postman or we picked up at the Post Office. The only monitor we knew was the kid in class that the teacher appointed to write down the names of those who misbehaved while she/he was out of the room. "Hardware" was a thing we went to the store to buy when we were fixing something at home. You might guess that "software" was something made of cloth or some other soft material, BUT IT ISN'T. These familiar terms have all been redefined by our young people to stand for something much different from the meanings that we are so familiar with.

This book will lead you through this maze of jargon and people "friendly devices." I will help you make these computers do your bidding. The tasks will be quite foreign to everything you have done in the past. But, I will do my best to help you by using familiar terms to define the altered meanings of today. To make it easier to understand, I will try to repeat familiar words and relate them to the today's altered words. The Glossary (Appendix C) lists many present-day uses of words and redefines them in Klutz terms. I also tell you how to find special dictionaries so you can look up things you see and hear at home that are not explained in this book. It takes awhile ... to absorb so many things. You won't learn all these new terms right away but don't be discouraged. Give yourself a chance to let your memory absorb them.

I have learned from my research that older people like us have trouble doing things that require manipulation of mechanical devices. The computer "mouse" is just one such contraption that is deemed to be "people friendly." However, it is quite unfriendly to many of us who have problems getting keys into locks or anything else that demands "eye/hand" coordination. For that reason, I give directions that you can use to run the computer by using only keyboard commands. Appendix A is a summary of keystroke (shortcut) commands that are repeated throughout the course. Just so your grandchildren won't get too upset, I also tell how these same commands are given using the mouse. I want you to try to use **only** the keyboard commands during the first two lessons unless the keyboard gives you more problems than the mouse. You will be able to make the computer work right from the start. **Try to use the**

keyboard for giving commands, you will find it quite easy ... and very accurate.

Each of the lessons in this book should take you a couple of hours to finish. Do the best you can and you will find the work rewarding. This course gives you an idea about how to use your personal computer. It is divided into three distinct sections … word processing, email, and using the Internet (check the Glossary in the Appendix if you don't understand the meaning of any of these words). It is best to do the lessons in the order in which they appear. However, you skip about and do the lesson groups in a different order.

The two lessons in word processing teach you how to begin using a computer much like you have used a typewriter in the past. They demonstrate how easy it is to get the computer to do simple tasks like letter writing. Since people make mistakes, I teach you how to correct some of the normal errors that you will probably make.

The two lessons on use of email tell you how to get a free email account, learn how to keep from making email addressing mistakes (using the address book), how to send emails to groups of people, and how to do many other things with a good email program.

The last two lessons deal with use of the Internet to get information about something that interests you. It might be that you want to check to see if the medicines that you take will not have bad interactions with one another. You may not be able to go to Paris, France to see the Louvre Museum but you may be interested in seeing pictures of some of its exhibits (such as the Mona Lisa). So many things can be done on the Internet. You will learn how to do them.

Many keyboard commands (shortcuts) are listed in Appendix A along with equivalent mouse commands to make running the computer easier. Frequently used Command sequences that you use throughout this book are repeated in Appendix B. This single reference area for such information ends the need to thumb through the text each time you forget how to give a particular set of commands.

The Glossary (Appendix C) defines computerese in Klutz terms. The Index section at the end of this book can help you find out how you learned to perform many computer tasks. Use it to refresh your memory.

Once you finish these six "quick start" lessons you may need to go back over all of them once again. The simple tasks presented in this book are so basic that remembering them will be easy. However, don't be discouraged if you discover that you need to go back to a particular lesson to refresh your mind on its details. **Check the Index to see if you fix a problem faster.**

Getting Started

Lesson 1

The Computer Revolution.

Christopher Evans in his book *The Micro Millennium* which was first published in 1980 begins with:

> THIS BOOK is about the future. Not some distant future which we and our descendants can blissfully ignore, but one which is imminent and whose progress can be plotted with some degree of precision. It is a future which will involve a transformation of world society at all kinds of levels, and while taking place slowly at first, will gather pace with sudden force. It's a future which is largely moulded by a single, startling development in technology whose impact is just beginning to be felt. The piece of technology I'm talking about is, of course, the computer.

Basic Computer Skills is designed to bring a little understanding to those who have missed the opportunity to learn how to use this intimidating machine. Much of the fear of this truly stupid device comes as a result of the highly specialized language that has sprung up around it. We start by defining some of the more basic terms and adding a few new ones with each lesson.

An explanation of all of the terms that follow plus many more can be found in Appendix C ... the Glossary.

All computers are divided into two parts.

Hardware ... the electronic machine which performs assigned tasks. This is the part which has a chord that plugs into an electric outlet, can be turned on and off, and physically delivers the expected results.

Software ... the instructions which control the machine's performance. It is the group of instructions which tell the device how to complete a required task. These assignments must be broken down into many simple tasks. The electronic computer seems to do its work, sometimes quite complicated work, in a fleck of time. Perhaps it is this performance of only an assigned task that confuses people about its abilities.

<u>Some hardware items</u>.

Keyboard ... a device which is used to put material into the computer one character at a time. Computer keyboards are similar to those used by mechanical or electric typewriters even to the extent that the letter arrangements were designed to slow fast typists down to keep them from jamming the original mechanical devices.

Monitor or Video ... a device which is used to display characters and/or pictures in black and white or in color. These are so-called *digital* devices are the forerunners of the newest television technology.

Hard disk ... a device which is usually permanently mounted inside a computer that is capable of recording, storing, and retrieving words, pictures, or sound. These devices have large capacities. Several billion characters of written material can be stored on a single hard disk. There are miniature storage units available now which can be easily inserted and removed improving data security and portability.

Flexible, diskette, or floppy disk ... a portable device which is small enough to be transported and stored easily. It is used in much the same way as the hard disk for storing computer material ... either character or picture forms. Today's *floppy* disks are most often about 3-1/2" square with a metal slide on one side which protects the flexible magnetic medium inside.

CD ROM ... this storage medium was originally designed to produce music. The name *CD ROM* is an acronym made by taking the first letter of each of the several words which make up its definition ... Compact Disk Read Only Memory (read only memory in this case is the recorded digital marks which cannot be erased or rewritten). It worked so well because discrete digital marks were used to generate sound that the computer industry investigate the technique and found that computer characters and pictures could be placed on them.

Some general software.

Program ... a group of instructions which the computer can understand and which when followed will perform tasks.

DOS ... an acronym -- Disk Operating System ... in rather cryptic terms it means what it says. It is the program that permits the computer to send and record material on a disk or read the recorded material from the disk and bring it into the computer's memory. It works with hard disks, floppy disks, or CD ROMs. The CD ROM must be recorded in a way that DOS can understand.

Windows 95, 98, NT, 2000, XT. ... these are the names of programs (the numbers or letters that follow the name "Windows" merely indicate "version number") which controls how and when other programs can run. These programs make it possible for the computer to be running several programs at the same time. *Windows* is the name given by its manufacturer, Microsoft, it permits opening "*windows*" to view what is happening in one or more programs that may be running at the moment.

This book will help those who have a Windows XP, 2000, ME, 98, or 95 version of the operating system. A large majority of the information in this book will be useful even though you have older versions such as 95, 98, or ME.

Word Processing ... the name given to programs that accept instructions from input devices (keyboards or microphones) and record them or display them as characters, numbers or drawings. These can then be formed into letters, brochures, posters or other items. Word processors are the easiest of programs to use. They produce results similar to that which one can get from a typewriter. Names for such programs are: Microsoft WordPad, Microsoft Works, Microsoft Word, Word Perfect, and Claris Works. While it is possible to exchange material among the several different word processing programs, the operator must give special instructions (commands) to the computer so it will know what to do.

Spreadsheet ... the name given to programs which create displays that are similar to an accountant's *spreadsheet* which is used for "what if" and other types of financial analysis.

Data base ... very similar to the spreadsheet except that only a single record (line of a spread sheet) is usually kept in memory at one time. Data bases usually contain too many records to permit it.

Some computer commands that we will be using throughout this course.

SaveAs... name the document (when you tell the program to start a New Document the computer gives that document a general name like **WordPad - DOCUMENT**. To make sure that you won't store anything else in the same place on your disk, you need to give the new document a special name. This "command" (a direction that you give the computer to have it do the things you want it to do) also lets you tell the computer where to put it and any other special thing you wish done to it.

Save ... send material to a permanent storage device ... floppy disk, hard disk, or optical disk. You must already have told it how and where to do the saving with a **SaveAs...** command (Windows 98, ME, & XP automatically force you to perform a **SaveAs...** if you forgot to do it).

Open ... find and make available material from a permanent storage device ... floppy disk, hard disk, optical disk, or CD-ROM.

Close ... stop using a document or file ... get it off of the screen.

Special computer terms which we will use quite frequently.

Memory ... an area inside the computer hardware that can hold material which the computer can use as long as a program that uses it is running and the computer is turned on.

File ... a group of related records (material about one particular topic such as a mailing list).

Record ... a collection of related material about a single topic used mostly to refer to items in a **Data Base**.

First we must learn where the keys are on the keyboard.

Today's most popular keyboard design came from Digital Equipment Company of Maynard, Massachusetts. You may have heard of the VT 101 keyboard but most likely not. This design has changed little over the last almost 30 years. It features a row of "function keys" across the top, a "numeric pad" on the right hand side and an assortment of special purpose keys between the pad and the keyboard arrangement that resembles that of a typewriter. Many of the keys you will be asked to use in the lessons that follow are identified by "callout" boxes that surround the picture on the next page.

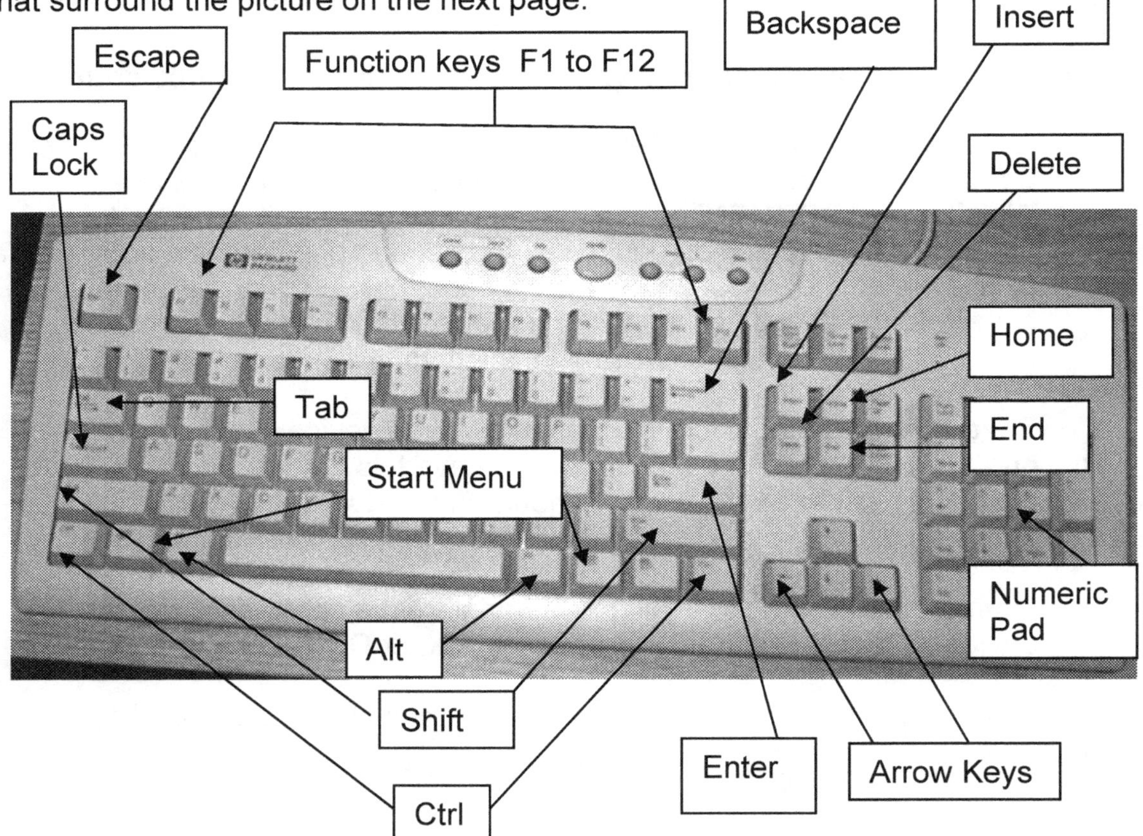

Now a few conventions

We will abbreviate the name for each key and separate these names with a slash (/) or tell you what to point at and press (click) the left hand button on the mouse.

Using keyboard commands, for example:

So the computer program can understand that you are giving a command and not just entering information, you must hold down one or two keys and press an additional key or position the mouse pointer and press the mouse button. We will give the name for each key the same way it is given on your keyboard and separate these names with a slash (/) or tell you what to point at and press (click) the left hand button on the mouse.

Most keys on your keyboard are all set to repeat if you hold them down for a short time. To keep them from doing this and causing you a problem be sure to push them down and let them up them quickly. Three keys will not repeat or do any damage to your work. You can hold them down for long periods of time. These three keys are: **Shift, Alt, Ctrl**.

Just to remind you that you can hold a particular key down, I will give you the name of that key and follow it with a slash. For instance, **Alt/** means to *hold down the* **Alt** key. A letter such as **F** without a slash following it means to *momentarily press or "tap"* that key because it will repeat. For instance, **Alt/F** tells you to hold the **Alt** key down and "tap" or momentarily press the **F** key.

Ctrl/Shift/F means to *hold down both* the **Ctrl** key and the **Shift** key while *momentarily pressing* or "tapping" the letter **F**. e.g. **Ctrl/Shift/F**.

Key commands are given by holding down the first one, two, or three keys and momentarily pressing the last key. Do not hold all of the keys down for any period of time because the computer is set to automatically repeat all but certain special keys such as **Ctrl, Alt,** and **Shift** keys.

Using the mouse to issue commands:

Click on **File** means to *put the* mouse pointer on the word **File** then press the left mouse button while still on the word **File**.

Starting the computer for the first time.

For those of you who have never done this it can be a scary situation. What do you do so you don't mess it up? What makes this thing turn on, where is the switch, or what happens after I turn it on? Well … not much. The machine turns on, you hear a fan start running, and you see something start to come up on your monitor's screen (if you have also turned the monitor on or if the monitor is set to turn on when the computer does.

So we can get started, we will assume that your computer has something like Windows 95, 98, NT, 2000 or XP in it as an operating system. Remember what we just said a page or two ago, a computer cannot work unless it has an operating system of some type installed. But.... the operating system only sets the thing up so it can use what we called "application programs". Application programs are what helps you (the operator) make the computer perform work for you. The operating system connects the application program to all the parts of the computer that it needs to do the different tasks that you want it to do.

Turn it on ...

You will have to look around for the main switch. In the newer machines there is a button on the front that you press in to make it start. If your monitor is not set so it will turn on at the same time as the computer, you will have to turn that on as well. The monitor's switch is usually in the front. However, some of the older computers and older monitors had their switches on the side or in the back. So, it you can't find a switch on the front of either your computer or your monitor, you will have to look either on the side or the back to locate it.

It will take a little while for the computer and monitor to start. The monitor usually is ready before the computer finishes its starting routine. Probably the hardest this to understand is that once you have turned on the switch, the computer spends a lot of time just getting ready to accept your next instruction. So ..... you just have to learn to wait.

Manufacturer Logo

Windows XT Logo

Desktop ready to use

If you look on the monitor screen, once the "desktop" ... the screen has a lot of little pictures scattered all over it with a name under each picture (many computer geeks like to call these pictures "icons" while others call them "gui's" ... Graphical Unit Interfaces). You will know that everything is ready to go when the mouse pointer (which is usually an arrow but seems to have an hour glass with it while the computer is not ready to accept a command) loses the little hour glass that is right next to it. The mouse pointer changes to an hour glass when the computer is busy finishing a task and is not ready for new commands. *You just have to wait until the system is ready to go to work for you.*

Bring in your processing program … WordPad.

	Keyboard	Mouse
1.	Press the **Start Menu** button or **Ctrl/Esc**	Point to **Start button** and press the **left Mouse** button (**Click**).
2.	Press **P** one or more times to **Programs** to **highlight** it (**surround with dark blue**) and press **Right Arrow** if the menu doesn't expand.	Point to **Programs** to **highlight** it (**surround with dark blue**) … the **Mouse pointer** usually causes the Start menu. to expand if it doesn't, click the **left Mouse** button.
3.	Press **A** one or more times until you highlight Accessories, then press the **Right Arrow** if the **Accessories** menu doesn't expand.	Point to **Accessories** … **Accessories** usually expands if it doesn't, click the **left Mouse** button.
4.	Press **W** one or more times to highlight **WordPad** and press **Enter** if it doesn't start right away.	Point to and click the (**press left**) **Mouse** button.

Start Menu Styles

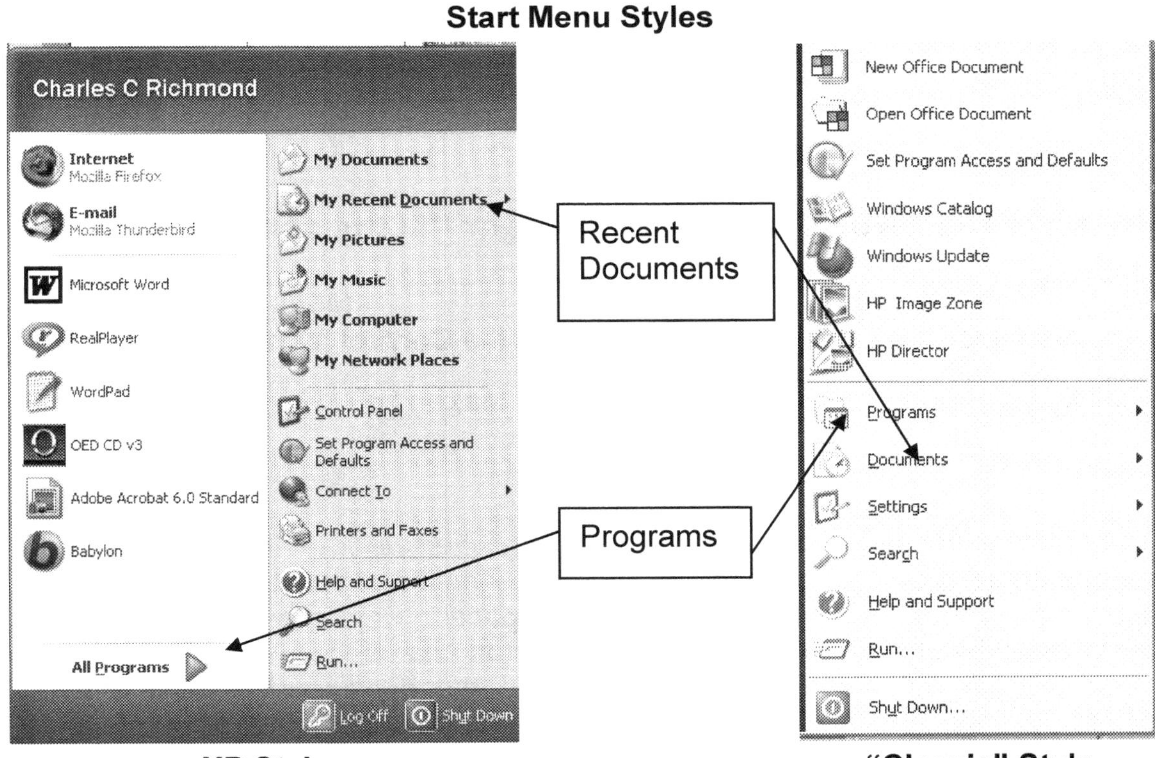

XP Style **"Classic" Style**

When WordPad first comes in, it sometimes does not cover the entire screen.

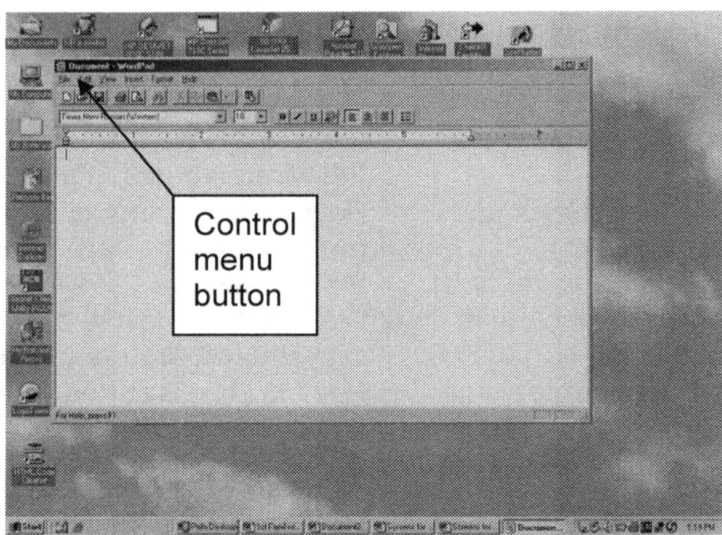

Here is what your **Microsoft® WordPad** "window" looks like. You will notice that it starts out as one of two "windows" on your **monitor**. Before we start to work with this word processor we should have the computer make the **WordPad** "window" larger so it is easier to see what we are doing. It will work just as well if we leave it at this small size but I find it easier when the letters and pictures are larger.

To make the "WordPad window" larger (fill the screen) …

Keyboard		Mouse
1.	**Alt/Space**	Click the **Control Menu button**
2.	**X**	Click **Maximize**

The first time we see what we are to work with when we want to write a letter, memo, or just a note. Confusion is not the description of our feelings. Its more like panic. There seems to be such a small space to write in and this space is surrounded by all manner of rulers, sunny rectangular pieces, even more peculiar areas with a series of pictures on them that don't seem to make any sense. We will try to explain a few of them here and will continue to point out more of them as we go to use them.

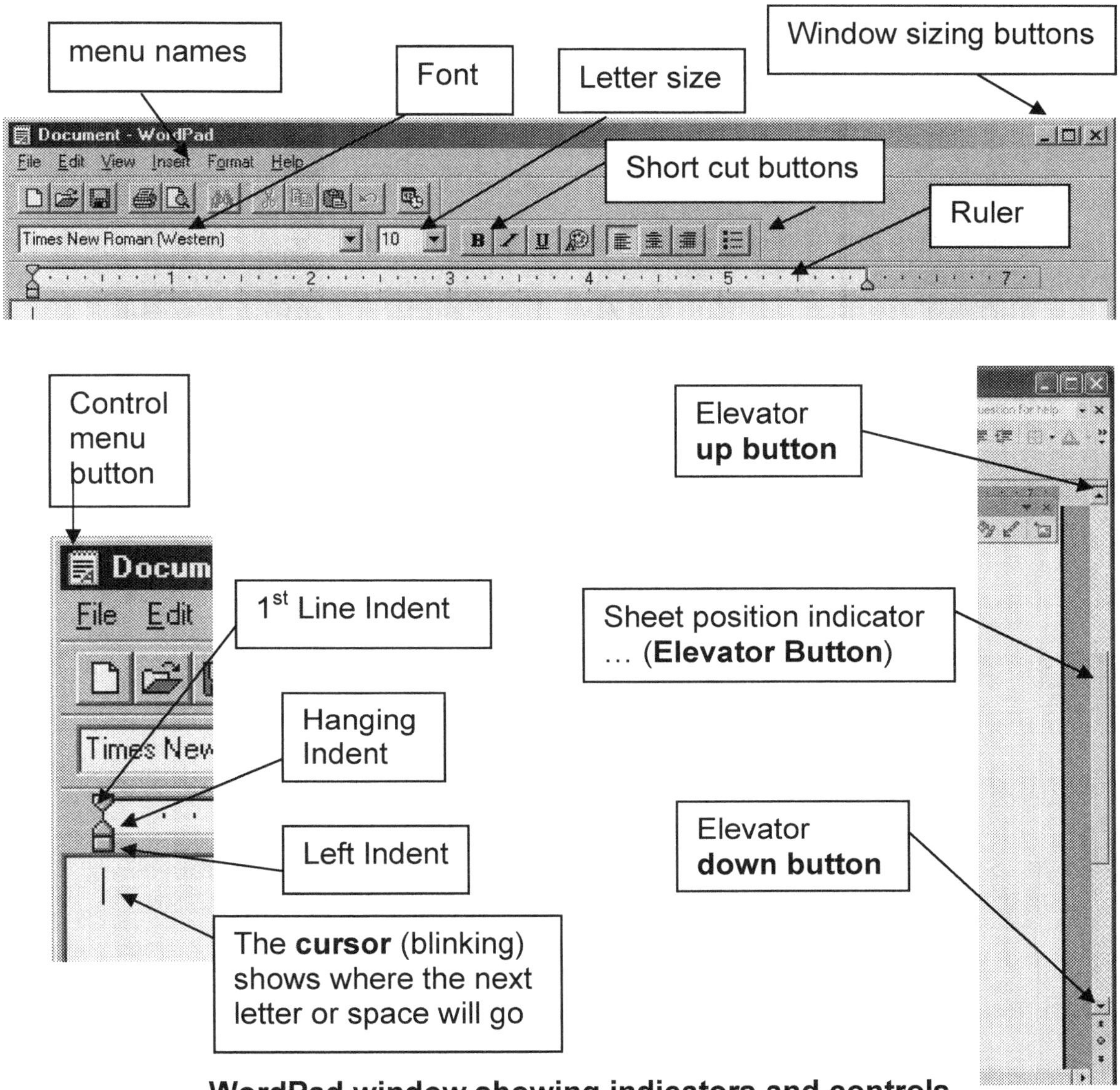

menu names

Font

Letter size

Window sizing buttons

Short cut buttons

Ruler

Control menu button

1st Line Indent

Hanging Indent

Left Indent

The **cursor** (blinking) shows where the next letter or space will go

Elevator **up button**

Sheet position indicator … (**Elevator Button**)

Elevator **down button**

WordPad window showing indicators and controls

Since **Microsoft® WordPad** is a word-processing program, when you start typing, the letter keys you press on the keyboard will appear on the screen. The blinking vertical line (**cursor**) is there to show you where the next keyboard entry will appear.

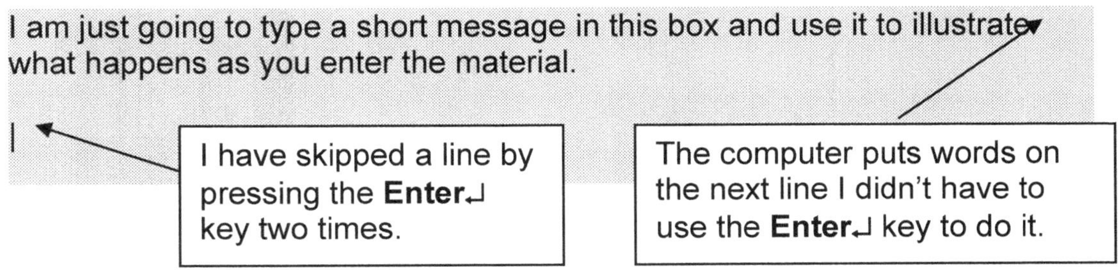

You will need to move around inside a document.

- You may want to get your **cursor** to a particular place to start putting in or taking out something.
- You need to know how to go from one end of a document to another as quickly as possible.
- You will want to move around inside paragraphs or sentences … moving the **cursor** one character or one line at a time can be annoying.
- You will want to change many words at one time … take them out or replace them, etc.

Move the cursor around inside a document

Task	Keyboard	Mouse
Move one character at a time	Press the **Right** or **Left Arrow key**	Move the **Mouse pointer** to the place you want the **cursor** to be and press the **Left Mouse button**
Move one word at a time	Hold the **Ctrl** key down while pressing the **Right** or **Left Arrow key**	Same as above
Move one line at a time	Press **Up** or **Down Arrow key**	Same as above
Move to the end of a line	Press the **End** key	Same as above
Move to the beginning of a line	Press the **Home** key	Same as above
Move to the beginning of a document	Hold the **Ctrl** key down while pressing the **Home** key	Same as above except when your **Mouse pointer** is far from the place you want to reach, then it will take some time to move up or down through a document
Move to the end of a document	Hold the **Ctrl** key down while pressing the **End** key	Same as moving to the end of a document … above

What is the difference between the Backspace key and the Delete key???

If you press the **Backspace** key, you erase the "**a**".

If you press the **Delete** key, you erase the "**k**".

The **cursor** is here between the **a** and the **k**

You need to ma|ke a correction

I don't always do a perfect job of typing but I don't have to worry about it because correcting mistakes is something the computer can fix quite easily. Here's how it works.

Move the **cursor** to the mistake … use the arrow keys or put the mouse pointer on the letter that's wrong and click it … if you don't get it quite right, use the arrow keys to move it the rest of the way. Just **Backspace** if the **cursor** is to the right of the mistake or **Delete** if it's to the left of the mistake. Then type in the correct letter. The program is set to **insert** all new letters.

I don't always do a puirfect job of typing but I don't have to worry because correcting mistakes is something the computer can fix quite easitly.

Put your mouse pointer on the incorrect word, **right click** it, then click the correct word. Sometimes the computer can't figure out what it should be so you must do it yourself by moving the **cursor**, erasing, and retyping.

Once you have finished your message you can save it for later use, erase it and throw it away, or you can print it and then save it or throw it away. If you try to "**Save**" a document whose name is a general one like "**Document - WordPad**", the program won't let you use that name because it is going to use it again at some other time. At that time the computer would put the next document right over the older one so you would lose the old document that you didn't give a name to. The program will put it in a place of its choosing unless you tell the computer where to put it. However, Word documents are usually placed in a file called "My Documents," but not always. It is a good idea to tell the computer where to put it as well as give it a name.

Name a document and save it for later viewing

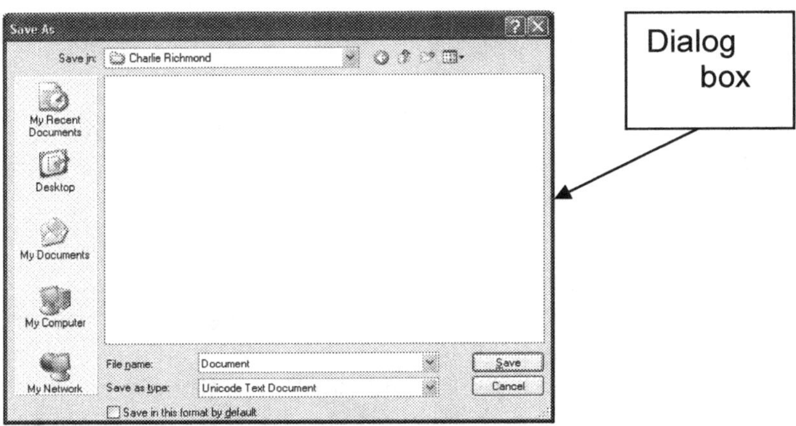

SaveAs... dialog box

The **WordPad** program puts a **dialog box** on the screen (a box that contains questions you should answer before you "**save**" the document). If you let the computer pick where to save it, you may have trouble finding it later. The computer uses a file called **My Documents** so if you don't put many documents there, they won't be too hard to find. You will learn later in this lesson how to tell the computer *exactly* where to put your work.

Save a document for the first time (SaveAs...)

	Keyboard	Mouse
1.	**Ctrl/S**	Click the **Save** button
2.	Type in the name you want for the document	Type in the name you want for the document
3.	**Enter↵**	Click **Save**

All you have to do is type in the name you want to remember the document by and press **Enter**. When you want to get it back, be sure **My Documents** shows in the **Look in** box then type the document name into the **File name** box and press **Enter**.

If you have given the document a name but you have made some changes in it, you want to save it again … The program will remind you about saving it before you erase it and ask you if you want to save the changes.

Saving a document.

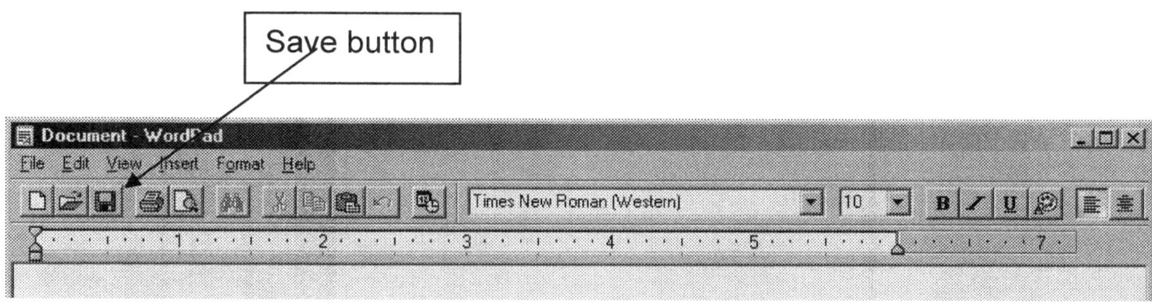

	Keyboard	Mouse
1.	**Ctrl/S**	Click the **Save button**

Once you have put an old document away and you want to start another one …

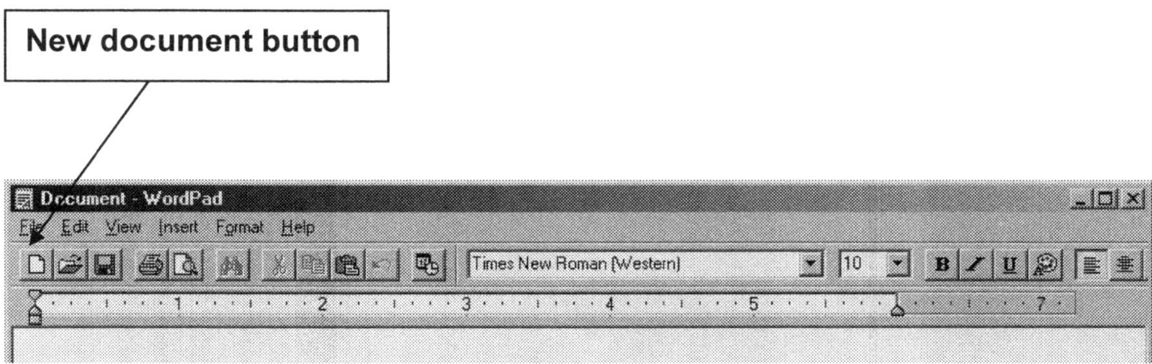

Starting a new document.

Keyboard		Mouse
1.	**Ctrl/N**	Click **New document** button
2.	**Enter↵**	Click **OK**

You can bring back one of your older documents …

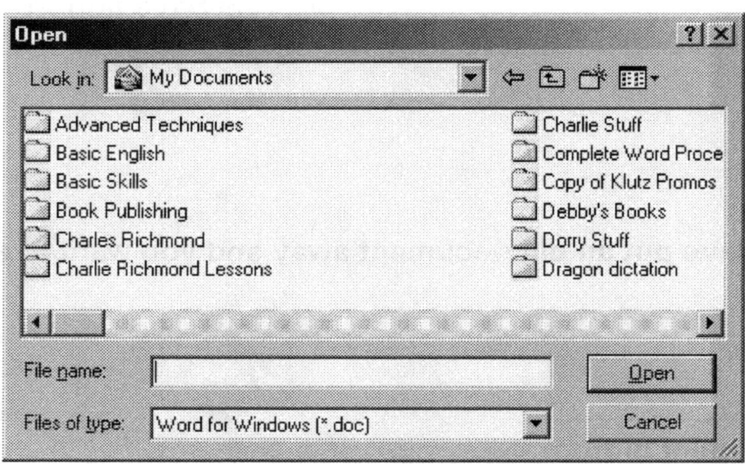

"Open" dialog box

Open an old document.

	Keyboard	Mouse
1.	**Ctrl/O**	Click **Open** button
2.	**Shift/Tab**	Click on the **document's name** twice
3.	**Arrow keys** down to the **document's name**	
4.	**Enter↵**	

I just brought back an old document that I want to add something to …

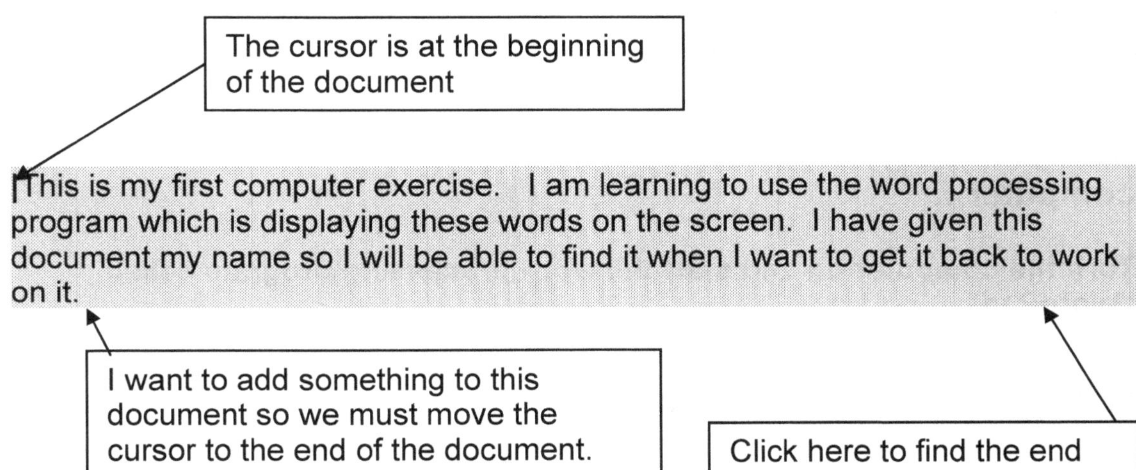
The cursor is at the beginning of the document
This is my first computer exercise. I am learning to use the word processing program which is displaying these words on the screen. I have given this document my name so I will be able to find it when I want to get it back to work on it.
I want to add something to this document so we must move the cursor to the end of the document.
Click here to find the end

	Keyboard	Mouse
1.	**Ctrl/End** … check page 4 to find the **End** key if you have forgotten where the **End Key** is.	Click somewhere below the end of the last line that you see on the screen
2.	If you want to add to the paragraph, just type in the new words. If you want to put the new words into another paragraph, press **Enter↵** twice then begin typing.	If you want to add to the paragraph, just type in the new words. If you want to put the new words into another paragraph, press **Enter↵** twice then begin typing.

Making your words or letters stand out. There are three ways that a word or letter may be made to stand out from those around it. Give the command before you type and give the "turn off" command when you have finished typing.

1. Make it darker (bolder) than the other words.
2. Italicize it so it looks different from the other words.
3. Underline it so it will stand out better.

	Keyboard	Mouse
1.	**Ctrl/B** … make **bold**	Click "**B**" button … make **bold**
	Ctrl/B … turn off **bold**	Click "**B**" button … turn off **bold**
2.	**Ctrl/I** … ***Italicize***	Click "I" button … ***Italicize***
	Ctrl/I … turn off ***Italicize***	Click "I" button … turn off ***Italicize***
3.	**Ctrl/U** … **Underline**	Click "**U**" button … **Underline**
	Ctrl/U … turn off **Underline**	Click "**U**" button … turn off **Underline**

Now you are going to start doing a few things with your computer …

Turn the computer on and start the word processing program called "WordPad".

	Keyboard	Mouse
1.	Turn the computer on … the Switch is usually in the front. When you push the button, a green light should turn on on both the computer and the keyboard.	Turn the computer on … the Switch is usually in the front. When you push the button, a green light should turn on on both the computer and the keyboard.

Microsoft Windows is what is called an **operating system.** It helps the **application programs** by performing tasks like moving material from the disk to memory and from memory back to the disk. That is why the original operating systems were called **DOS** (Disk Operating System). Most of its work consisted of taking things from the keyboard or disk and putting them into memory. Then taking them from memory and putting them back on the disk or on the monitor screen.

Get your word processing program … Microsoft WordPad. As soon as your word processing program comes in, the rest of the commands you give will be given to that program.

	Keyboard	Mouse
1.	Press the **Start Menu** button or **Ctrl/Esc**	Point to **Start button** and press the **left Mouse** button (**Click**).
2.	Press **P** one or more times to **Programs** to **highlight** it (**surround with dark blue**) and press **Right Arrow** if the menu doesn't expand.	Point to **Programs** to **highlight** it (**surround with dark blue**) … the **Mouse pointer** usually causes the Start menu. to expand if it doesn't, click the **left Mouse** button.
3.	Press **A** one or more times until you highlight **Accessories**, then press the **Right Arrow** if the **Accessories** menu doesn't expand.	Point to **Accessories** … **Accessories** usually expands if it doesn't, click the **left Mouse** button.
4.	Press **W** one or more times to highlight **WordPad** and press **Enter** if it doesn't start right away.	Point to and click the (**press left**) **Mouse** button.

Let's make a place to keep all your practise work.

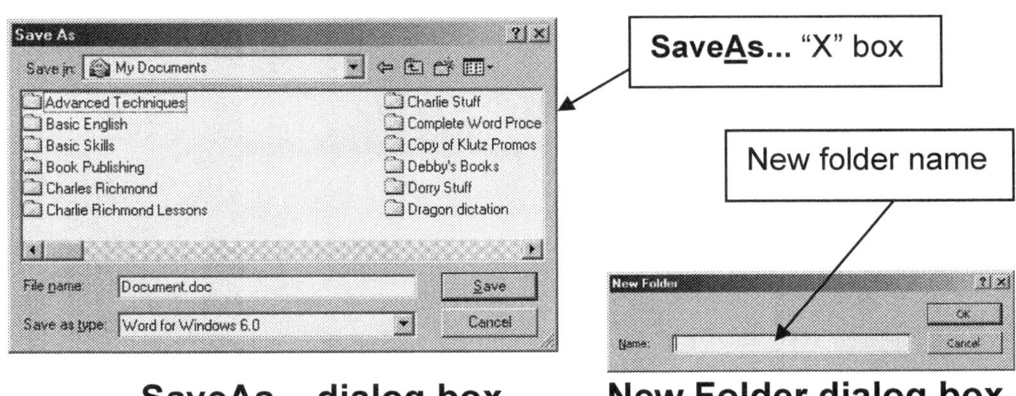

SaveAs... dialog box **New Folder dialog box**

Create a new folder for your work.

	Keyboard	Mouse
1.	**Ctrl/S**	Click on the **Save** button
2.	**Alt/I**	
3.	**Tab**	
4.	**Right Arrow** to **New Folder** button	Click the **New Folder** button
5.	**Space**	
6.	Type in your **first** and **last names** plus the word "**lessons**"	Type in your **first** and **last names** plus the word "**lessons**"
7.	**Enter** or **Alt/O**	Click **Open**
8.	**Esc**	Click the **SaveAs... "X"** box

Starting a new document using Microsoft WordPad.

When WordPad is first started, it shows a screen/window for a new document. The remainder of the time during these lessons you will have to tell the computer to start a new page.

General name ...
Document - WordPad

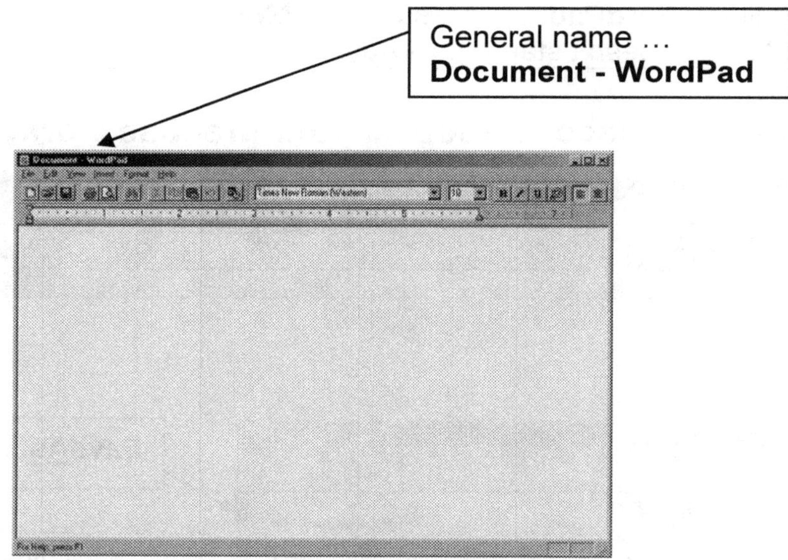

This is a New Document that is ready to take your material

Give the document a name and tell the computer where to put it ... SaveAs

The blue line at the top of your screen should shows " **Document –.WordPad**" You must give this document the name that you want it to be known by and you must tell the computer where you want to put it. To do this you use a procedure called "**SaveAs...**".

Keyboard		Mouse
1.	**Ctrl/S**	Click the **Save** button
2.	If **Save in...** box already shows your **full name** ... skip to step 7 .	If **Save in...** box already shows your **full name** ... skip to step 7.
3.	**Shift/Tab**	Click twice on the folder with your **full name** on it.
4.	**Arrow key** move blue "highlight" to the folder with your **full name** on it.	
5.	**Enter↵**	
6.	**Alt/N**	Click in the **File name** box
7.	Type in your **first name**	Type in your **first name**
8.	**Enter↵**	Click **Save**

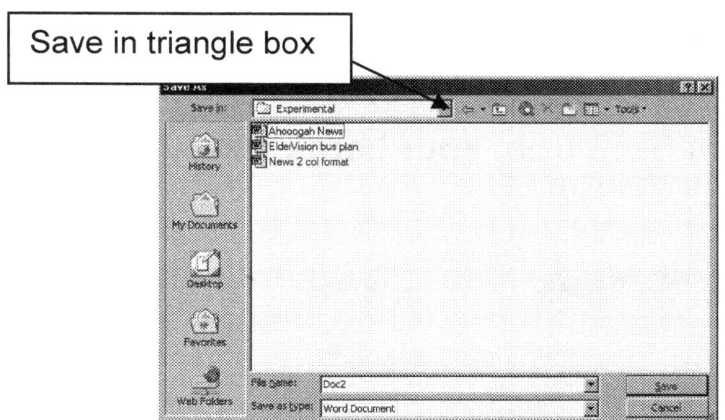

SaveAs... screen ready for entries

If you have done each step correctly, your first name will appear at the top of your screen near the words "WordPad". This is the name that "WordPad" will use to find your document.

Type in the words from the shaded area below ... learn how easy it is to have the computer type something for you!

Don't bother to try to make your screen look like the typing in the shaded area. Let the computer decide when to end a line. It does this quite easily. It is just one of the little things that a computer can do for you that makes your work simpler.

> This is my first computer exercise. I am learning to use the word processing program which is displaying these words on the screen. I have given this document my name so I will be able to find it when I want to get it back to work on it.

Save your document ... put it onto your hard disk.

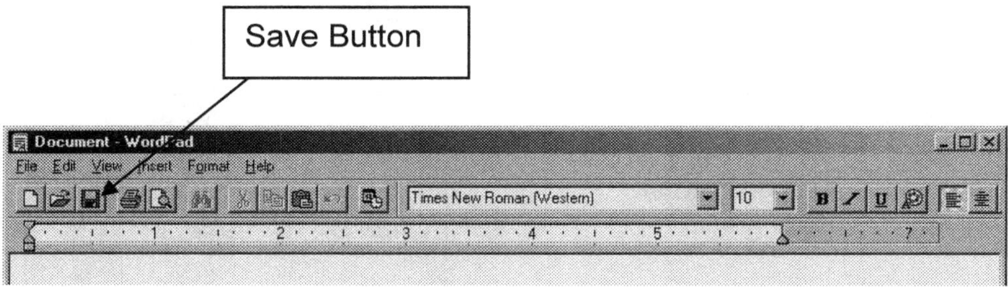

	Keyboard	Mouse
1.	**Ctrl/S**	Click the **Save** button

Bring a document back from your hard disk.

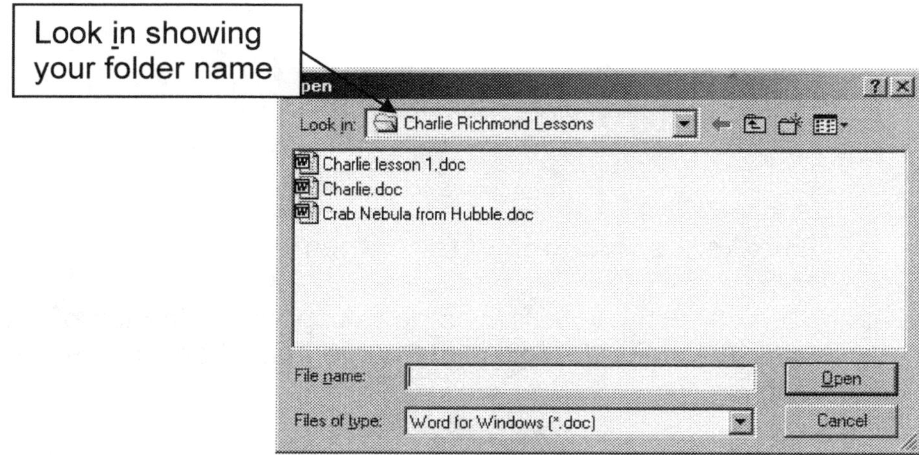

File Open Dialog Box

Open a File procedure … bring back a "saved" document

Keyboard		Mouse
1.	**Ctrl/O**	**Click the** Open button **(looks like a file folder**)
2.	If **Look in** already shows your **first** & **last names** skip to step 6.	If **Look in** already shows your **first** & **last names** skip to step 7.
3.	**Shift/Tab**	Click on the folder with **your name** on it
4.	**Arrow key** move blue "highlight" to the folder with **your name** on it	
5.	**Enter↵** and skip to step 7.	Click **OK**
6.	**Shift/Tab**	
7.	**Arrow key** to the document that shows your **first name**	Click on the document that shows your **first name**
8.	**Enter↵**	

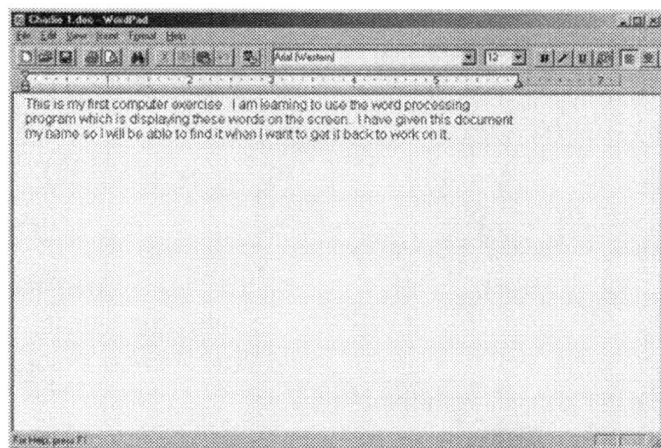

Your first exercise as you bring it back from the hard disk

Make some changes to your document.

Put your "|" blinking cursor at the end of the paragraph …

1. **Ctrl/End**
2. Press **Enter** twice to skip a line

This is my first computer exercise. I am learning to use the word processing program which is displaying these words on the screen. I have given this document my name so I will be able to find it when I want to get it back to work on it.

Type in this new line

This is a sentence that I have added to my original document.

Save your document again.

	Keyboard	Mouse
1.	**Ctrl/S**	Click the **Save** button

Start another document.

	Keyboard	Mouse
1.	**Ctrl/N**	Click the **New Document** button
2.	**Enter↵**	Click **OK**

Give the document a name … SaveAs

	Keyboard	Mouse
1.	**Ctrl/S**	Click the **Save** button
2.	If **Save in...** box already shows your **full name** ... skip to step 7 .	If **Save in...** box already shows your **full name** ... skip to step 7.
3.	**Shift/Tab**	Click twice on the folder with your **full name** on it.
4.	**Arrow key** move blue "highlight" to the folder with your **full name** on it.	
5.	**Enter↵**	
6.	**Alt/N**	Click in the **File name** box
7.	Type in your **last name**	Type in your **last name**
8.	**Enter↵**	Click **Save**

This time try copying the short paragraphs below.

I am really having the computer write something that makes a little sense. I haven't been able to do anything like this before but after just a few pages of this "Computers for Klutzes" book, I am actually making the computer do what I want it to do.

I have already learned many things that I can continue to use if I will only keep working with the computer and learning how it can be made to do things that I want it to do.

Once you have finished the note **Save** it, get it off of the screen and turn your computer off.

Save your document.

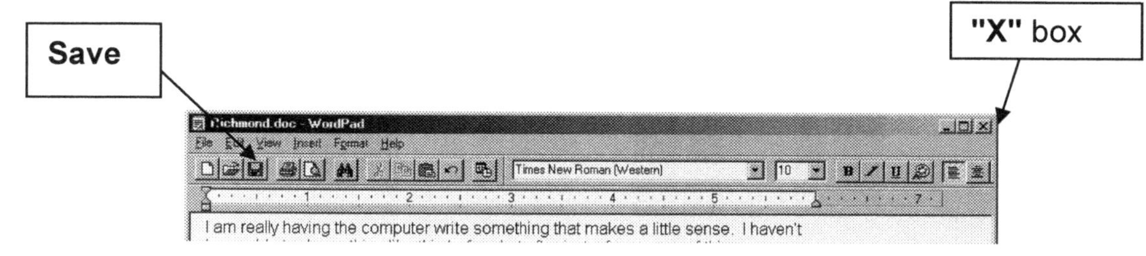

	Keyboard	Mouse
1.	**Ctrl/S**	Click the **Save** button

It's time to turn off the computer, the lesson is finished ...

Turn the program off.

	Keyboard	Mouse
1.	**Alt/F4**	Click the topmost right hand "**X**" box

Turn the computer off.

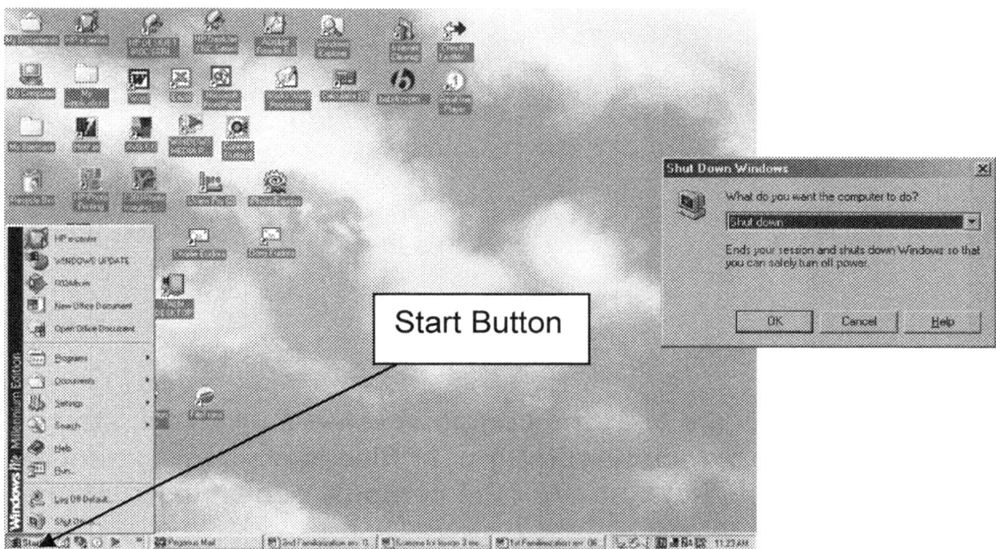

Turn the Computer off procedure

	Keyboard	Mouse
1.	**Start Menu** button or **Ctrl/Esc**	Click **Start** button
2.	**U**	Click the **Shut Down** command
3.	**Enter↵**	Click **OK**

Note: Appendix B repeats start the computer, start a program, start a new document, open (get) a document from your files, save a document as, save a document (put it in a file), and shut the computer down instructions.

Creating, Changing, Saving, and Resaving

Lesson 2

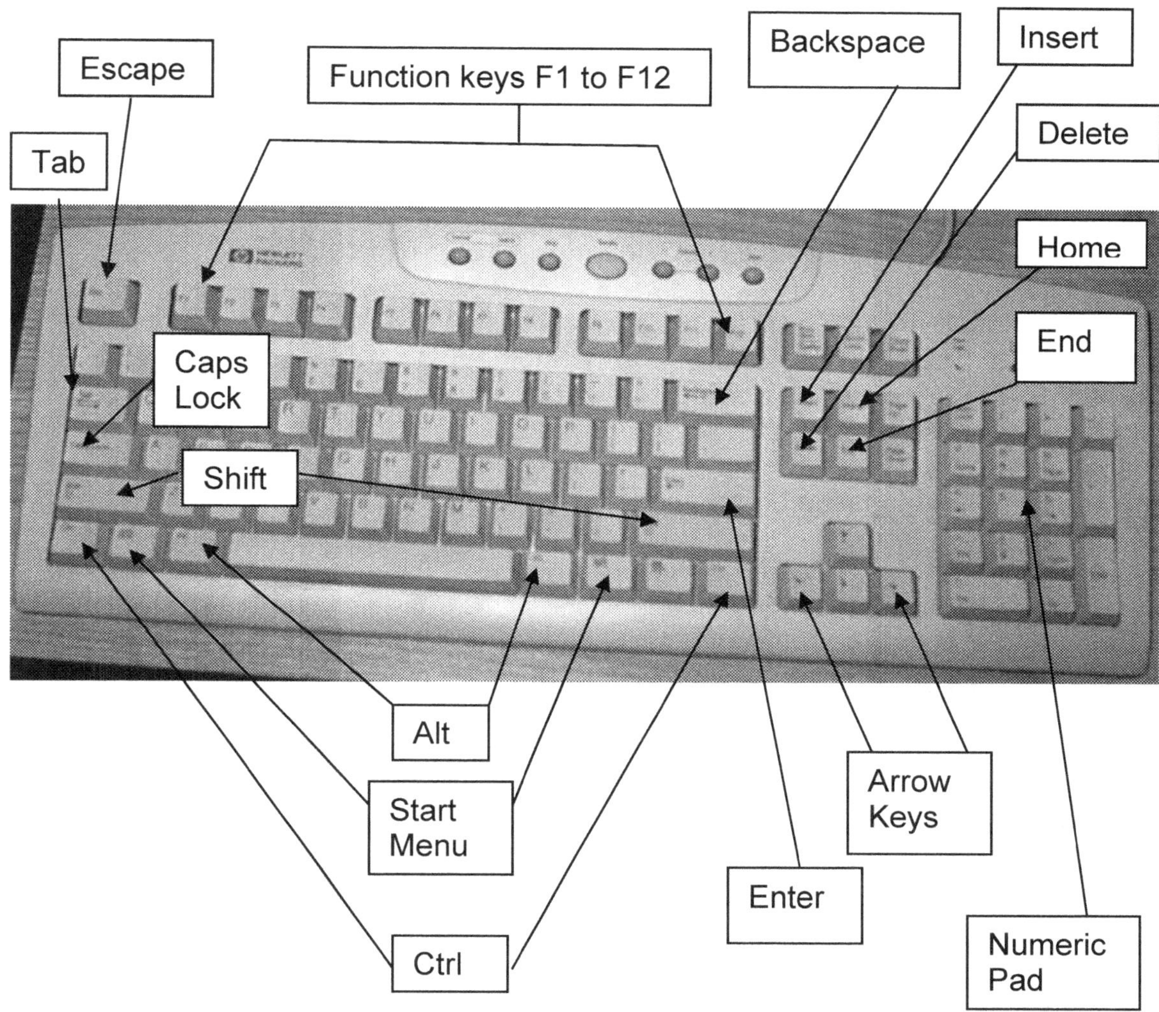

Let's review the conventions

So the computer program can understand that you are giving a command and not just entering information, you must hold down one or two keys and press an additional key or position the mouse pointer and press the mouse button. We will abbreviate the name for each key and separate these names with a slash (/) or tell you what to point at and press (click) the left hand button on the mouse.

Using keyboard commands, for example:

Most keys on your keyboard are all set to repeat if you hold them down for a short time. To keep them from doing this and causing you a problem be sure to push them down and let them up them quickly. Three keys will not repeat or do any damage to your work. You can hold them down for long periods of time. These three keys are: **Shift, Alt, Ctrl**.

Just to remind you that you can hold a particular key down, I will give you the name of that key and follow it with a slash. For instance, **Alt/** means to *hold down the* **Alt** key. A letter such as **F** without a slash following it means to *momentarily press or "tap"* that key because it will repeat. For instance, **Alt/F** tells you to hold the **Alt** key down and "tap" or momentarily press the **F** key.

Ctrl/Shift/F means to *hold down both* the **Ctrl** key and the **Shift** key while *momentarily pressing* or "tapping" the letter **F**. e.g. **Ctrl/Shift/F**.

Key commands are given by holding down the first one, two, or three keys and momentarily pressing the last key. Do not hold all of the keys down for any period of time because the computer is set to automatically repeat all but certain special keys such as **Ctrl, Alt,** and **Shift** keys.

Using the mouse to issue commands, for example:

Click on **File** means to *point the* **mouse pointer** at the word **File** then press the **left mouse button** while still pointing to the word **File**.

Turn the computer on and start your program

	Keyboard	Mouse
1.	Turn the computer on … the Switch is usually in the front. When you push the button a green light should turn on on the computer and the keyboard	Turn the computer on … the Switch is usually in the front. When you push the button a green light should turn on on the computer and the keyboard
2.	Press the **Start Menu** button or **Ctrl/Esc**	Click **Start**
3.	Press **P** one or more times to **Programs** to **highlight** it (**surround with dark blue**) and press **Right Arrow** if the menu doesn't expand.	Point to **Programs**
4.	Press **A** one or more times until you highlight Accessories, then press the **Right Arrow** if the **Accessories** menu doesn't expand.	Move the pointer to **Accessories**
5.	Press **W** until **WordPad** is highlighted (surrounded by dark blue)	Move the pointer to **WordPad**
6.	**Enter↵**	Click the **left mouse button**

If this picture (icon) is on your computer screen when you first turn it on, you can click twice on it or you can click anywhere on your screen and move the "**highlight**" with the arrow keys until this "**icon**" is highlighted and then press **Enter** to start **Microsoft® WordPad**.

Exercise 1

Start a new document

When you first start **WordPad**, the program automatically brings in a new document so you won't have to get one for this exercise. In Exercise 2, however, you will need to bring in a new, blank document to work on.

Give the document a name and say where it goes ... SaveAs

The blue (dark colored) band at the top of your screen should shows "**Document - WordPad**." You must give this document the name which you want it to be known by so you can find it later on when you want to look at it again or you want to change it. You must also tell the computer where you want it put so you will know where to look for it later. To do this you use a procedure called "**SaveAs...**".

In Lesson 1 you set up a folder to hold the documents that you would write during this course. If you did not do this, go to **page 18** and set the folder up now. Keeping your work in a folder is important because such a folder will be easy to find and that will make it easier for you to do your work.

Name your document procedure

	Keyboard	Mouse
1.	**Ctrl/S**	Click **Save** button
2.	If your **full name** is in the **Save in** box go to step 7.	If your **full name** is in the **Save in** box go to step 7.
3.	**Shift/Tab**	
4.	**Arrow key** move the blue **highlight** to the folder with **your full name** on it	Click the folder with **your full name** on it
5.	**Enter↵**	Click **OK**
6.	**Alt/N**	Click in the **File name** box
7.	Type in **Lesson 2 exercise 1**	Type in **Lesson 2 exercise 1**
8.	**Enter↵**	Click **Save**

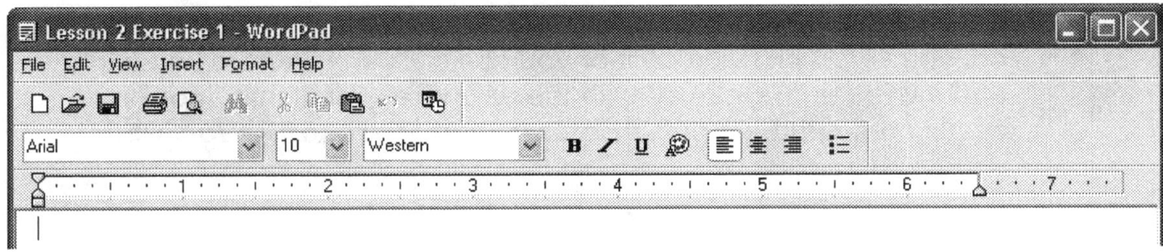

If you have performed each step correctly, **Lesson 2 exercise 1 – WordPad** will appear at the top of your screen. You may have to wait for a short time until the computer finishes writing information on your hard disk.

Type the material below ... **do not try to make your document look like what is given for you to copy**. Just let the computer decide when to go to the next line and what type face to use. **Use Backspace to erase mistakes you make.**

Now you are ready to type a new document. You don't have to worry about when to go to the next line. The computer figures this out for you. The "computerese" name for this action is "wraparound." When you used a typewriter, you had to decide when to go to the next line.

Save your finished document

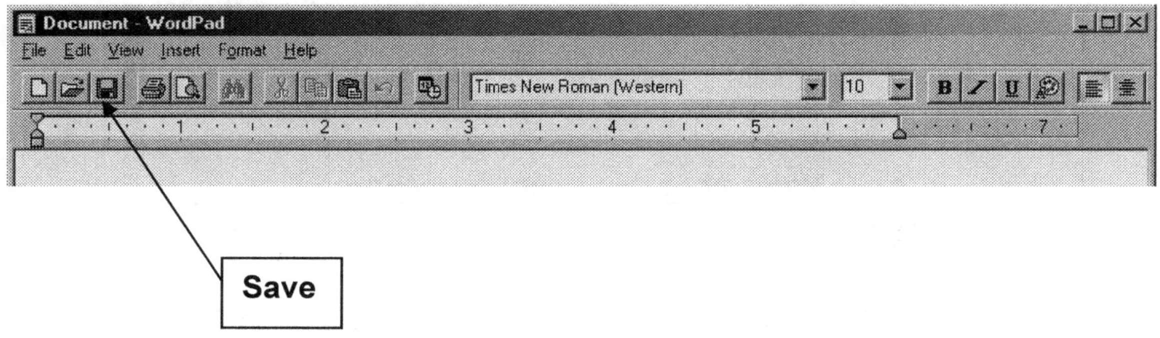

Save document procedure

	Keyboard	**Mouse**
1.	**Ctrl/S**	Click the **Save** button

Exercise 2

Create a New document.

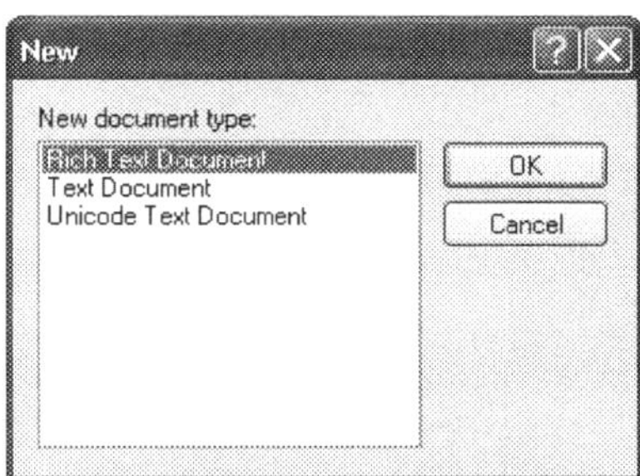

New document type dialog box

New Document procedure

	Keyboard	**Mouse**
1.	**Ctrl/N**	Click the **New Document** button
2.	**Enter↵**	Click **OK** button

Give the document a name … SaveAs

SaveAs procedure

	Keyboard	**Mouse**
1.	**Ctrl/S**	Click **Save** button
2.	If your **full name** is in the **Save in** box go to step 7.	If your **full name** is in the **Save in** box go to step 7.
3.	**Shift/Tab**	
4.	**Arrow key** move the blue **highlight** to the folder with **your full name** on it	Click the folder with **your full name** on it
5.	**Enter↵**	Click **OK**
6.	**Alt/N**	Click in the **File name** box
7.	Type in **Lesson 2 exercise 2**	Type in **Lesson 2 exercise 2**
8.	**Enter↵**	Click **Save**

If you have performed each step correctly, **Lesson 2 exercise 2** will appear at the top of your screen followed by "**WordPad**". You may have to wait for a short time until the computer finishes writing this information on your hard disk.

Now tell your computer that you want a particular type face and type size for this document.

Though many people just accept the type face and size that is set by "default" (because overlook the possibility that the document might look better if a different face and size are used for it.

Set the type face to `Courier New` and type size to 12 pt. …

It will make what you type look like it was done on a typewriter.

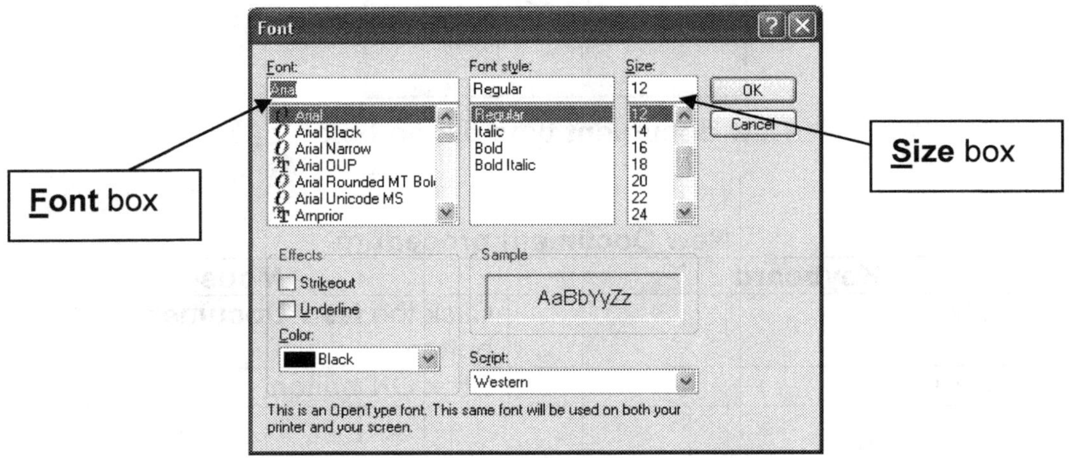

Font dialog box

Set the type face and size procedure

	Keyboard	Mouse
1.	**Alt/O** and then **F** to go to the **Font** box	Click the **down box** next to the box that shows a typeface
2.	Type in **`Courier New`** or **Down Arrow** to **`Courier New`**	Click **`Courier New`**
3.	**Alt/S**, type in **12** or **Down Arrow** to the **12**	Click the **down box** next to **Size**
3.	**Enter↵**	Click **12**

Ways to make something stand out … get your attention!

Make something Bold

Keyboard		Mouse
Before you start	**Ctrl/B**	Click **B** button
After you finish	**Ctrl/B**	Click **B** button

Underline something

Keyboard		Mouse
Before you start	**Ctrl/U**	Click **U** button
After you finish	**Ctrl/U**	Click **U** button

Italicize something

Keyboard		Mouse
Before you start	**Ctrl/I**	Click **I** button
After you finish	**Ctrl/I**	Click **I** button

You can always change what you have done … See Appendix B page 137.

Type the material below ...

Do not try to end the sentences where they are ended below. Just let the computer decide when to go to the next line. You will be asked to emphasize several words … follow the directions and see if they get your attention more.

The way you can make your computer put them into your documents is given above.

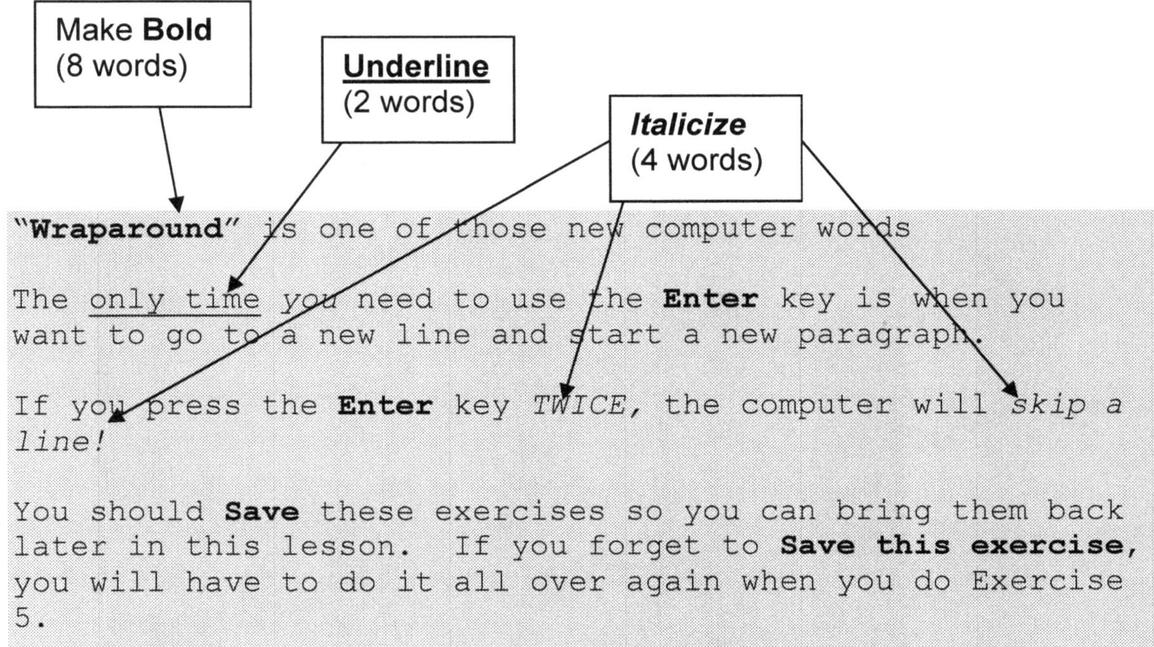

"**Wraparound**" is one of those new computer words

The only time you need to use the **Enter** key is when you want to go to a new line and start a new paragraph.

If you press the **Enter** key *TWICE*, the computer will *skip a line!*

You should **Save** these exercises so you can bring them back later in this lesson. If you forget to **Save this exercise**, you will have to do it all over again when you do Exercise 5.

It is <u>good practise</u> to do two things when you finish a document: (1) **Save** your work. (2) Close it so you won't make changes to it by mistake.

Underline (2 Words)

Save your document

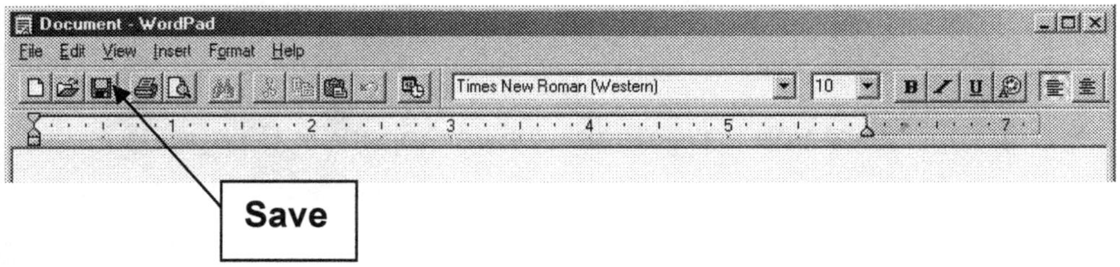

	Keyboard	Mouse
1.	**Ctrl/S**	Click the **Save** button

Exercise 3

Create a New... document.

	Keyboard	Mouse
1.	**Ctrl/N**	Click the **New Document** button
2.	**Enter**	Click **OK**

Give the document a name … SaveAs

	Keyboard	Mouse
1.	**Ctrl/S**	Click **Save** button
2.	If **Save in** already shows your **full name** go to step 7.	If your **full name** is in the **Save in** box go to step 7.
3.	**Shift/Tab**	
4.	**Arrow key** move the blue **highlight** to the folder with **your full name** on it	Click the folder with **your full name** on it
5.	**Enter↵**	Click **OK**
6.	**Alt/N**	Click in the **File name** box
7.	Type in **Lesson 2 exercise 3**	Type in **Lesson 2 exercise 3**
8.	**Enter↵**	Click **Save**

Set the typeface to Times New Roman …

it will make what you type look like a newspaper or magazine printing.

	Keyboard	Mouse
1.	**Alt/O** and then **F** to go to the **Font** box	Click the **down box** next to the box that shows a typeface
2.	Type in **Times New Roman**	Click **Times New Roman**
3.	**Alt/S** and **Arrow Key** to the **12**	Click the **down box** next to **Size**
3.	**Enter↵**	Click **12**

Paragraph indentation ...

When you write newsletters, reports or business letters, you will want to alter indentations to give the document a special appearance. In this exercise you will be asked to type things for the body of a business letter. You will prepare three different paragraph styles.

Microsoft defines a paragraph as beginning at the upper left of a word/line group and continuing until an **Enter↵** is found. By this definition a paragraph can be less than one full line.

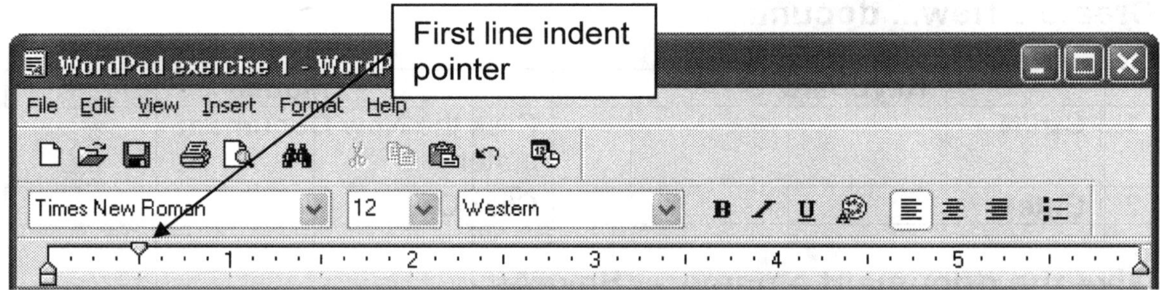

A paragraph whose first line is indented

Keyboard	Mouse
Tab	Put **Mouse pointer** on the first line Indent pointer, hold the **left Mouse button** down, move the indent pointer to the wanted location and let go of the **Mouse button**.

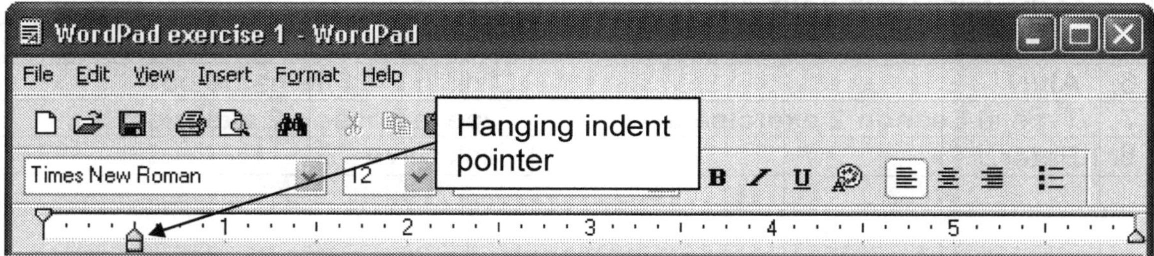

A paragraph whose first line is longer than following lines in the paragraph

Keyboard		Mouse
1.	**Alt/O** **P** **Alt/F** Type in **-0.5”** **Enter↵**	Put **Mouse pointer** on the hanging Indent pointer, hold the **left Mouse button** down, move the indent pointer to the wanted location and let go of the **Mouse button**.

Type the material on the next page ... do not try to end the sentences where they are ended below. Just let the computer decide when to go to the next line. Type the text below as well as you can. Use **Backspace** to erase mistakes you make.

See above for how to do each **indent** type.

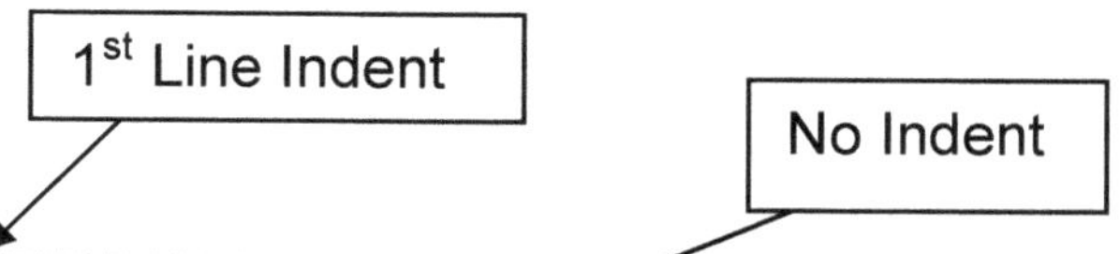

We would like to have you stop at our new regional warehouse.

We understand that you have been looking for a local source to care for your computer needs.

A visit would give you a better understanding of just how complete our inventory is and that it surely will handle most of your immediate needs.

If you would give us a couple of days notice and tell us what you particularly wish to look at, we will see that a good assortment of equipment, parts, and service manuals are available to be examined.

Please feel free to bring any of your associates whom you feel can advise you about the utility and quality of these items.

Hanging Indent

Save your work

	Keyboard	Mouse
1.	**Ctrl/S**	Click the **Save** button

Exercise 4

Bring back (Open) a document you have saved

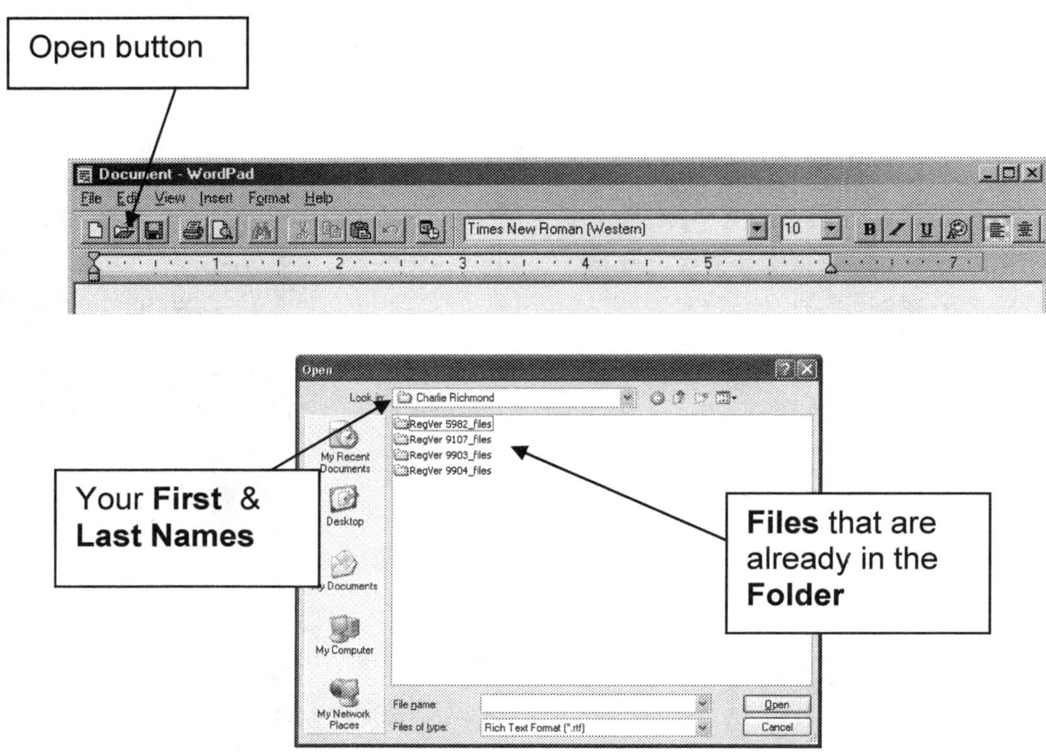

File Open Dialog Box

	Keyboard	Mouse
1.	**Ctrl/O**	**Click the** Open button **(looks like a file folder)**
2.	If **Look in** already shows your **first** & **last names** skip to step 6.	If **Look in** already shows your **first** & **last names** skip to step 7.
3.	**Shift/Tab**	Click on the folder with **your name** on it
4.	**Arrow key** move blue “highlight” to the folder with **your name** on it	
5.	**Enter↵** skip to step 7.	Click **OK**
6.	**Shift/Tab**	
7.	**Arrow key** to **Lesson 2 exercise 1** document	Click on **Lesson 2 exercise 1** document
8.	**Enter↵**	

Check Page 10 for correcting mistakes …

either adding information or erasing something that isn't wanted.

Make some changes to your old document.

Move the cursor left of "**Now**" (**Ctrl/Home**) with the **Arrow keys** or the **Mouse …** Press Delete 5 times, then type: the letter "**Y**"

Move the cursor here with the **Arrow keys** or the **Mouse …**Type 2 spaces followed by: **Let the computer do the work**

Now you are ready to type a new document. You don't have to worry about when to go to the next line. The computer figures this out for you. The "computerese" name for this action is "wraparound." When you used a typewriter, you had to decide when to go to the next line.

Move the cursor to the end of the last line (**Ctrl/End**) with the **Arrow keys** or the **Mouse** and type: **2 spaces** then type**: Now you no longer have to.**

Here's what it should look like when you are done.

You are ready to type a new document. You don't have to worry about when to go to the next line. The computer figures this out for you. Let the computer do the work. The "computerese" name for this action is "wraparound." When you used a typewriter, you had to decide when to go to the next line. Now you no longer have to.

Save your document

	Keyboard	Mouse
1.	**Ctrl/S**	Click the **Save** button

Exercise 5

Bring back (Open) a document that you have saved.

Open button

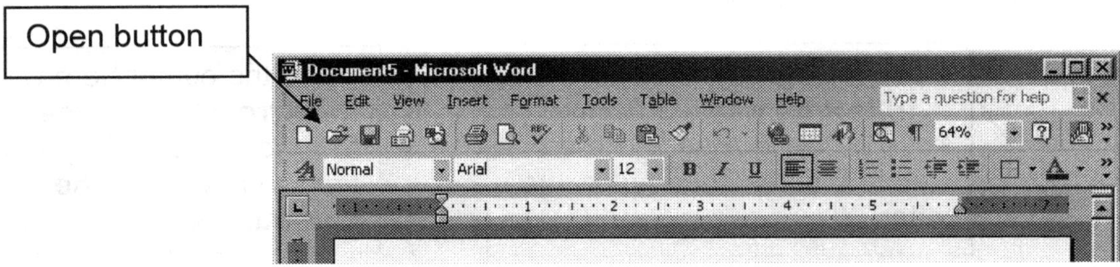

Bring a document back so you can work on it

	Keyboard	Mouse
1.	**Ctrl/O**	**Click the** Open button **(looks like a file folder)**
2.	If **Look in** already shows your **first** & **last names** skip to step 6.	If **Look in** already shows your **first** & **last names** skip to step 7.
3.	**Shift/Tab**	Click on the folder with **your name** on it
4.	**Arrow key** move blue "highlight" to the folder with **your name** on it	
5.	**Enter**↵ and skip step 7.	Click **OK**
6.	**Shift/Tab**	
7.	**Arrow key** to **Lesson 2 exercise 2** document	Click on **Lesson 2 exercise 2** document
8.	**Enter**↵	

Here is what you saved in Exercise 2 of this lesson. Now we will make some changes to it.

Move the **cursor** to the beginning of the second paragraph, **Shift/Down Arrow** twice … the lines are "**highlighted**," now change the type face to **Times New Roman** (see p. 33).

"**Wraparound**" is one of those new computer words

The only time *you* need to use the **Enter** key is when you want to go to a new line and start a new paragraph.

If you press the **Enter** key *TWICE,* the computer will *skip a line!*

You should **Save** these exercises so you can bring them back later in this lesson. If you forget to **Save this exercise,** you will have to do it all over again when you do Exercise 5.

It is good practise to do two things when you finish a document: (1) **Save** your work. (2) Close it so you won't make changes to it or add another exercise to it by mistake.

Move the **cursor** to the parenthesis that is to the left of "**1**" and **Enter**↵ twice

Move the **cursor** to the parenthesis that is to the left of "**2**" and **Enter**↵

Results of your changes ...

The second paragraph in **Times New Roman**.

The numbered list.

"**Wraparound**" is one of those new computer words

The only time *you* need to use the **Enter** key is when you want to go to a new line and start a new paragraph.

If you press the **Enter** key *TWICE,* the computer will *skip a line!*

You should **Save** these exercises so you can bring them back later in this lesson. If you forget to **Save this exercise,** you will have to do it all over again when you do Exercise 5.

It is good practise to do two things when you finish a document:

(1) **Save** your work.
(2) Close it so you won't make changes to it or add another exercise to it by mistake.

Highlighting tells the computer what it is that you want it to work on. In this case the entire second paragraph was rewritten in Times New Roman type. You could have done many other things with that paragraph:

- Changed the type size
- Italicized it or underlined it.
- Erased it.
- Moved it … by cutting and pasting.
- Changed the indent, or the margins.
- Attached it to another paragraph.

Whatever you want to do to just that paragraph, can be done. **Highlighting** can be very useful but **highlighting** can cause you some problems if the highlight is not turned off properly. The reason is very basic. The highlight identifies a character, paragraph, many paragraphs, etc. as a group that the computer is to perform one operation on … if you press any key on the keyboard other than the **Arrow keys**, the character that key generates will replace everything that is highlighted. If you press the **Space bar**, everything highlighted will be replaced by a space (it will disappear).

Fortunately, there is a key combination and an **Undo** button that will put everything back the way it was before you pressed the offending key. The key combination is: **Ctrl/Z**. The **Undo** button is up at the top of the screen, it looks like this: .

Let's see how it really looks before we put it away.

Preview what it would look like if you printed it

Keyboard	Mouse
Alt/F and **V**	Click the **Print Preview** button

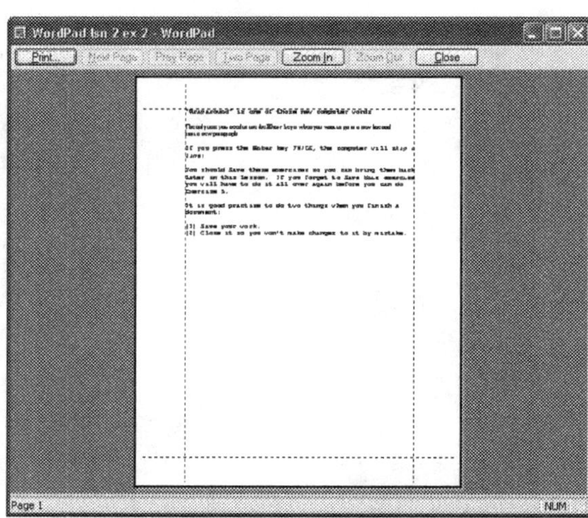

Print preview screen

You can print it if you like. Then you can see how it looks like on paper.

	Keyboard	Mouse
1.	**Ctrl/P** and **Enter**↵	Click the **Print** button

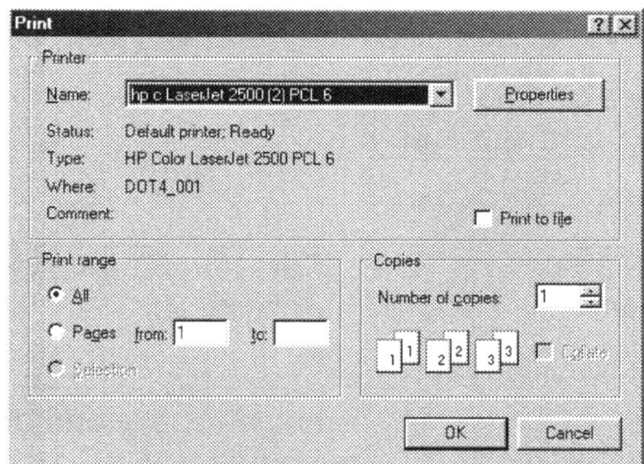

Print Dialog Box

Save your changed document.

	Keyboard	Mouse
1.	**Ctrl/S**	Click the **Save** button

Exercise 6

Open (bring back) a document you have saved

	Keyboard	Mouse
1.	**Ctrl/O**	**Click the** Open button **(looks like a file folder)**
2.	If **Look in** already shows your **first** & **last names** skip to step 6.	If **Look in** already shows your **first** & **last names** skip to step 7.
3.	**Shift/Tab**	Click on the folder with **your name** on it
4.	**Arrow key** move blue "highlight" to the folder with **your name** on it	
5.	**Enter↵** and skip step 7.	Click **OK**
6.	**Shift/Tab**	
7.	**Arrow key** to the **Lesson 2 exercise 3** document	Click on the **Lesson 2 exercise 3** document
8.	**Enter↵**	

Rearrange a document.

Combine the second and third paragraphs

We would like to have you stop at our new regional warehouse.

We understand that you have been looking for a local source to care for your computer needs.

A visit would give you a better understanding of just how complete our inventory is and that it surely will handle most of your immediate needs.

If you would give us a couple of days notice and tell us what you particularly wish to look at, we will see that a good assortment of equipment, parts, and service manuals are available to be examined.

Please feel free to bring any of your associates whom you feel can advise you about the utility and quality of these items.

Combine two paragraphs that are next to eachother

	Keyboard	Mouse
1.	Move the **cursor** to the beginning of the third paragraph with the **Arrow keys**	Put the **Mouse pointer** to the left of the 1st letter of the third paragraph
2.	**Backspace** until the third paragraph moves up and joins the end of the second paragraph	Place the **Mouse pointer** anywhere on one of the **highlighted** lines and press and hold the **left Mouse button** while you move the third paragraph up to meet the end of the second paragraph

Keyboard		Mouse
3.	Type in two **spaces**	Type in two **spaces**

Join the first and fourth paragraphs

We would like to have you stop at our new regional warehouse.

We understand that you have been looking for a local source to care for your computer needs. A visit would give you a better understanding of just how complete our inventory is and that it surely will handle most of your immediate needs.

Attach paragraph four to paragraph one

If you would give us a couple of days notice and tell us what you particularly wish to look at, we will see that a good assortment of equipment, parts, and service manuals are available to be examined.

Please feel free to bring any of your associates whom you feel can advise you about the utility and quality of these items.

Combine paragraphs one and four

Keyboard		Mouse
1.	Move the **cursor** to the beginning of the fourth paragraph with the **Arrow keys**	Put the **Mouse pointer** to the left of the 1st letter of the fourth paragraph
2.	**Shift/Down Arrow** three times to **highlight** three lines of the fourth paragraph	Hold the **left Mouse button** down while you move the **Mouse pointer** down to **highlight** all three lines of the fourth paragraph and let go of the button
3.	**Ctrl/X**	Click the **Cut button**
4.	Move the **cursor** to the end of the first paragraph using the **Arrow keys**	Click the **Paste button**
5.	**Ctrl/V**	
6.	Type in two **spaces**	Type in two **spaces**

The first and fourth paragraphs are joined

We would like to have you stop at our new regional warehouse. If you would give us a couple of days notice and tell us what you particularly wish to look at, we will see that a good assortment of equipment, parts, and service manuals are available to be examined.

We understand that you have been looking for a local source to care for your computer needs. A visit would give you a better understanding of just how complete our inventory is and that it surely will handle most of your immediate needs.

Please feel free to bring any of your associates whom you feel can advise you about the utility and quality of these items.

This is a mess …

The paragraphs are indented differently.
There are too many lines skipped between paragraphs.

Your job now is to make all paragraphs with no first line indent or overhang and to remove the extra skipped lines in between paragraphs. Make yours look like mine below …

This can be done by using the **Backspace** or **Delete** keys

We would like to have you stop at our new regional warehouse. If you would give us a couple of days notice and tell us what you particularly wish to look at, we will see that a good assortment of equipment, parts, and service manuals are available to be examined.

We understand that you have been looking for a local source to care for your computer needs. A visit would give you a better understanding of just how complete our inventory is and that it surely will handle most of your immediate needs.

Please feel free to bring any of your associates whom you feel can advise you about the utility and quality of these items.

Save your document.

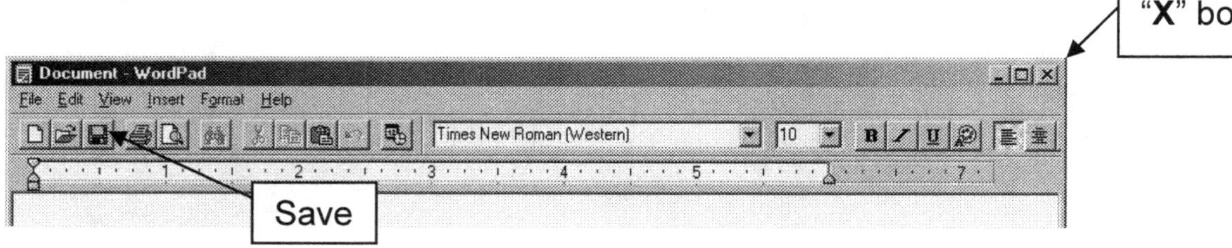

	Keyboard	Mouse
1.	**Ctrl/S**	Click the **Save** button

It's time to turn off the computer, the lesson is finished …

Turn the program off.

Keyboard		Mouse
1.	**Alt/F4**	Click the topmost right hand "**X**" box

Turn the computer off.

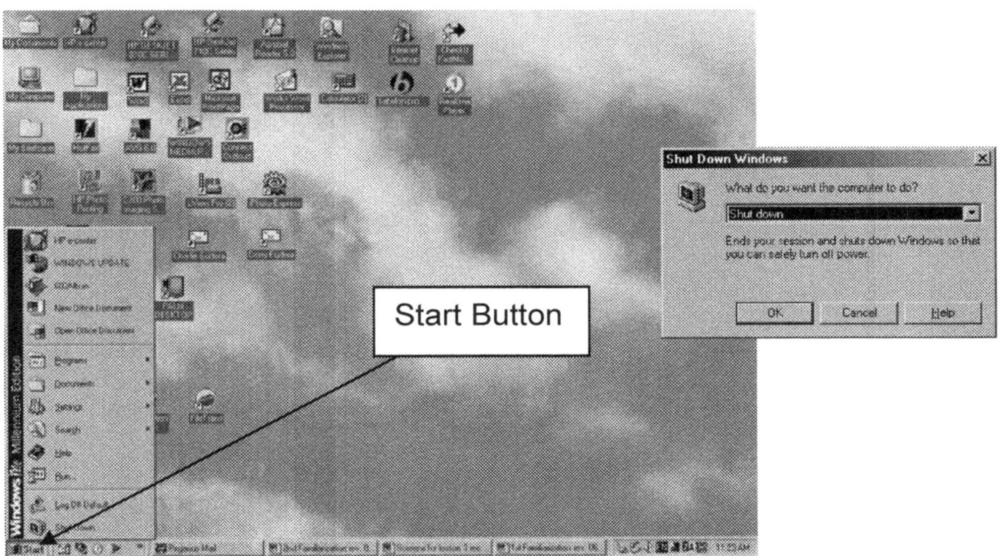

Keyboard		Mouse
1.	**Start Menu** button or **Ctrl/Esc**	Click **Start** button
2.	**U**	Click the **Shut Down** command
3.	**Enter↵**	Click **OK**

Note: Appendix B repeats start the computer, start a program, start a new document, open (get) a document from your files, save a document as, save a document (put it in a file), and shut the computer down instructions.

Introduction to Internet and Email

Lesson 3

The Information Age

The first successful digital computer of the forties heralded the end of the mechanical age and commenced what we are calling today ... **the Information Age.** We are finding that information in quantity, with accuracy, and with timeliness can indeed alter lifestyles and ways of living. Instead of speeding up our physical work we are making our production and transportation much more efficient.

We are learning about how to control this seeming genius. That is what this course is all about. You will learn how to make this machine do your bidding so you personally can utilize its power.

You are not here to learn about how to handle shipments of materials, though what you learn could certainly be used for such a task. You will learn about some of the many tools that are available for us to use. Tools that, when correctly used, will make our lives better and much more fun. You will learn how to communicate with people who live anywhere on this planet. You will learn how to reach people down town or around the world. You will learn that the meaning of words that you hear so frequently are part of today's **computer jargon**. You will find that these words are really quite commonplace and that computer "experts" like the members of academia delight in using ordinary words of our language in strange ways.

Most computer related words are put together from a definition of what a particular item or part does or looks like. These made up words are called **acronyms**. I will attempt to define each new one when I use it. Ones that I miss will be in the **Glossary** ... Appendix C.

Internet is what makes it all happen. It all started when our Defense Department asked our research institutions to design a communications system that could overcome service interruptions and not lose messages that were coursing over the wires or through the satellites. The first full scale design was called ARPANET (Army Research & Planning Agency Network). The key to its success was the development of "store and forward" procedures.

Following ARPANET was CSNET (Computer Science Network) and NSFNET (National Science Foundation Network). The last was the forerunner of the internet as we know it today. NSF funded five supercomputer centers at five universities in the 1980's. This network proved to be so successful that the system was expanded to include fifteen sites. The net then reached outside the United States.

An artist's conception of the electronic superhighway

With the switching, store and forward power of the system now made available to the world, the system grew from the five original computers to the fifteen supercomputers which were capable of connecting many thousands, even millions of computers. The system has grown from a few hundred computers connected to internet to many million. Yes, even our small home microcomputers (dubbed "personal computers" by IBM when it introduced its first micro).

Hypertext This is the breakthrough that really ignited internet use. The capability of formatting displays and being able to reproduce them at a great distance resulted in millions of people, universities, governments, and businesses putting *Home Pages* on the internet. Hypertext was developed in CERN Switzerland as a method for writing academic and scientific papers with their numerous references in such a way that these references could be called up by someone reading the paper just by pointing a mouse pointer at a transfer point and clicking. The source material could be brought in for the reader to examine.

It didn't take long for internet technicians to realize that this technique had many other values. These values are still being exploited and expanded.

Start Internet Explorer

If your screen does not have the Internet Explorer icon on it page 49 has the directions for doing it!

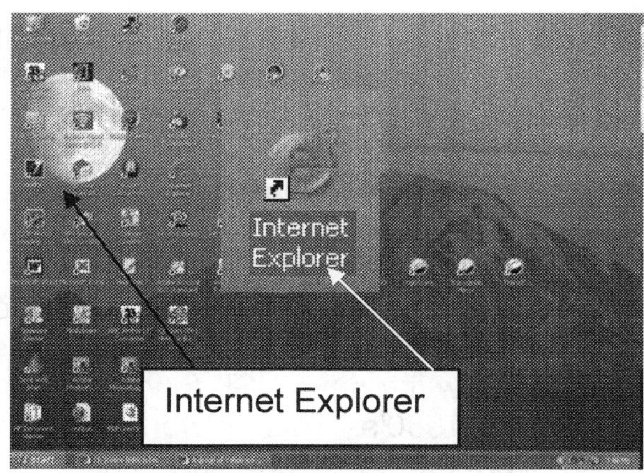

"Desktop" opening screen

If you don't have the icon (picture symbol) for Internet Explorer on your "Desktop" here is an easy way to put one there.

Procedure to put an Internet Explorer icon on your Desktop when you are using the new "Category View."

	Keyboard	Mouse
1.	**Start Menu** button or **Ctrl/Esc**	Click **Start Menu** button
2.	**C** to **Control Panel**	Click **Control Panel** button
3.	**Tab** 5 times to **Appearance & Themes** and **Enter↵**	Click **Appearance & Themes**
4.	**Tab** 9 times to **Display** and **Enter↵**	Click **Display**
5.	**Ctrl/Tab** to **Desktop** tab	Click **Desktop** tab
6.	**Alt/D** (Customize Desktop button)	Click **Customize Desktop** button
7.	**Alt/I**	Click box next to **Internet Explorer**

Internet Explorer icon to the Desktop when using the Classic View

	Keyboard	Mouse
1.	**Start Menu** button or **Ctrl/Esc**	Click **Start Menu** button
2.	**Down Arrow**, then **Right Arrow** to **Display** icon and **Enter↵**	Click **Display**
3.	**Ctrl/Tab** to **Desktop** tab	Click **Desktop** tab
4.	**Alt/D** (Customize Desktop button)	Click **Customize Desktop** button
4.	**Alt/I**	Click box next to **Internet Explorer**

Start Internet Explorer procedure.

	Keyboard	Mouse
1.	**Start menu** key or **Ctrl/Esc**	Click **Internet Explorer** icon (picture)
2.	**P** … may take several presses	
3.	Press **I** until **Internet Explorer** is highlighted (surrounded by blue)	
4.	**Enter↵**	

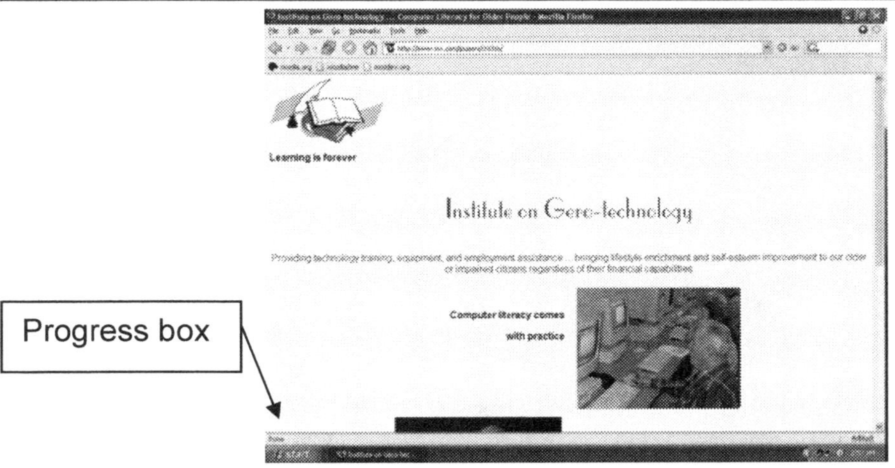

Homepage of the Institute on Gero-technology

Once your chosen **homepage** is displayed and the **progress box** says "**done**", you are ready to tell **Internet Explorer** where you want it to go next.

Go to Yahoo! Mail's homepage.

	Keyboard	Mouse
1.	**Alt/D**	Click in the right hand end of the **Address** box
2.	Type in **WWW.Mail.Yahoo.com**	Type in **WWW.Mail.Yahoo.com**
3.	**Enter↵**	Click the **Go** button

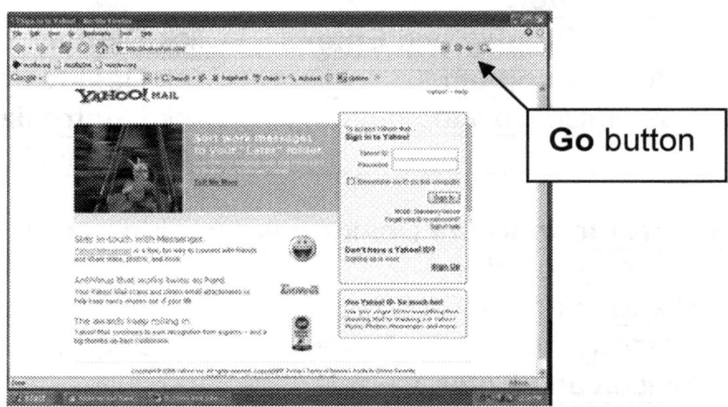

Yahoo! Mail Login Page

Sign up procedure

	Keyboard	Mouse
	Wait until Yahoo!'s mail page is in	
1.	**Tab** 7 times to **Sign up**	Click **Sign up**
2.	**Enter↵**	
3.	**Tab** 7 times to **Sign Up**	Click **Sign Up**
4.	**Enter↵**	

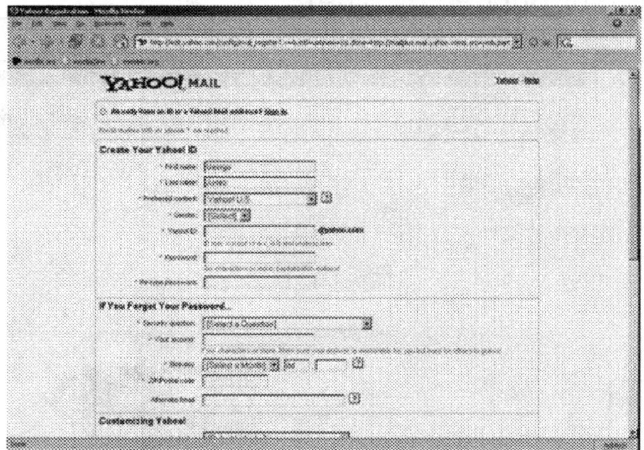

Fill in the your ID and Password Information

ID and Password procedure

	Keyboard	Mouse
1.	**Tab** 5 times to **First Name:** box	Click **First Name:** box
2.	Type in your **First Name**	Type in your **First Name**
3.	**Tab** and type in your **Last Name**	Click the **Password** box and type in your **Last Name**
4.	**Tab** twice to **Gender** and type in **M** or **F**	Click the [v] box and click either **Male** or **Female**
5.	**Tab** once & type in the 1st 6 letters of your last name, first & middle name initials and your year of birth.	Click once & type in the 1st 6 letters of your last name, first & middle name initials and your year of birth.
6.	**Tab** to **Check Availability of this ID** and press **Enter**↵	Click **Check Availability of this ID**
7.	If the **ID** you entered is **OK** go to step 8 otherwise repeat step 5 or choose a different **ID** using Yahoo's "ID helper."	If the **ID** you entered is **OK** go to step 8 otherwise repeat step 5 or choose a different **ID** using Yahoo's "ID helper."
8.	**Tab** to the **Password:** box and type in a mix of 8 letters and numbers	Click the **Password:** box and type in a mix of 8 letters and numbers
9.	**Tab** & retype the **Password**	Click the **Re-type password:** box & retype your **password**

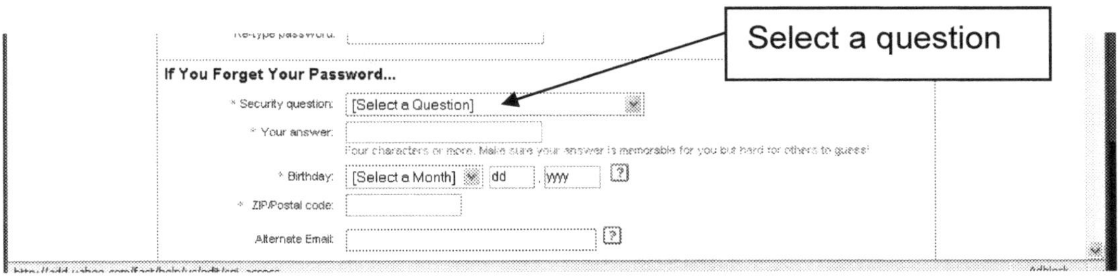

Fill in your "secret question" information … in case you forget the password

	Keyboard	Mouse
1.	**Tab** to **Security Question**	Click the button next to the **Security Question:** or just click the box
2.	Press the **Down Arrow** on your keyboard until a question appears that you would like to use whose answer is one that you will always know.	Click the question that you would like to use whose answer is one that you will always know.
3.	**Tab** to the **Your Answer:** box and type in the answer you will to give.	Click in the **Your Answer:** box and type in the answer you will to give.

Keyboard		Mouse
4.	**Tab** and press the **Down Arrow** until your month of birth appears.	Click the button next to the **(select one)** box or just click the box and then the month of your birth
5.	**Tab** to the next box and type in your **birth day** … 2 numbers	Click the next box and click your **birth day** … 2 numbers
6.	**Tab** and Type in your **birth year …** 4 numbers	Click the next box and type in your **birth year …** 4 numbers
7.	**Tab** to the **Zip/Postal Code** box and type in your zip code	Click the **Zip/Postal Code** box and type in your zip code
8.	**Tab** and type in your current email address if you wish	Click **Alternate Email** and type in your current email address if you wish

Customize Yahoo! Email … give information about your work and what you do to give Yahoo! an idea about what topics might interest you. Just **Tab** over the ones you don't wish to fill in and fill in the ones you would like to supply.

Verify your registration … This step is necessary to keep electronic sign-up programs from getting a group of email accounts at one time … such accounts are used by spammers (people who send email advertising that is generally unwanted).

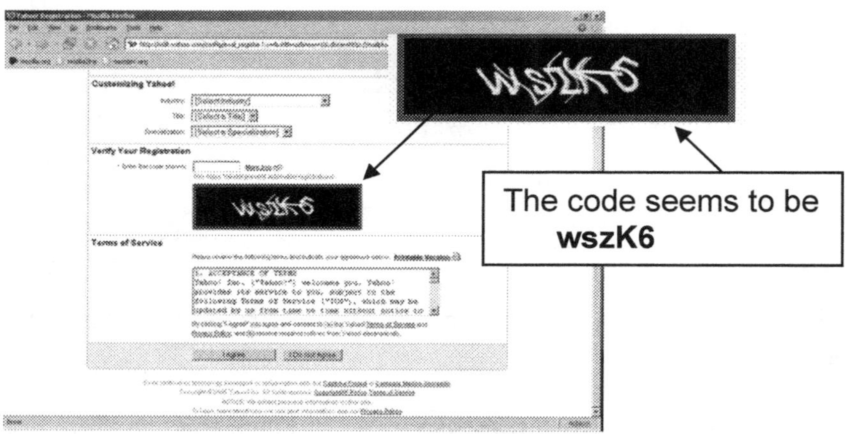

Verify your registration screen

Verify your registration procedure

Keyboard		Mouse
1.	**Tab** to the **Enter the code shown** box and type in what you can recognize from the **black boxed code.**	Click the **Enter the code shown** box and type in what you can recognize from the **black boxed code.**
2.	**Tab** 8 times until you reach the **I Agree** box and press **Enter↵**	Click the **I Agree** box

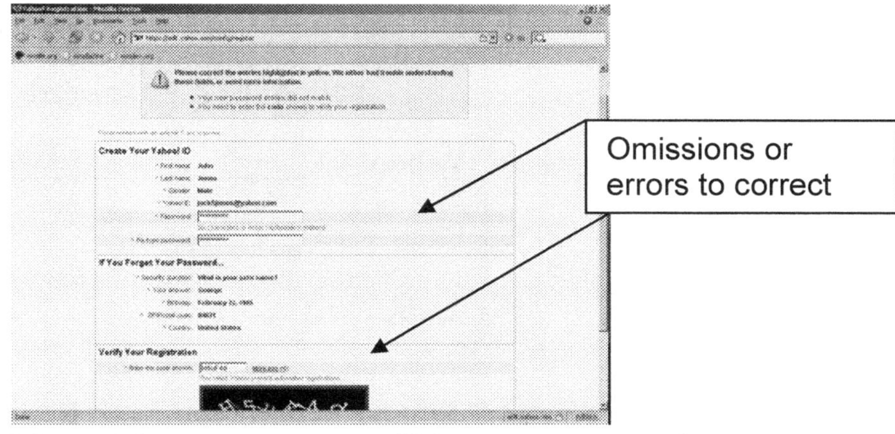

If you did anything wrong, you will have to correct them before Yahoo! accepts you

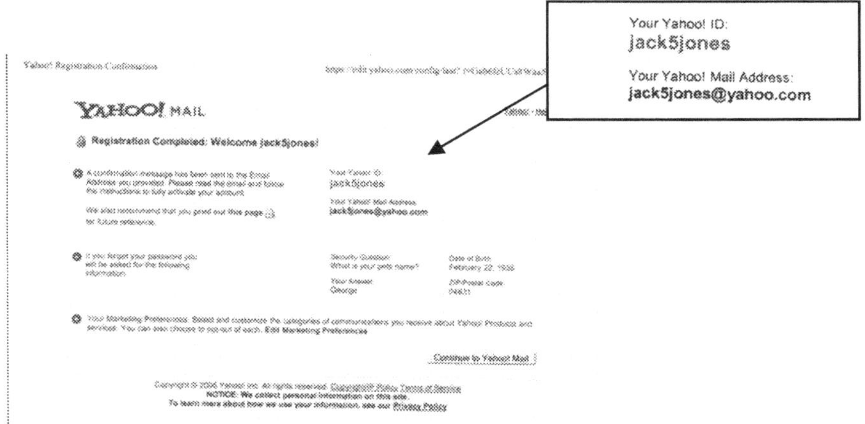

Yahoo! confirms your "Yahoo ID" and shows you what your email address looks like

Start your work with Yahoo! Mail …

	Keyboard	Mouse
1.	**Tab** 6 times to **Continue to Yahoo! Mail**	Click **Continue to Yahoo! Mail**

The Welcome Screen

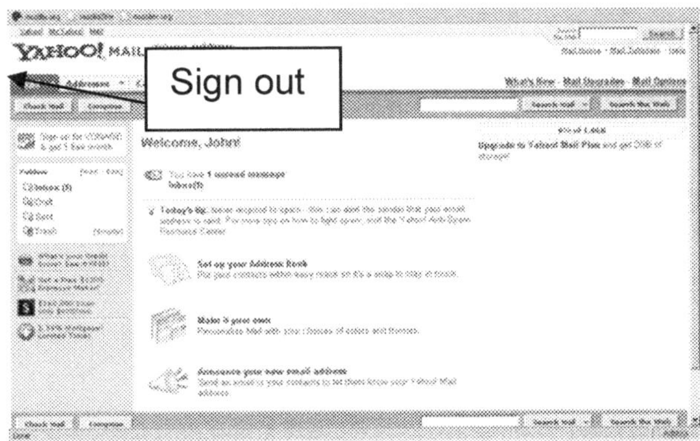

Make sure you write down your Yahoo ID and the Password you chose … use the box below …

Yahoo! ID & Password
Yahoo! ID ____________________
Password ____________________

Now that you have a Yahoo! Email Account you need to practice starting it.

Starting Yahoo! Mail

	Keyboard	Mouse
1.	**Tab** to **Sign Out** and press **Enter**↵	Click **Sign Out**
2.	**Alt/Home**	Click the **Home** button
3.	**Alt/D** and type in **Mail.Yahoo.com**	Click anywhere in the **Address box** and type in **Mail.Yahoo.com**
4.	**Enter**↵	Click **Go**

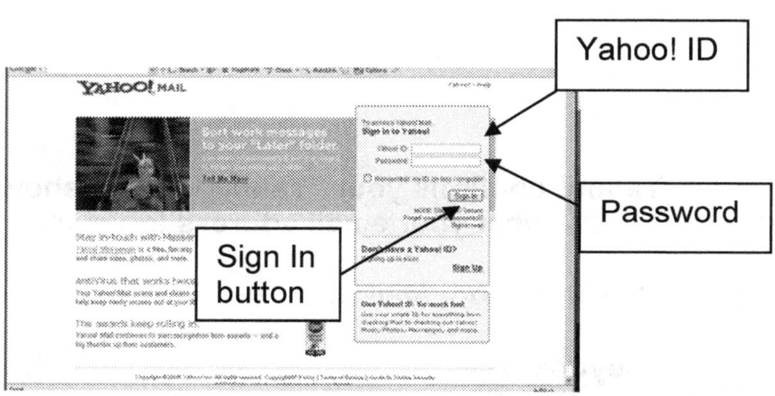

Sign in for Yahoo! Mail

	Keyboard	Mouse
1.	Type in your **Yahoo! ID** … above	Type in your **Yahoo! ID** … above
2.	**Tab** to the **Password:** box	Click the **Password:** box
3.	Type in your **Password** … above	Type in your **Password** … above
4.	**Tab** twice to the **Sign In** button	Click the **Sign In** button
5.	**Enter**↵	

If you type in your **Yahoo! ID** and **Password** correctly, you will get the **Welcome Page.**

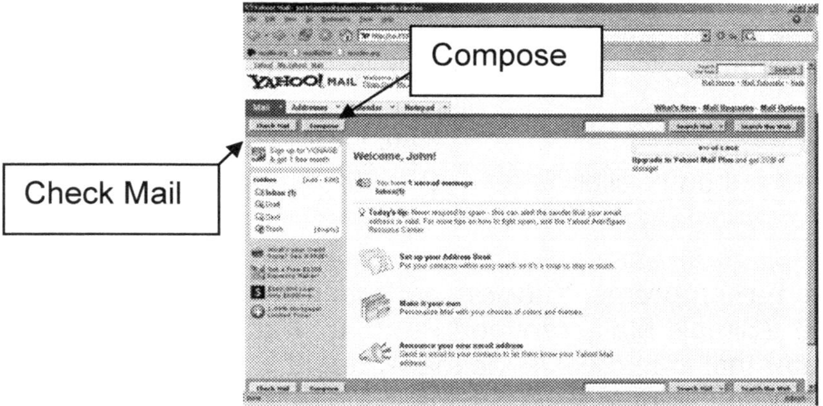

Welcome Page

Now write an email letter using your new Yahoo! account and send it off …

Keyboard		Mouse
1.	**Crtl/Shift/P**	Click **Compose** the pointer becomes a hand with a pointing finger

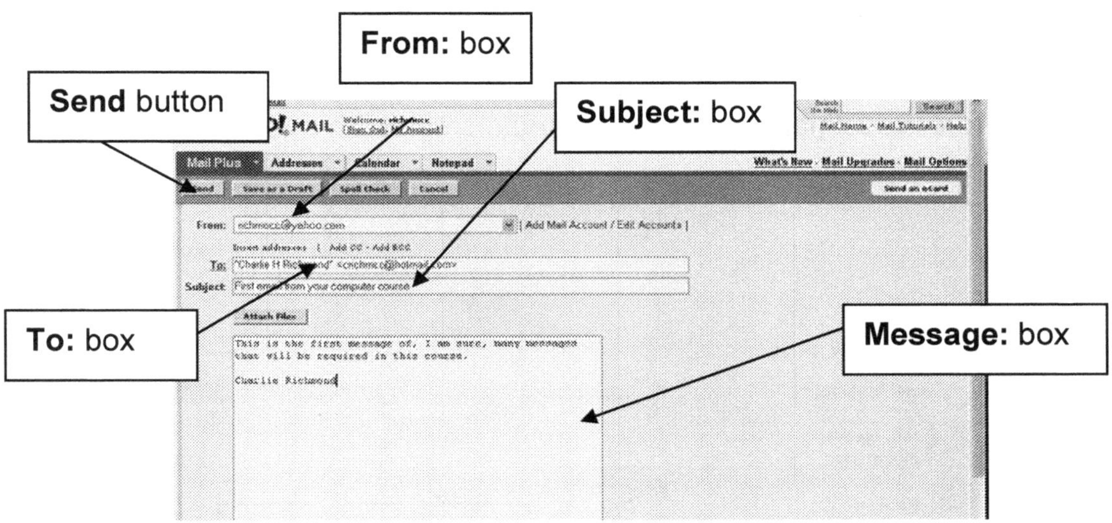

Compose screen showing a message ready to send

Write your first email message and send it.

Keyboard		Mouse
1.	Type in "**Charlie Richmond**" **<richmocc@yahoo.com>**	Type in "**Charlie Richmond**" **<richmocc@yahoo.com>**
2.	**Tab** to the **Subject** box and type in "First email from your computer class"	Click in the **Subject** box and type in "First email from your computer

	Keyboard	Mouse
4.	**Tab** to the **Message** box and type in: "**This is the first message of, I am sure, many messages that will be required in this course.** Now type **your name**"	Click in the **Message** box and type in: "**This is the first message of, I am sure, many messages that will be required in this course.** Now type **your name**"
5.	**Tab** to the **Send** button or click **Send**	Click the **Send** button
6.	**Enter**↵	

Unlike some other email programs, **Yahoo!** sends its messages off right away, sends it to the SMTP (Simple Mail Transport Program) that is. This program contacts the computer that is to receive the message. If it can't find that computer or the place you want to send the message to, the program sends your message back with a note that it couldn't deliver the message. If it finds some other condition that does not permit the delivery of the message right away, it holds onto the message, keeps checking with the receiving computer, and holds the message until it gets permission to send. If the message is not delivered for several days, it gives you the choice of canceling or permitting a further delay of the delivery.

Once your computer receives permission to send, it splits the message into "message packets" and sends it out one packet at a time. The receiving computer keeps track of each packet and asks your computer to resend any that are missing or are not complete. All the packets do not have to travel over the same route to the destination … other computers send the packets by the best and fastest way.

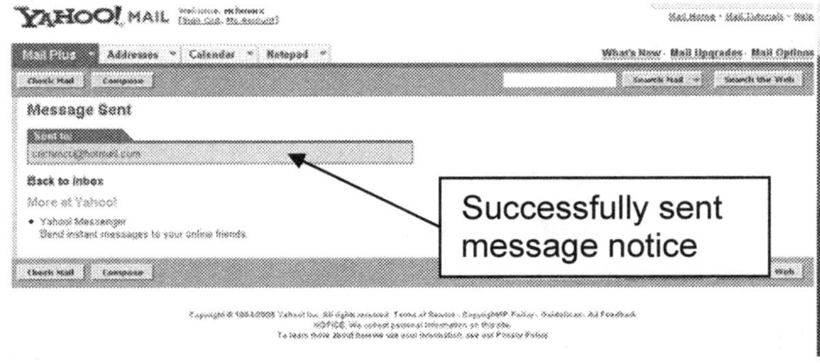

Your message was sent successfully

Write and send another message.

	Keyboard	Mouse
1.	**Ctrl/Shift/P**	Click the **Compose** button
2.	The **cursor** should be blinking in the **To:** box, if not **Tab** to it and type in the address given in the Exercise Material below	The **cursor** should be blinking in the **To:** box, if click it and type in the address given in the Exercise Material below
3.	**Tab** to the **Subject** box and type in the subject from the Exercise Material below.	Click in the **Subject** box and type in the subject from the Exercise Material below
4.	**Tab** to the **Message** box and type in: the Message from the Exercise Material below. Now type **your name**"	Click in the **Message** box and type in: the Message from the Exercise Material below. Now type **your name**"
5.	**Tab** to the **Send** button or click **Send**	Click the **Send** button
6.	**Enter↵**	

Use the directions given above to help you fill in the *Compose* form and to send the message.

Exercise 1

To: <dbr@example.com>
Subject: Practice Internet message

Email can get to the other side of the world in less than 30 seconds. I like email because I can send a message to someone and I know that it has reached them. They can answer and know that their answer has been received.

(your name)

Exercise 2

To: <rel@example.com>
Subject: Another chance to communicate over Internet

I don't have any problems with writing email and sending it. It is the other stuff that has me worried.

(your name)

Just one more exercise, then we are through with this lesson.

Send Charlie Richmond a message telling him why you are taking this course and what you hope to learn from it.

Charlie's email address is: richmocc@yahoo.com

Sign out of Yahoo! mail.

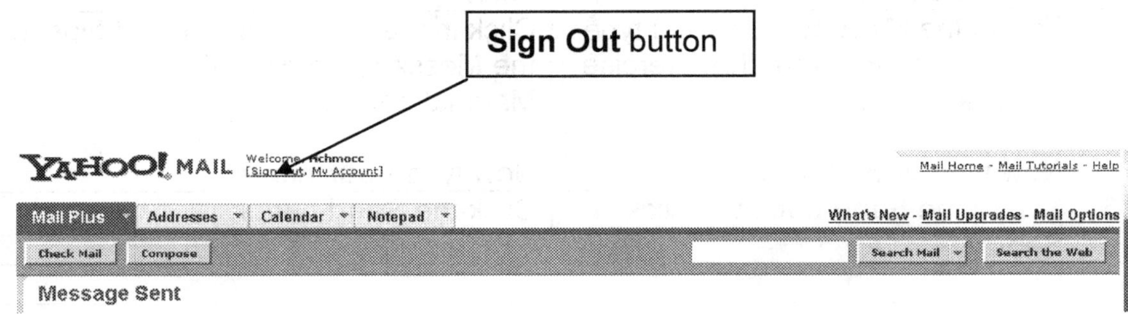

Sign out procedure

Keyboard		Mouse
1.	**Tab** to **Sign Out**	Click **Sign Out**
2.	**Enter**↵	

It's time to turn off the computer, the lesson is finished …

Turn the program off.

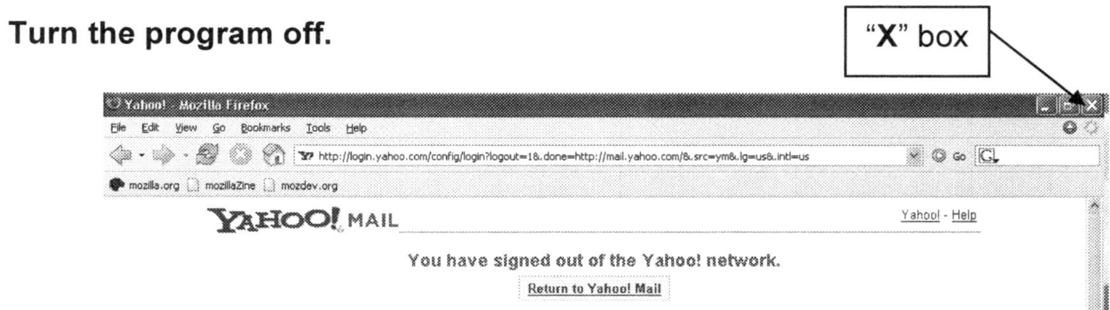

	Keyboard	Mouse
1.	**Alt/F4**	Click the topmost right hand "**X**" box

Turn the computer off.

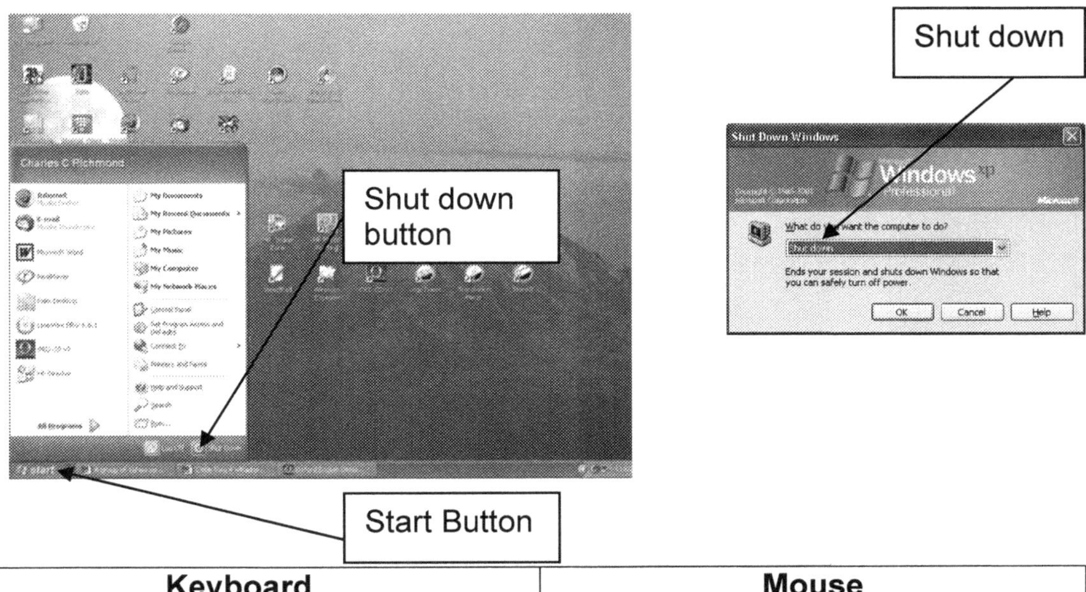

	Keyboard	Mouse
1.	**Start Menu** key or **Ctrl/Esc** key	Click **Start** button
2.	**U**	Click the **Shut Down** button
3.	**Enter**↵	Click **OK**

Using Email Features

Lesson 4

Email programs.

Earliest communications over the Internet were what we call email today. This single component accounts for most of the current traffic. It is simple to use. It is convenient and it can be utilized free of charge.

Start Internet Explorer

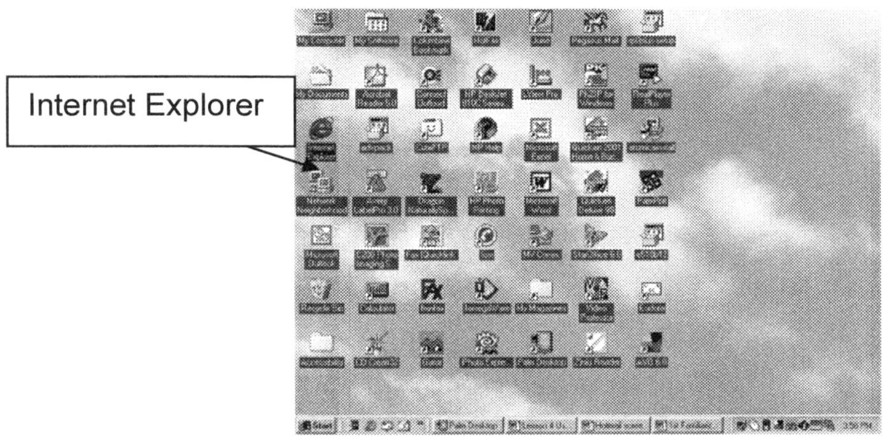

"Desktop" opening screen

Start Internet Explorer procedure

Keyboard		Mouse
1.	**Start** button	Click **Internet Explorer** icon (picture), if there is no icon on your Desktop page 49 tells you how to put it there.
2.	**P** until **<u>P</u>rograms** is highlighted	
3.	**Right Arrow**	
3.	**I** until **Internet Explorer** is highlighted (surrounded by blue)	
4.	**Enter↵**	

Get the Yahoo! Mail page

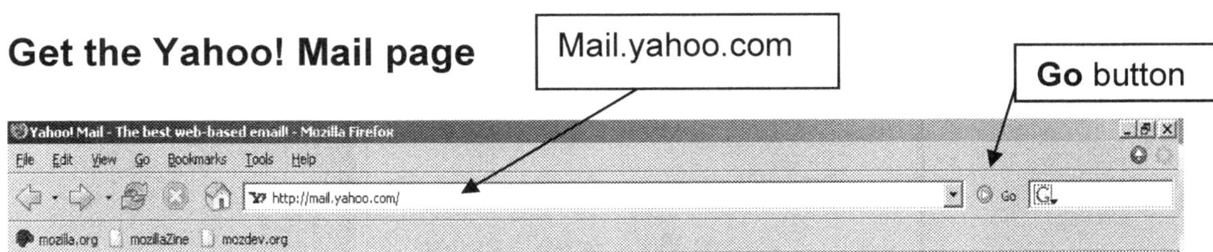

Add<u>d</u>ress Box after typing in the Yahoo! Mail address
Go to Yahoo! Mail

Go to Yahoo! Mail procedure

	Keyboard	Mouse
1.	**Alt/D** and type in **Mail.Yahoo.com**	Click anywhere in the **Address** box and type in **Mail.Yahoo.com**
2.	**Enter↵**	Click the **Go** button

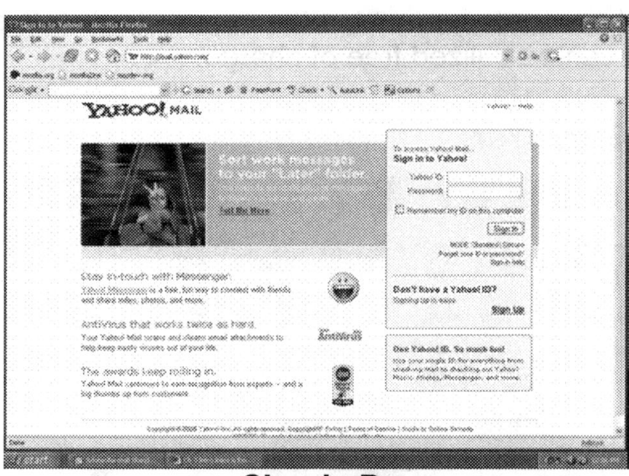

Sign-in Page

Sign-in procedure

	Keyboard	Mouse
Wait until Yahoo's! Sign In page is in and the cursor is blinking in the Yahoo! ID box		
3.	Type in your **Yahoo! ID:** see pg. 54	Type in your **Yahoo! ID:** see pg. 54
4.	**Tab** to **Password:** box	Click in the **Password:** box
5.	Type in your **Password:** see pg 54	Type in your **Password:** see pg. 54
6.	**Enter↵**	Click the **Sign In** button

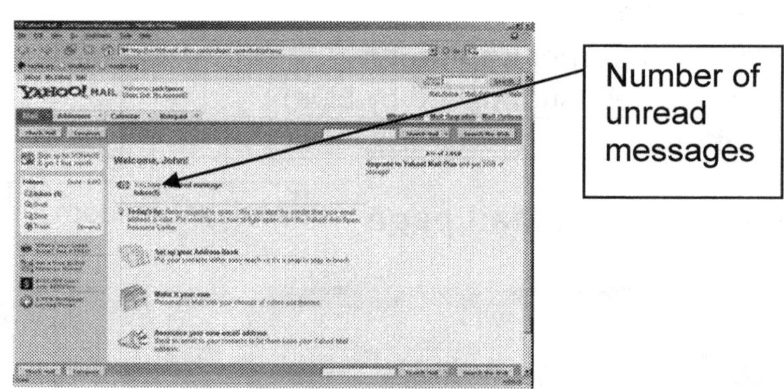

Yahoo! Welcome Screen

If Yahoo! says there is mail in your mailbox, go check it out.

Check for mail procedure

	Keyboard	Mouse
1.	**Ctrl/Shift/C**	Click the **Check Mail location**

Inbox with new mail

Read your mail

Bring a message in for reading

	Keyboard	Mouse
1.	**Tab** to the first **Subject** e.g. **failure notice**	Click the first **Subject** e.g. **failure notice!**
2.	**Enter↵**	

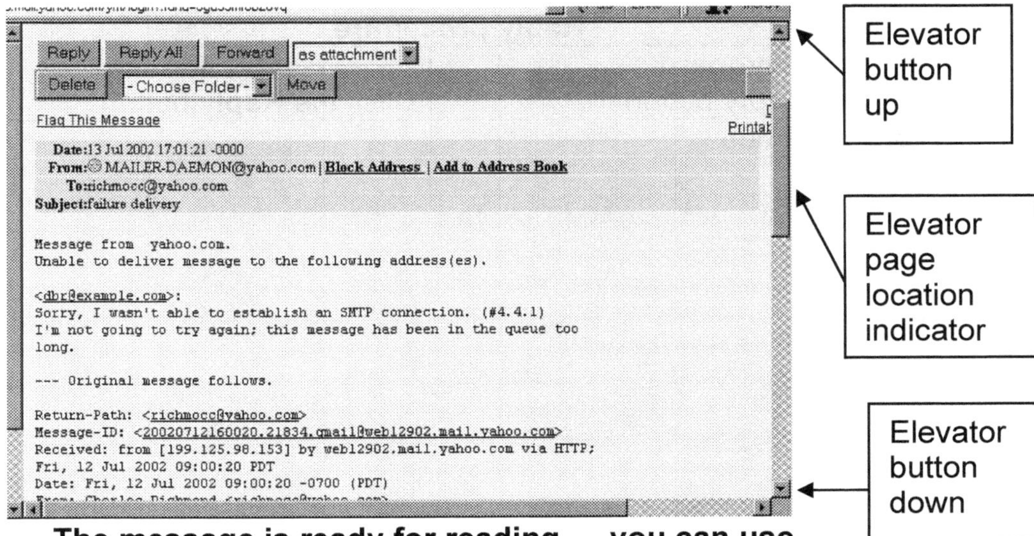

The message is ready for reading … you can use your up and down arrows or the "elevator" to get to all the text

Once you have read a message you may want to answer it....

The easiest way to email someone is to "**Reply**" to a message that someone sends you … email addresses are pretty tough to write down so letting the computer put them in is the safest thing to do … otherwise, you may get a message from Daemon just like you saw above if you don't put in the email address exactly correct..

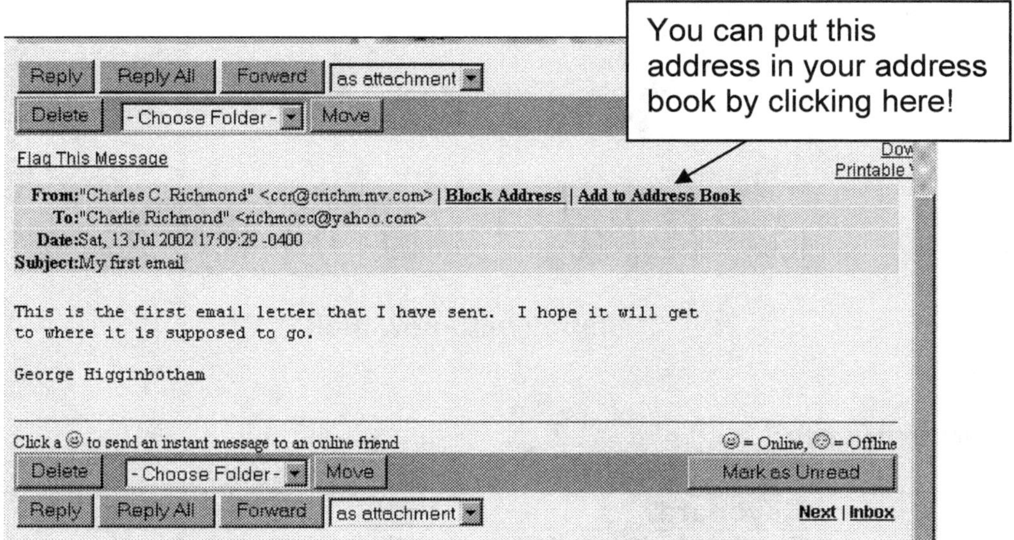

Here is a message from Charlie, let's answer it!

How to "reply" to a message.

Reply procedure

	Keyboard	**Mouse**
1.	**Tab** to the **Reply** button	Click the **Reply** button
2.	**Enter↵** or **Space**	

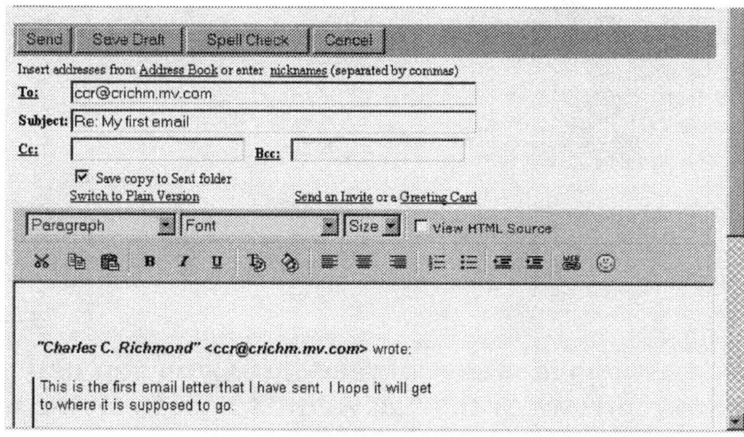

Your reply message is ready for you to add your message to it

Adding a message to your reply and sending it

	Keyboard	Mouse
3.	Type in your message or … "**Hello from computer class. We are using this message as a way to demonstrate how to send a reply to and email message. This is one way to make sure that your letter will make it to the person you want to receive it.**	Type in your message or … "**Hello from computer class. We are using this message as a way to demonstrate how to send a reply to and email message. This is one way to make sure that your letter will make it to the person you want to receive it.**
4.	**Tab** to the **Send** button	Click the **Send** button
5.	**Enter↵** or **Space**	

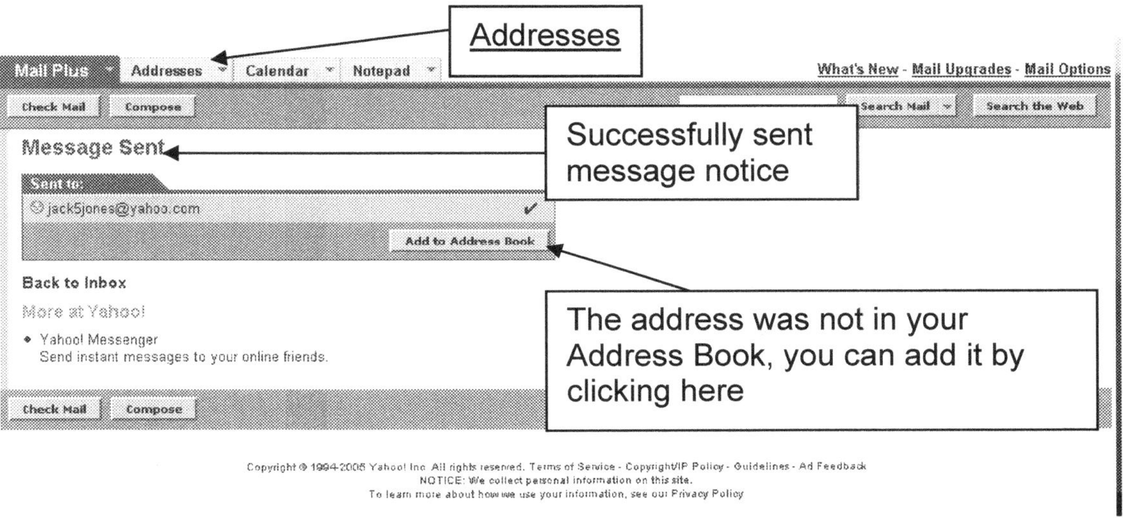

Sent message screen

When you are told that the message has been sent successfully … your message made it to its destination. Email addresses are most difficult to put in because they must be perfect to be delivered. You address book will save you many addressing errors. If you did not have the address in your Address Book a button will appear on the **Message Sent** screen. You can click **Add to the Address Book** and …

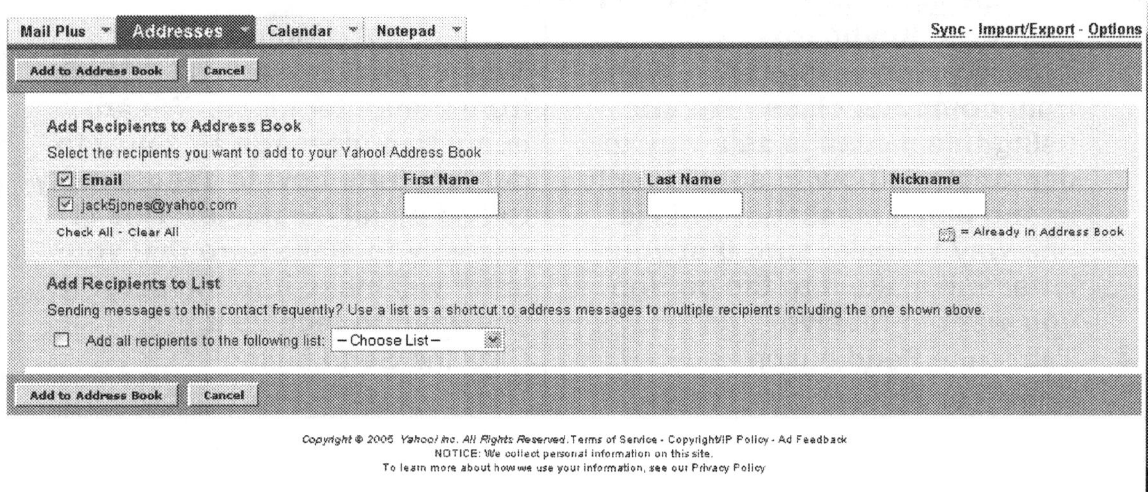

Add Recipient screen after clicking
the **"Add to Address Book"** button on the **Message Sent** screen

Fill in the "Add" form

Keyboard		Mouse
1.	**Tab** til you reach **First Name**	Click in **First Name** box
2.	Type in the **First Name**	Type in the **First Name**
3.	**Tab** and type in **Last Name**	**Tab** and type in **Last Name**
4.	**Tab** and type in a **Nickname**	**Tab** and type in a **Nickname**
5.	**Tab** to **Add to Address Book** button and **Enter**↵	Click **Add to Address Book** button

Now add people to your Address Book the hard way … by hand!

You have been shown two ways to have the computer save an email address for you … on the reading screen and on the . Here is a another way but it is most difficult because it relies upon you not to make any mistakes.

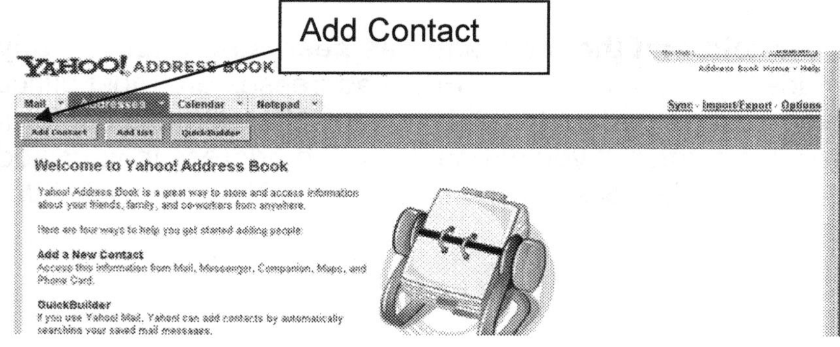

Address Book screen when book is empty

Add addresses procedure

	Keyboard	Mouse
1.	**Tab** to **Addresses** tab and **Enter↵**	Click **Addresses** tab
2.	**Tab** to **Add Contact** button and **Enter↵**	Click **Add Contact** button

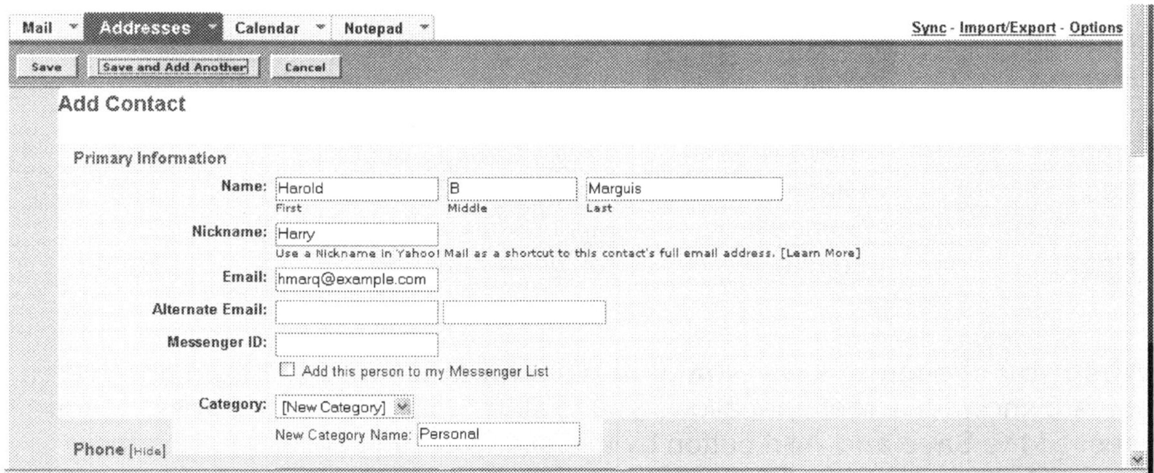

Add Contact screen

Add Contact procedure

	Keyboard	Mouse
1.	**Tab** to **Name:** First and type in **First Name**	Click **Name:** First box and type in **First Name**
2.	**Tab** and type in **Middle Name**	Click **Middle Name** box and type it in
3.	**Tab** and type in **Last Name**	Click **Last Name** box and type it in
4.	**Tab** and type in the **Nickname**	Click **Nickname** box and type it in
5.	**Tab** and type in the **Email:** address	Click **Email:** box and type in the address
6.	**Tab** to **Category:** box and **Arrow Down** 1st time to **[New Category]** and **Enter↵** after 1st time **Arrow Up** to **Personal** and go to step 9.	Click the down pointer box to the right of **Category:** box Click **[New Category]** 1st time only after 1st time go to step 8
7.	Type in **Personal** 1st time only	Type in **Personal** 1st time only
8.		Click **Personal**
9.	**Shift/Tab** to **Save and Add Another** or **Save** if you have no more to add.	Click **Save and Add Another** button or **Save** if you have no more to add
10.	**Enter↵**	
10.	**Shift/Tab** to **Done** and **Enter↵**	Click **Done**

Put in "New Contacts …

add all of the people listed below to your address book. Use the **Add Contact procedure** for each of the names in the table below.

New Contact Names to add to your Address Book

First Name	M. Init.	Last Name	Email	Nickname
Harold	B	Marquis	hmarq@example.com	Harry
Hannah	Z	Payter	hzpr@example.com	Nan
Marsha	C	Mellow	marshmellow@example.com	Marty
Charles	C	Richmond	ccr@acad.umass.edu	Chaz
Donald	W	Stewart	saberstrew@aol.com	Don
Leo		Glasheen	laglasheen@exampl.juno.com	Leo
Michael		Spinnelli	MI1123@worldnet.att.net	Mike
Ralph	E	Lavoie	rel@example.com	Ralph

When you choose to save what you have recorded and to begin another … you are shown a screen that allows you to start filling in a new address. If you pressed the **Save and Add** button by mistake, you can cancel by using the **Cancel** button. You can tab over to it and press **Enter↵** or you can click on it with the Mouse.

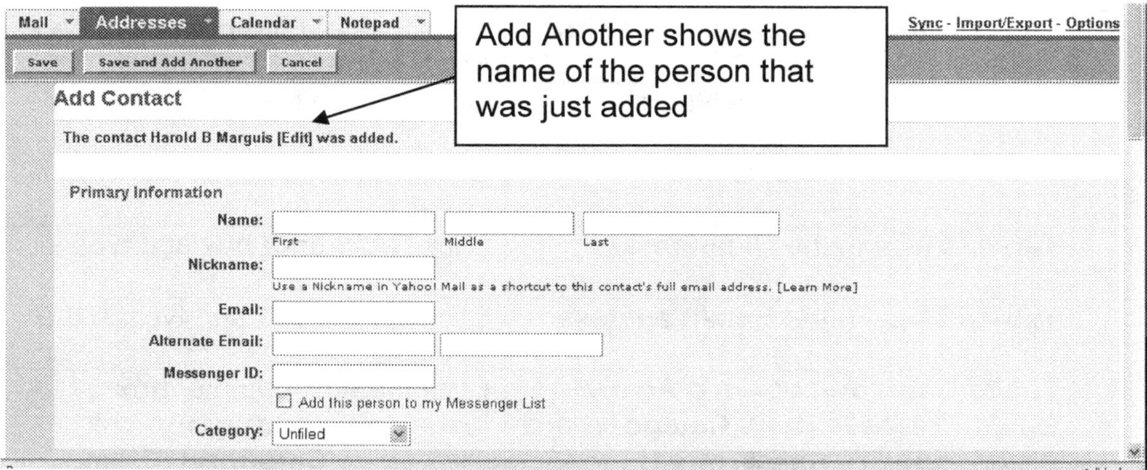

Add (Another) Contact screen

This is what you will see when you have finished your list of new contacts, chosen "Done" and pressed Enter or have clicked "Done."

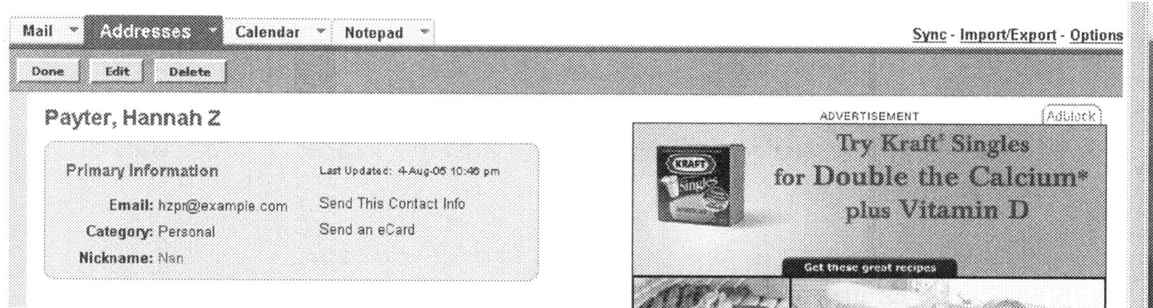

Save screen

Yahoo! Shows you your finished Address Book after you press Done or Tabbed to Done and pressed Enter.

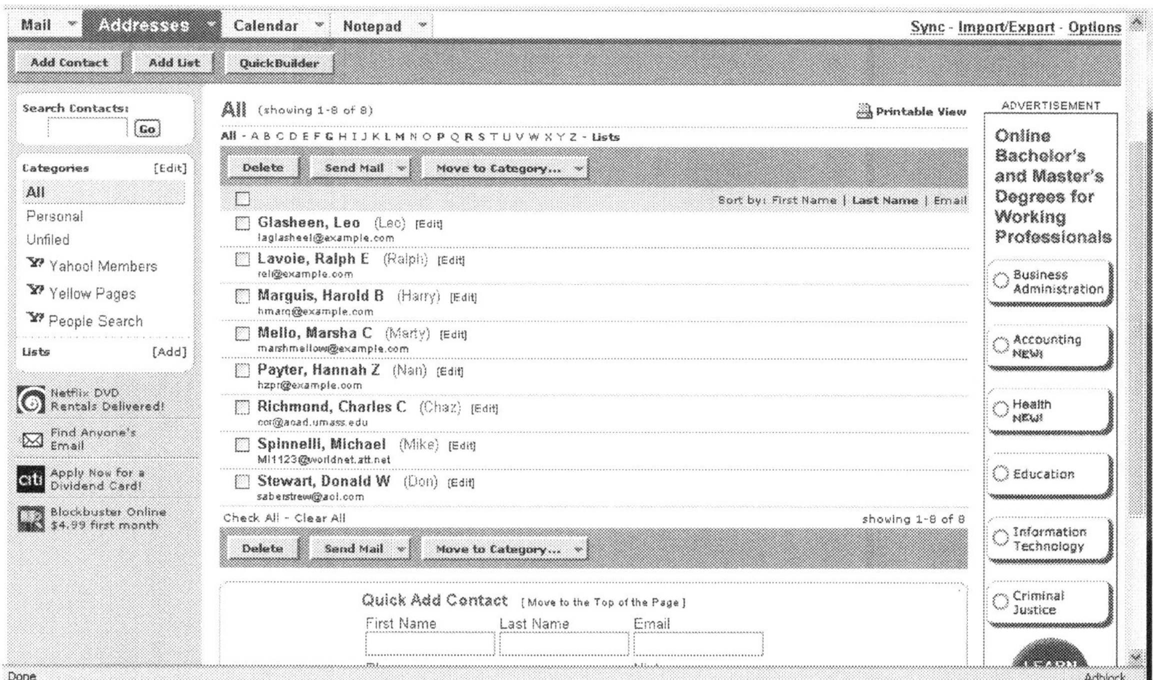

Finished Address Book

Close the Address Book procedure

	Keyboard	Mouse
1.	**Ctrl/Shift/C**	Click **Mail** button

Use the Address Book to put email addresses into your new email messages …

Addressing your emails using the Address Book start at the **Inbox** …
If you are in the **Address Book**, go back to the **Inbox** … click **Mail** or **Ctrl/Shift/C**.

Bring in the Compose form procedure

	Keyboard	Mouse
1.	**Ctrl/Shift/P**	Click on **Compose**

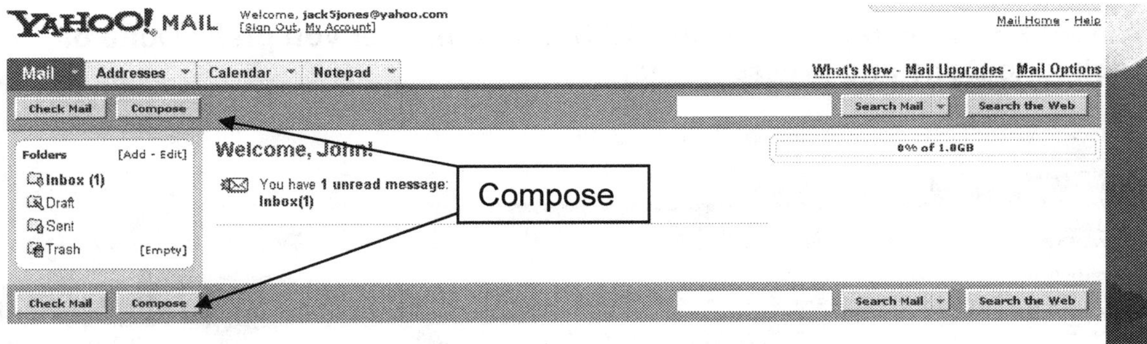

Inbox showing the location of the two places that Compose appears

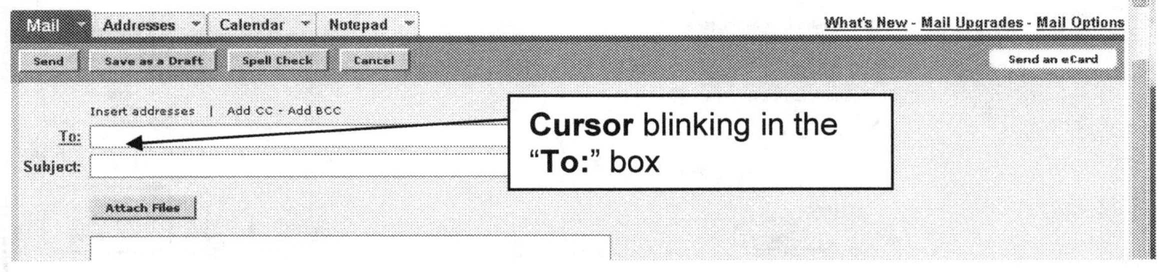

Compose form

Address an email message using the Address Book procedure

	Keyboard	Mouse
1.	Type in part of a **Name** or **Nickname** … a possible list drops down, you can use the **Down & Up Arrow** keys to choose the one you want then **Tab** or **Enter**	Type in part of a **Name** or **Nickname** … a possible list drops down. Click the one you want.

You can fill in the **CC:** and **BC:** addresses (you must **click** these "buttons") the same way … just type in the **Nickname** or some of it (you must **Down Arrow** to the one you want) and press **Tab**. If choices stay on the screen, clear them by pressing either the **Right** or **Left Arrow keys**.

If you forget any of the **Nickname**, you can address your email by clicking **Insert Addresses** and this **Dialog** box will appear:

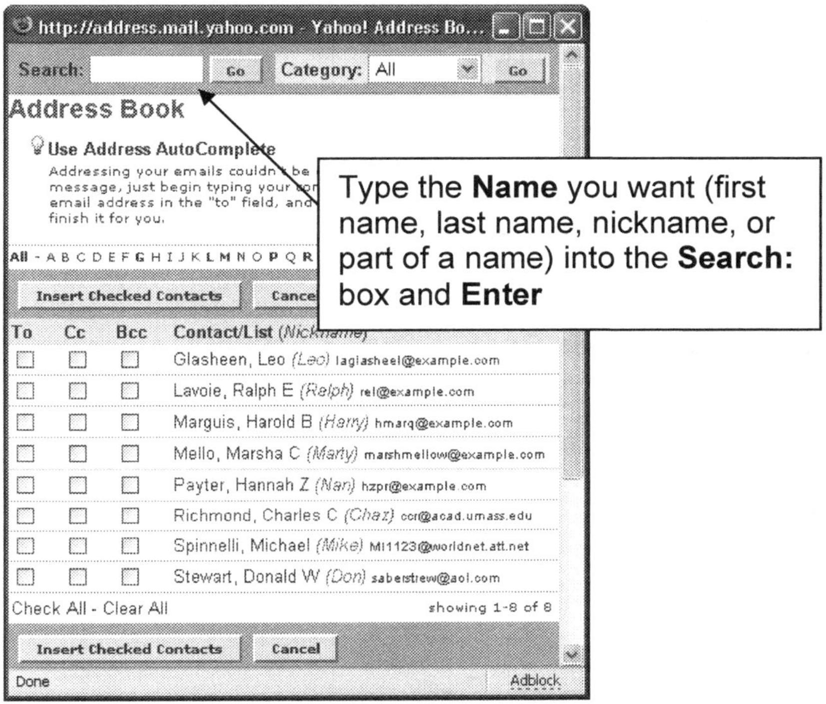

Insert Address screen

Find and insert an Address from the Address Book

	Keyboard	**Mouse**
1.	**Shift/Tab** to **Insert addresses** and **Enter↵** (you may have to click the **Insert addresses** button)	Click **Insert addresses**
2.	**Tab** and type in the name you want … part of the name, all of the first or last name, all the nickname … a partial name brings a list of possible addresses, you must choose the one you want.	Click the "**To**" box next the name
3.	**Tab** and press **Enter↵**	
4.	**Shift/Tab** to the "**To**" box next to the name you want and **Space**	
5.	**Tab** to **Insert Checked Contacts** and press **Enter↵**	Click **Insert Checked Contacts**

Finish the email by putting in a Subject and Message …

	Keyboard	Mouse
1.	**Tab** to the **Subject** box and type in the subject from the Exercise Material.	Click in the **Subject** box and type in the subject from the Exercise Material.
2.	**Tab** to the **Message** box and type in: the Message Now type **your name**"	**Tab** to the **Message** box and type in: the Message Now type **your name**"
3.	**Tab** to the **Send** button and **Enter↵**	Click the **Send** button

If you have several people that you want to send the same email to or just want to send a copy to … there are a couple of ways to do this.

Bring in the Address Book … Auto Complete … screen

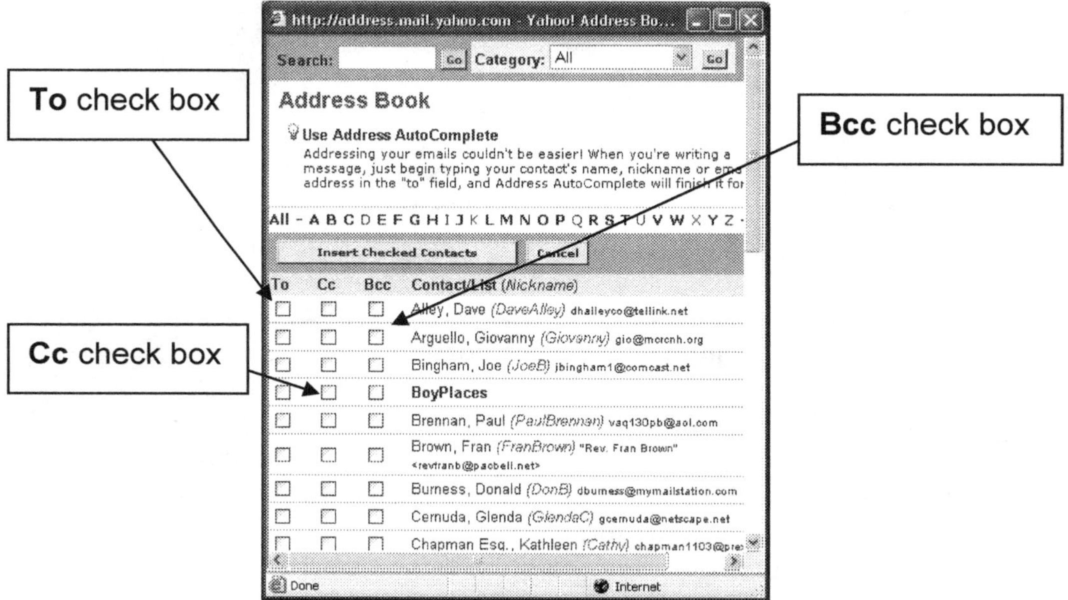

Choose and Insert each address procedure

	Keyboard	Mouse
1.	**Tab** to the **To**, **Cc**, or **Bcc** check box that is next to the address you want and **Space**	Click the **To**, **Cc**, or **Bcc** check box that is next to the address you want
2.	Repeat step 1 for each address you want to send your mail to	Repeat step 1 for each address you want to send your mail to
3.	**Tab** to **Insert Checked Contacts** button and **Enter**	Click **Insert Checked Contacts** button

If you want to send emails to the same group quite often, you can set up a **List** of people using addresses from your **Address Book**. You can then write or forward one email and send it to this group or **List**. The group's name is all you have to put in the "**To:**" box.

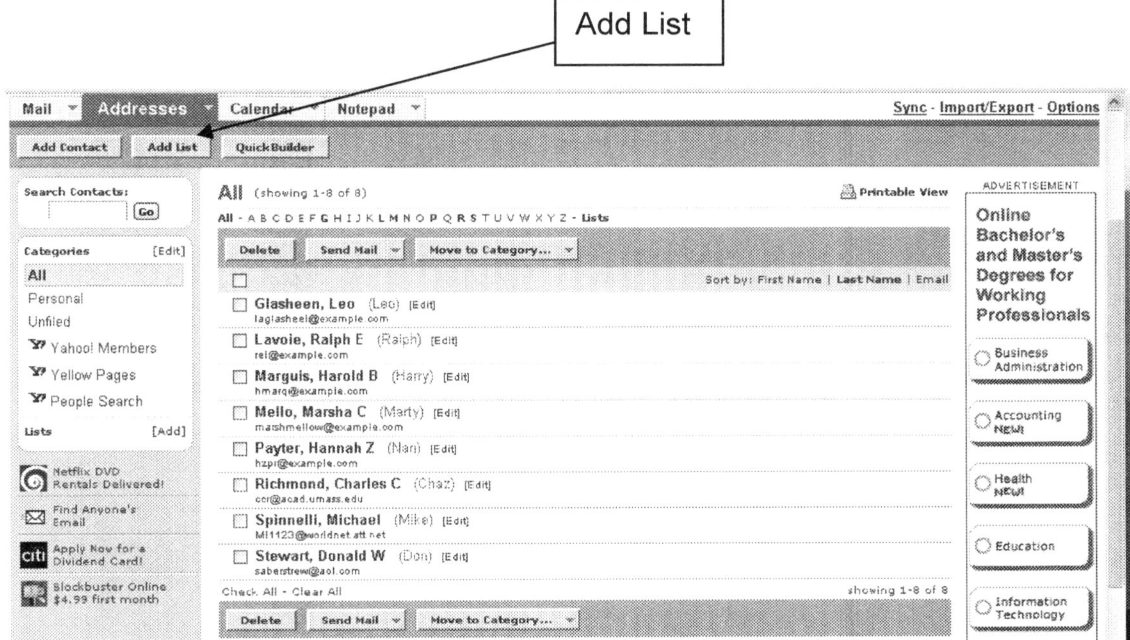

Address book page

Create a "Mailing List" procedure

	Keyboard	Mouse
1.	**Tab** to **Add List** button and **Space**	Click on **Add List** button

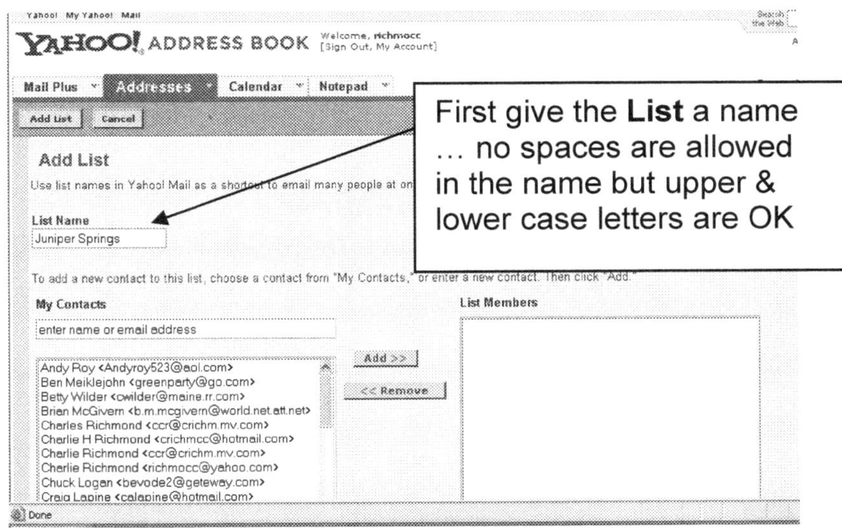

Address Book Add List screen

Prepare the List of people

	Keyboard	Mouse
1.	Type in the **List Name** "**BoysPlace**"	Type in the **List Name** "**BoysPlace**"
2.	**Tab** twice to the large box which shows a list of **My Contacts** .	
3.	Highlight a person you want in the list using an **Up** or **Down Arrow** Key and **Tab** then **Space**	Click on a person you want in the list
4.	**Tab**	Click **Add** » button
5.	**Space**	
6.	**Shift/Tab**	
4.	Repeat steps 3 to 6 for each new person you want on the **List**	Repeat step 3 & 4 for each new person you want on the **List**
5.	Once you have everyone you want in the **List**, **Tab** to **Add List** button	Once you have everyone you want in the **List** Click **Add List** button

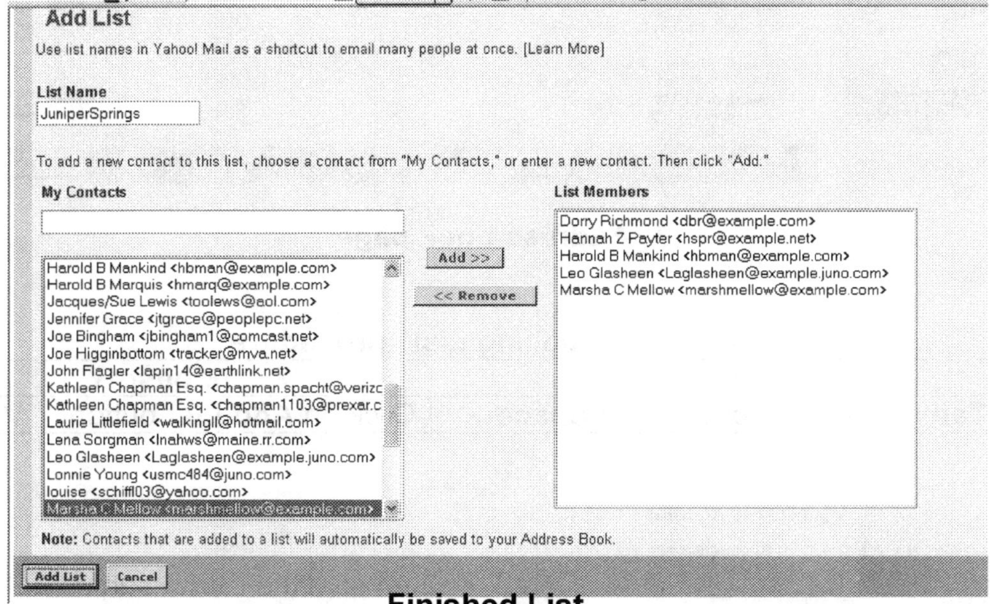

Finished List

Write and send some email messages …

Use your **Address Book** for putting in the email addresses by typing the person's **Nickname** in the "**To:**" box.

Write an email message procedure

	Keyboard	Mouse
1.	**Tab** to **Compose** and **Enter**↵	Click on **Compose**
2.	Type the person's **Nickname** in the "**To:**" box and **Tab****	Type the person's **Nickname** in the "**To:**" box and **Tab****
3.	**Tab** to the **Subject** box and type in a subject for the message	**Tab** to the **Subject** box and type in a subject for the message

	Keyboard	Mouse
4.	**Tab** to the **Message** box and type in what you want to say to the person and type in your name.	**Tab** to the **Message** box and type in what you want to say to the person and type in your name.

** Not all email programs will make the addressing of an email this easy. You may have to look for words like "**Insert Addresses**" to **Tab** to or to Click on and then choose the person from the **Address Book**.

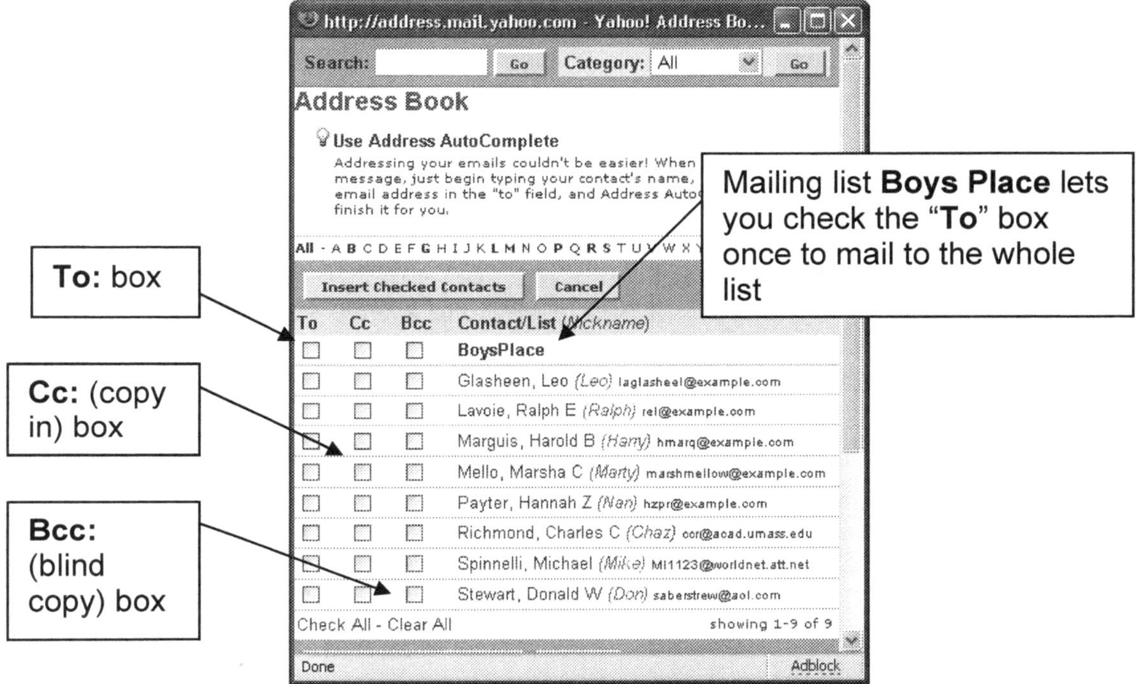

This is makes it easier to put many addresses on one email

You can mix lists in with individual addresses. There is no limit to what you can get the computer to do for you. However, even though you use the **Tab** key to go to a check box, you **must** use the **Mouse** to click a check mark into it.

I would like you to send this email to the **BoysPlace** list and copies to a couple of other people. And, you are not limited to the number of lists you wish to send a single email to.

Send an email to a list and copies to several different people

	Keyboard	Mouse
1.	Click **Insert Addresses**	Click **Insert Addresses**
2.	Click the **To** box for **BoysPlace**	Click the **To** box for **BoysPlace**

Keyboard		Mouse
3.	Click the **Cc** box for **Pat**	Click the **Cc** box for **Pat**
4.	Click the **Bcc** box for **CharlieR**	Click the **Bcc** box for **CharlieR**
5.	Type the words below into the correct places on the **Compose** form	Type the words below into the correct places on the **Compose** form
6.	**Tab** to the **Send** button (today you have to click the button because of a programming error)	Click the **Send** button
7.	**Enter↵**	

Here is the subject and the message to type into the Compose form …

Subject: Writing messages to new people before they send you a message

I just wanted to let you know that I am home now and that I would like t6o start exchanging messages with you. It has been quite awhile since we even talked on the phone. The trip was a lot of fun, however, but now that we are home, I must say that I am happy to be here.

Get back to me when you can. We can continue our conversation about where we go from here

Type your name here

As you become more familiar with email …

You will want to **attach things** like pictures you have taken of someone special or to send something like a news article that would interest someone who had moved out of town or is on vacation.

Here is how to send an attachment with a message.

Attaching something to an email message and sending it

Keyboard		Mouse
1.	Address and prepare the message as shown above "**Send an email**"	Address and prepare the message as shown above "**Send an email**"
2.	**Tab** many times to **Attach Files** button and **Enter↵**	Click **Attach Files** button

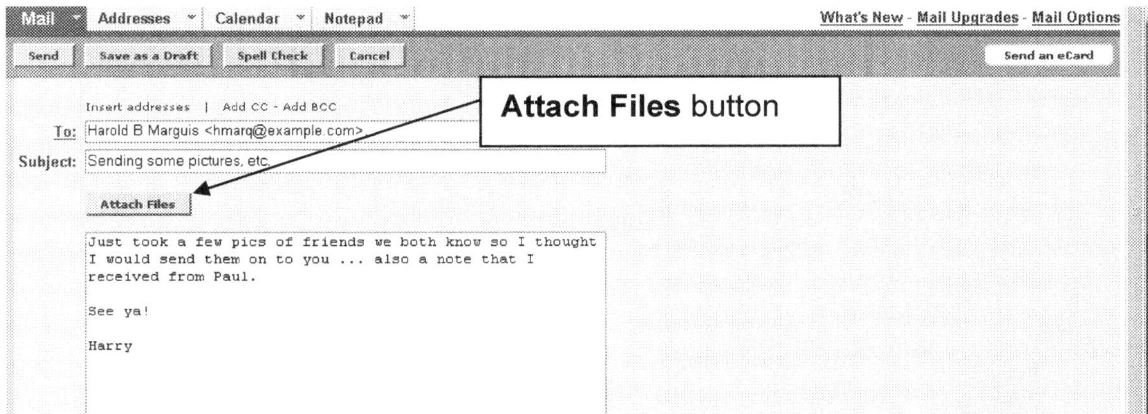

The Message is ready for the attachments!

Browse for the picture folders

	Keyboard	Mouse
3.	**Tab** to **File 1: Browse** button and **Enter↵** gets the **File Upload** dialog box	Click **File 1: Browse** button gets the **File Upload** dialog box

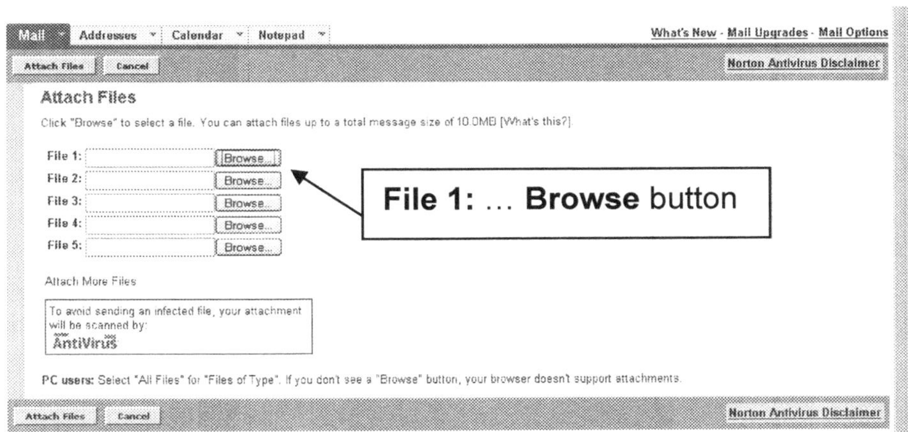

Attach Files screen

Move around My Documents to find My Pictures

	Keyboard	Mouse
4.	**Alt/I** and **Arrow Down**	Click the down pointer to the right end of **Look in** box
5.	**Arrow** to **My Documents** and **Enter↵**	Click **My Documents**
6.	**Alt/N**	Click twice **My Pictures** folder
7.	**Shift/Tab** and use **Arrow keys** to find **My Pictures** and **Enter↵**	

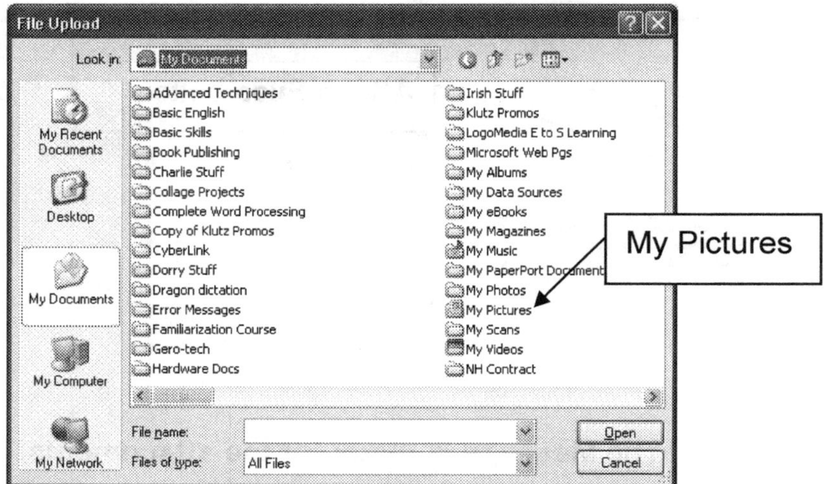

File Upload dialog box

Find a folder with a picture I want … it will be inside a sub-folder

Keyboard		Mouse
8.	**Arrow** key to **Demo Album**	Click **Demo Album** twice
9.	**Enter**	

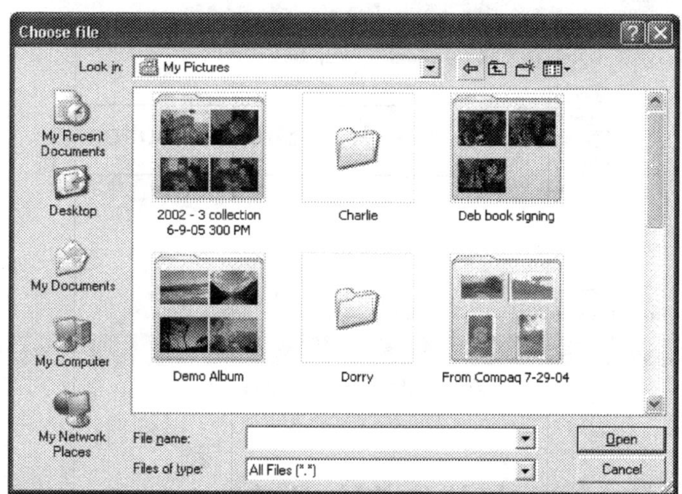

My Pictures showing many sub-folders

Choose the picture to attach

Keyboard		Mouse
10.	**Arrow** key to **Demo Album**	Click **Demo Album** twice
11.	**Enter**	

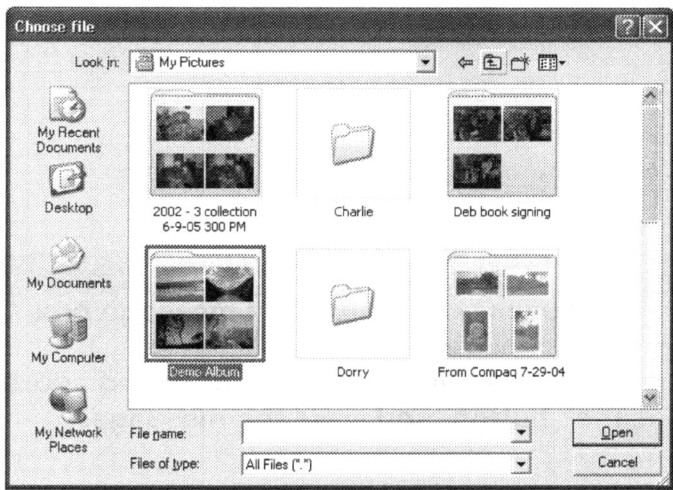

Choose File dialog box Demo Album chosen

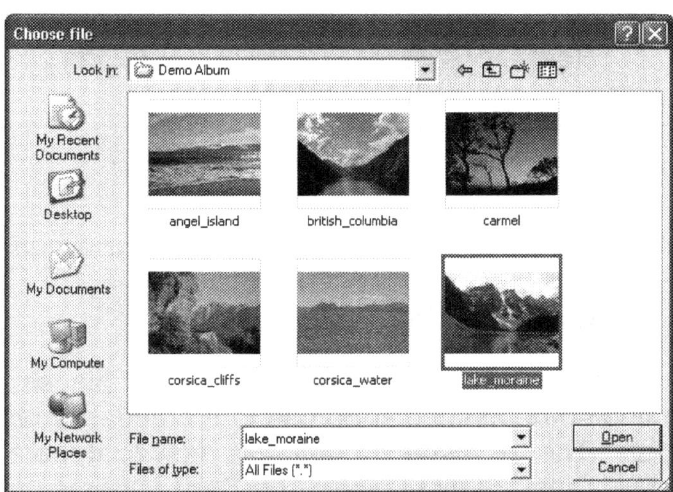

Choose File dialog box picture to attach chosen

	Keyboard	Mouse
12.	**Arrow** key to **Lake Moraine** picture	Click **Lake Moraine** picture
13.	**Enter**	
14.	**Tab** to **Attach Files** button	Click **Attach Files** button

Attach Files buttons

Address of the file to **Attach**

Attach Files dialog box

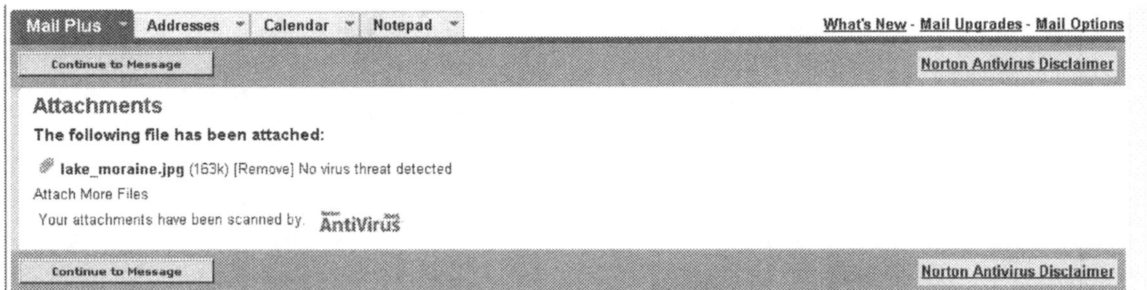

File successfully attached message box

The picture is ready to go, the message is written and addressed. Click the "Continue to Message" button, and send the message!

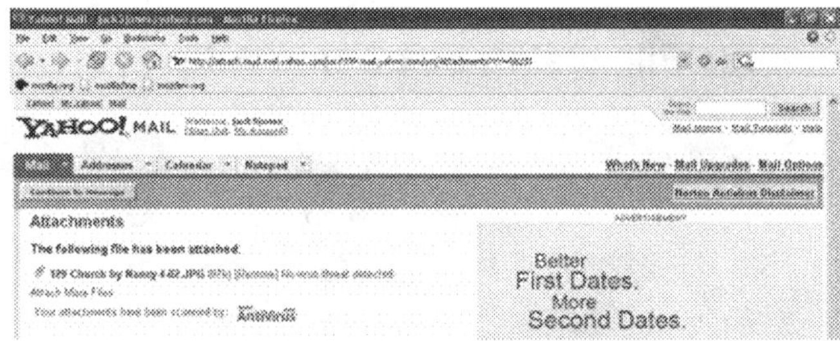

You have successfully attached things to your email message

Using folders to keep special messages.

Folders are places to put things that you wish to save or places you might look when you want to find something. Yahoo has four standard *mail folders* … In, sent, draft, and trash. The **In** folder's function is easy to understand … this is where your new messages are displayed. The **Sent** folder is used to hold messages that you send and want to keep a record of. The **Draft** folder may seem confusing … it is used to store emails that you haven't finished and want to keep until you are ready to finish them. The **Trash** folder is the place that Yahoo! sends messages you have deleted. The **Trash** folder is *emptied* every time you sign out.

Here is how to have Yahoo! make up special folders for you to use.

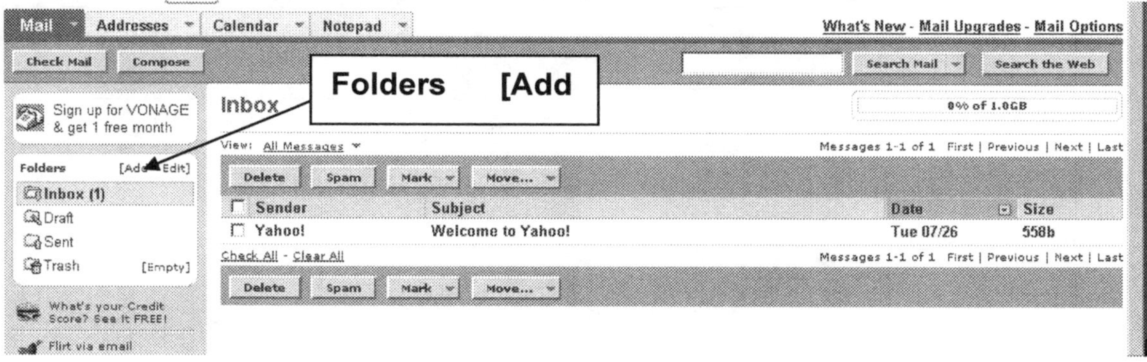

Add a Folder procedure

	Keyboard	Mouse
1.	**Tab** to **Folders** **[Add** and **Enter↵**	Click on **Folders** … **[Add**
2.	Type in the **Folder Name** and **Enter↵**	Type in the **Folder Name** and **Enter↵**

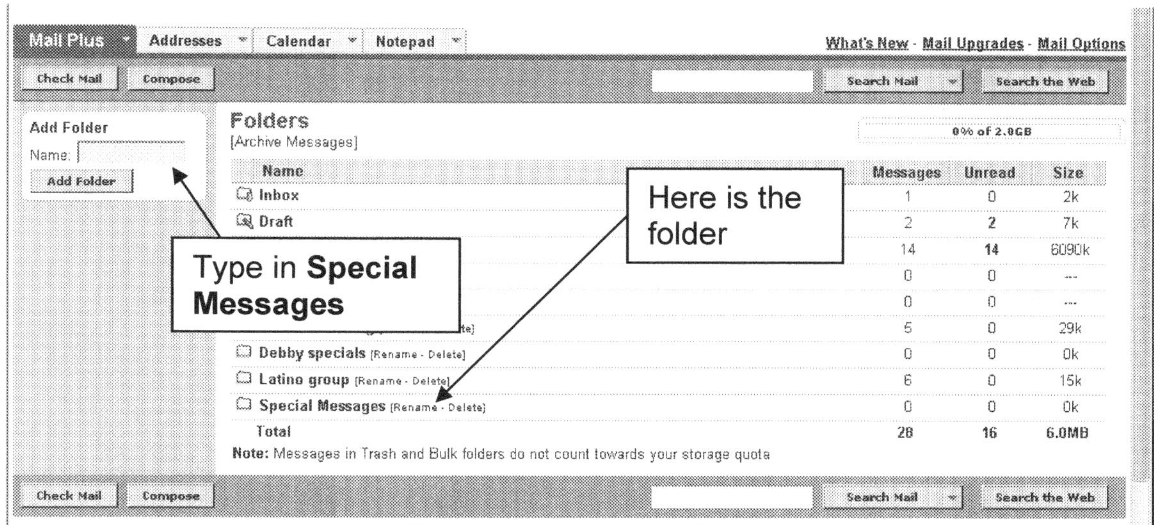

Setting up a new folder

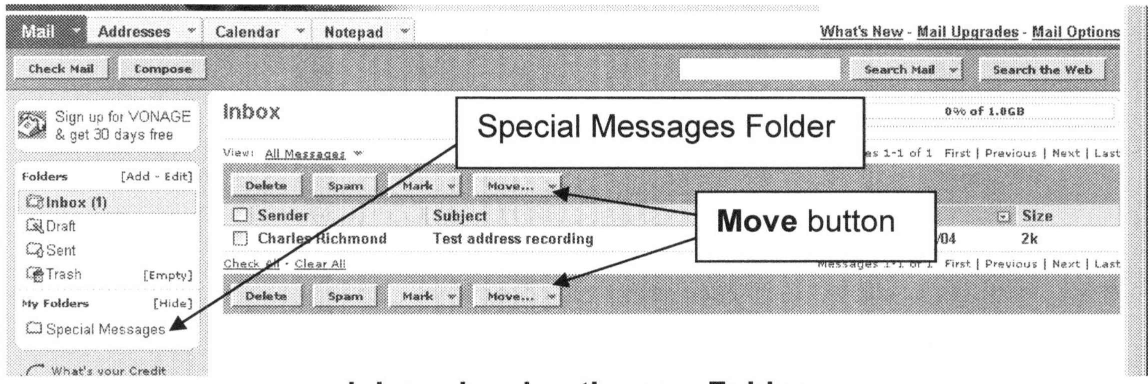

Inbox showing the new Folder

Both the **Inbox** and the **Reader** allow you to move a message to any of the **folders.**

The **Compose, Reply,** and **Forward** screens allow you to save a copy of the current message in the **Sent messages** and **Drafts** folder.

Options are available that do such things as:

- Allow you to change your password ... something you should do several times a year to keep your files secure.
- Change your secret question that substitutes for your password when you forget it.
- You can keep annoying emails from taking up your time by telling Yahoo! to block them.
- You can direct incoming mail into special folders so you only have to check a short list of messages if you have many mailings coming to you.
- You can have Yahoo! check your mail at other locations such as your ISP when you are out of town.
- You can create a special signature with ASCII pictures and other special items . This permits you to tell Yahoo! to attach the signature to your message when you wish it to do so.

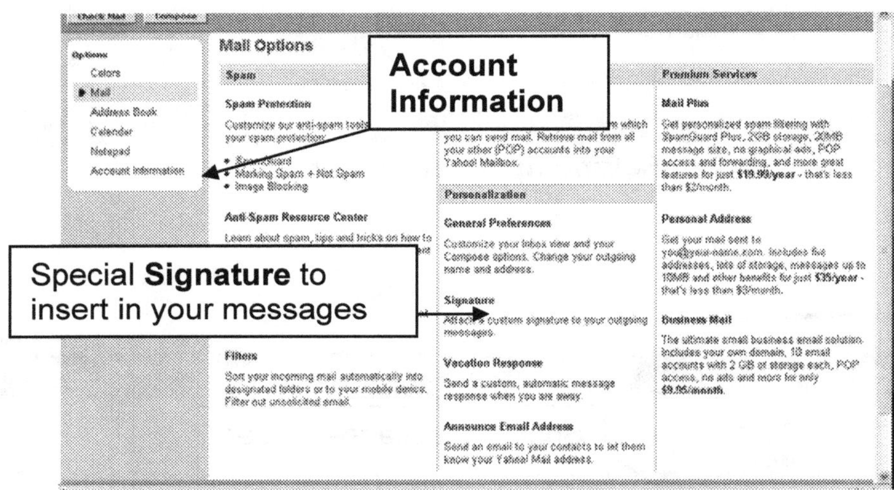

Options available with Yahoo! mail

It's a good idea to change your password several times a year.

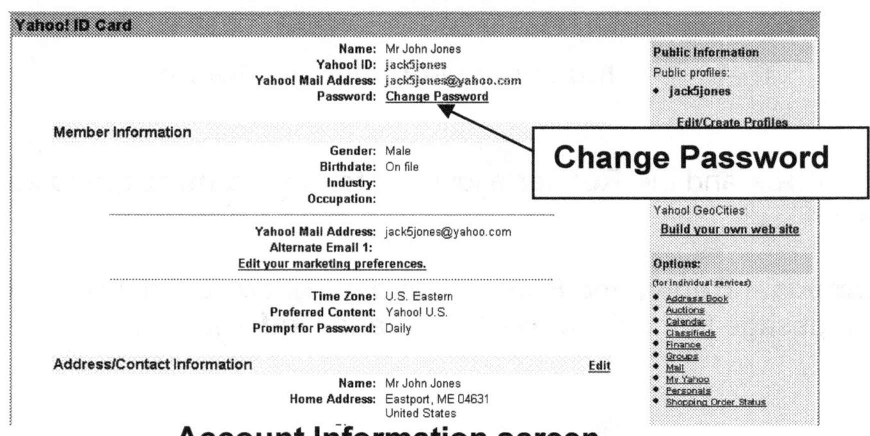

Account Information screen

Set up a signature to go on all your messages. The form allows you to have a signature that is 7 lines long. Such a size would allow you to draw a picture using ASCII characters. These sometimes take up much room.

Check out: http://users.inetw.net/~mullen/ascii.htm

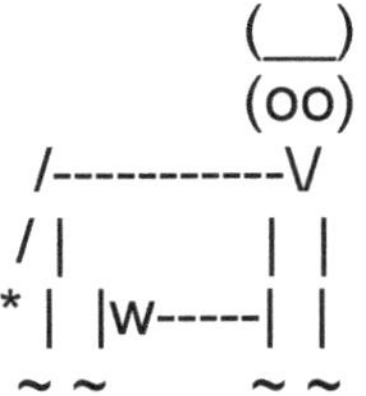

Once you do a masterpiece like this you won't want to do it many times more but you may want it as part of your signature.

Using Browsers

Lesson 5

Email, now Browsing the Web.

The World Wide Web (WWW) is the way we get information electronically from most places on the Earth. Early work on the Internet was quite confusing and difficult. Connecting one computer to another and sending information from one to another was well handled by the network. However, locating something stored was made difficult because location methods differed from computer system to computer system.

By incorporating different protocols … telnet to connect computers, gopher to organize and direct through the use of hypertext, file transport protocol (FTP) to insure complete and accurate transmission, and wide area information servers (WAIS) … Tim Berners-Lee and Robert Cailliau of CERN Laboratories, Switzerland developed addressing standards and a document coding method that could be used by the many diverse systems throughout the world. What you see on your computer screen is much different from what comes to you over the WWW via the Internet.

Browsing is the name that we use to describe our activities as we go about looking at or searching for things on the web. Information in the forms of text, pictures, or sound can be looked at. It's like being in a store, museum, or library and going about checking this and that until satisfied for the moment. Most of us have a pretty good idea about what we want to find. This lesson will start you on your way. It will be up to you to figure out what you want to do next.

Starting your Browser session.

I assume that you have an icon (a picture) on the "desktop" for the browser program that you want to use.

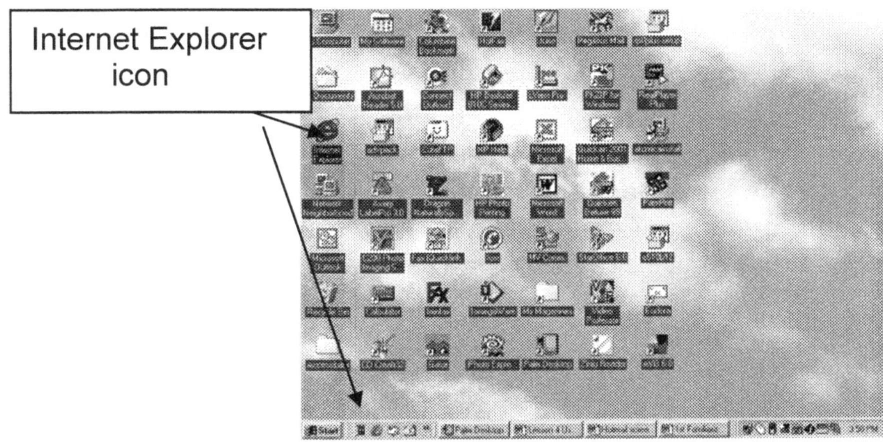

"Desktop" opening screen

Keyboard		Mouse
1.	Click anywhere on your "**desktop**"	Click **Internet Explorer** Icon twice
2.	Move the highlight around with the **arrow keys** until you highlight **Internet Explorer** or see **page 49**	
3.	**Enter↵**	

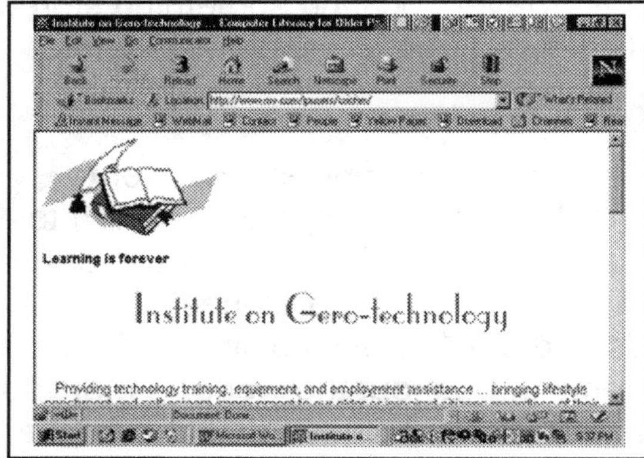

Mozilla/Firefox

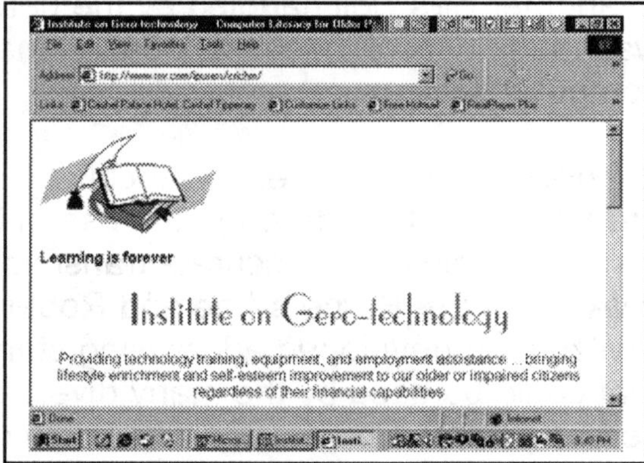

Internet Explorer

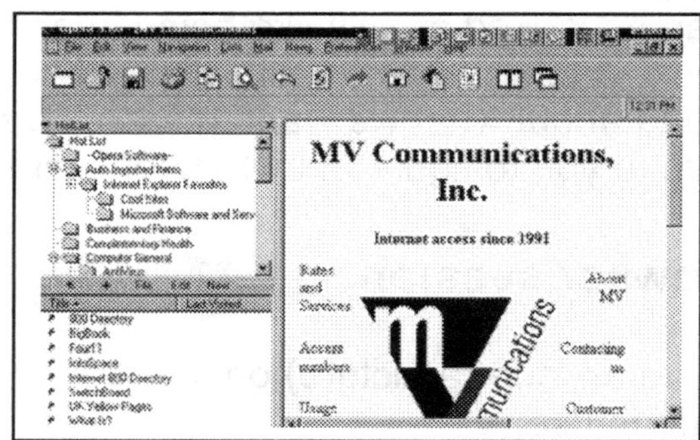

Opera

As you can see, from these illustrations each Browser has pretty much the same display. Each one has some feature to distinguish it from the others. Mozilla/Firefox has a very complex system for making many operations available. Opera (developed in Norway) is perhaps the fastest because it is not overloaded with special features. For instance, Opera does not have built in email but instead suggests you use one of the available email "clients". It does feature a listing of places to go.

Opera's Hotlist is displayed by **dragging** (placing the mouse pointer at a location shown above and when the pointer becomes a double line, holding down the left mouse button while moving the pointer) it open when you want to use it and by dragging it closed to make more room on the main screen when it is no longer wanted.

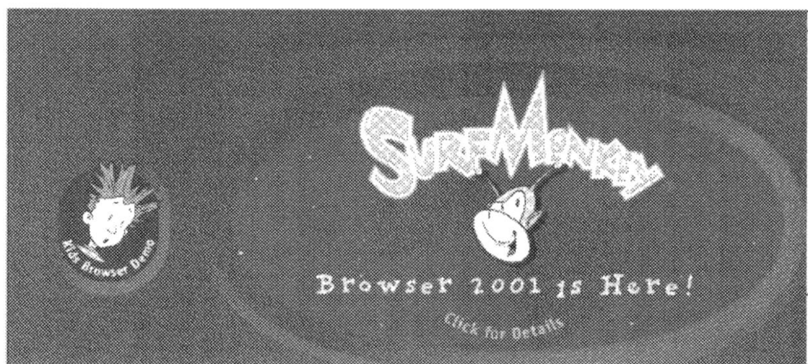

Surf Monkey

Surf Monkey is a program which works with your browser. It limits children's ability to cruise any place on the web. Its permitted sites are specially screened for use by young people. As you can see from the Surf Monkey screen above, its design is one that is friendly to children. It uses a password protected toggle switch to turn it off and on.

American Library Association has a page called, "Great Web Sites for Kids." You can visit it and use its classified listing of safe places for children to go. There are many other sites that offer child safe web addresses. But, many of these are sponsored by religious organizations.

Set up your own home page.

When you first turn your browser on, it displays what is called a home page. I like to use the list that I put together for the Institute on Gero-technology because it contains more than 600 places you can go to on the Web that appeal to older people. You may prefer to have some commercial site for your home page. You may want to start at Ebay for its auctions, Barnes & Noble for books, or the Smithsonian for historical information. You will find the starting place easy to get back to in case you get lost in cyber space and want to return to familiar territory. Click the "Home" button with your mouse or press **Alt/Home** on your keyboard to get there.

Make Gero-tech's Interesting Places your home page

Set up a personal homepage using Internet Explorer

Keyboard		Mouse
1.	**Alt/D**	Click **Address** box
2.	Type in **Gero-tech.org**	Type in **Gero-tech.org**
3.	**Enter**	Click **Go**

After the Gero-tech home page has finished "loading" (the next to the bottom line will say "Done")

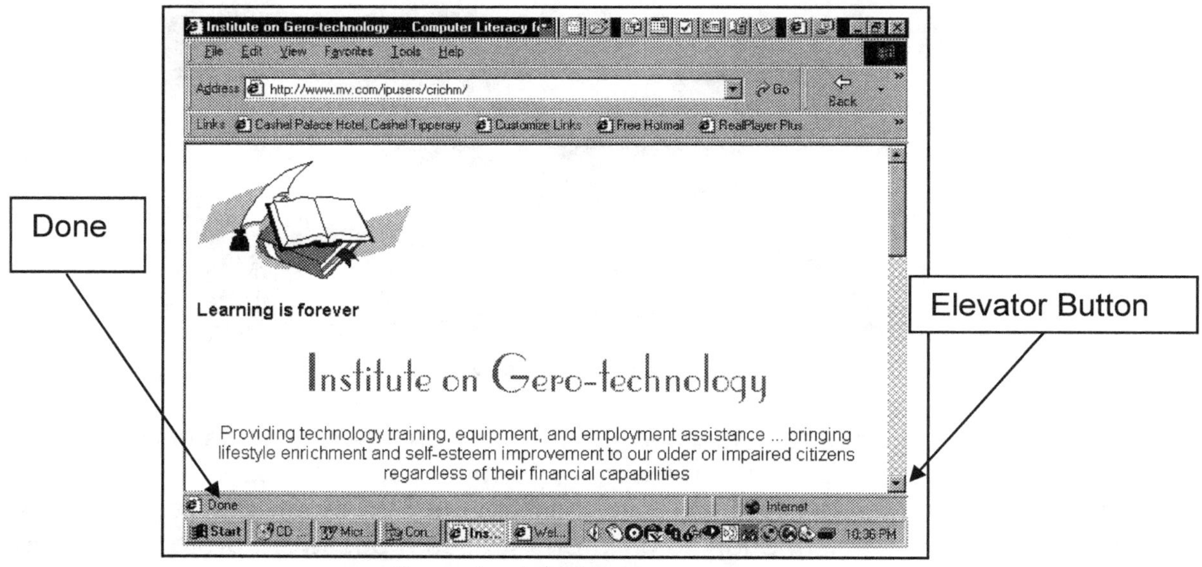

Gero-tech's Homepage

Set up Gero-tech's Interesting Places as your home page

	Keyboard	Mouse
4.	**Tab** to **Interesting Places** and **Enter**	Click **Interesting Places**
5.	**Alt/T**	Click **Tools**
6.	**O**	Click **Internet Options**
7.	**Alt/C**	Click **Use Current** button
8.	**Enter**	Click **OK**

Let's look at something on the Web ...

Gero-tech's **Interesting Places** list can be a good place to start. It is categorized to help you find things more easily. These categories are:

American Indians	Medical Resources	Software
Business & Finance	Older Americans	Sports
Government	Periodicals, Books, Publ.	Travel
K-12 Education	Schools & Colleges	Tutorials & Instruction
Libraries & Museums	Search Engines & Lists	TV & Radio Stations

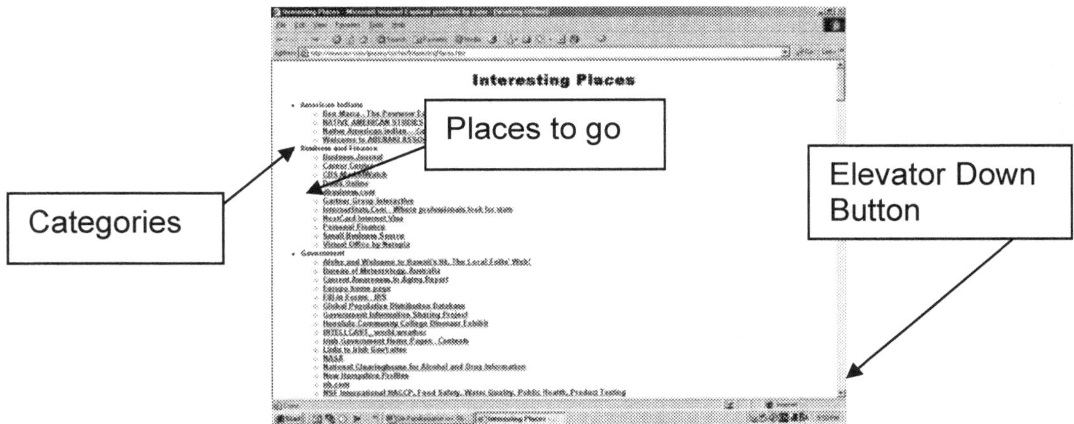

Now look at the list of places to go and pick a site to visit

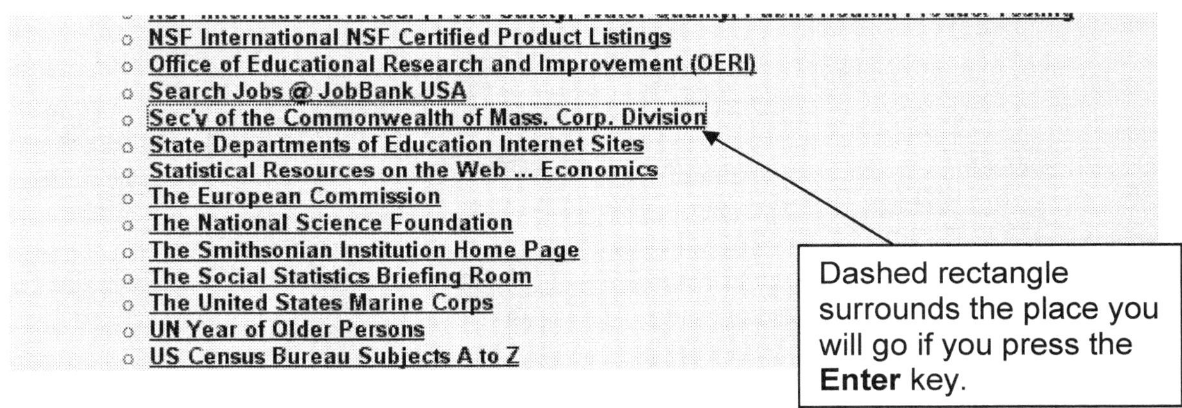

Interesting Places screen with rectangle surrounding a place to go

	Keyboard	Mouse
1.	**Tab** until you come to **RxList** it is in the **Medical Resources** Category … you can tell where you are because a blue colored topic is surrounded by a dashed rectangle. (It takes a lot of pushes)	Use the **Elevator** down button until you see **Medical Resources**
2.	**Enter**↵	Continue with the **Elevator** until you see **RxList**
3.		Click **RxList** (the pointer will turn into a hand with a finger pointing up when it is in the correct place)

I will to walk you through steps you can take to get the most information from sites you visit. I have chosen medications because they are very important to older people. The available information is excellent and quite complete. It is up to you to check out each of the site's options that seem to have any relevance to your interests. I will try to show you how to do this.

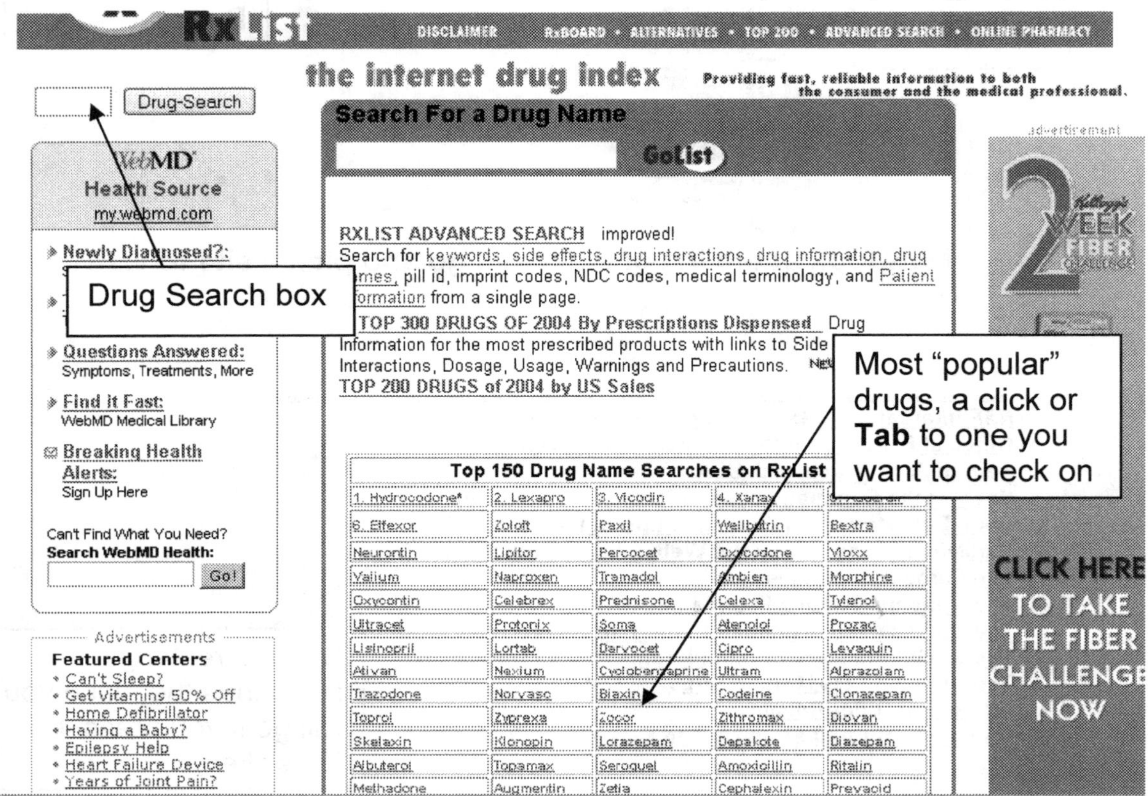

Rx List Homepage

Look for a drug

	Keyboard	Mouse
1.	**Tab** about 13 times until the cursor is in the rectangle to the left of the **Drug Search** button	Click in **Drug Search** box
2.	Type in the name of a drug use **Zocor** for this demonstration	Type in the name of a drug use **Zocor** for this demonstration or pick it from the "popular" list.
3.	**Enter↵**	Click the **Drug Search** button
5.	Find your specific drug from the list that appears on the screen … use **Page Dn** or **Down Arrow**	Find your specific drug from the list that appears on the screen … use your mouse pointer to get there
5.	**Enter↵**	Click the **Name** you want

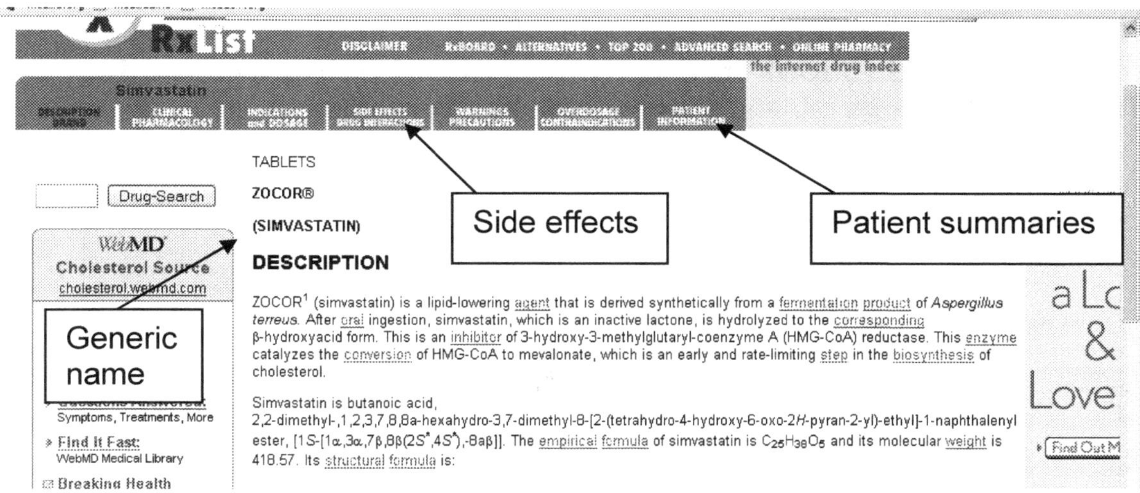

Drug Description

This first information gives you a good description of the drug. What it is. What it looks like and how you take it. It does not describe the shape or color of the different concentrations of the several dosage sizes.

Now Tab & Enter or click on the Side Effects tab to find out things to be careful about when taking this drug

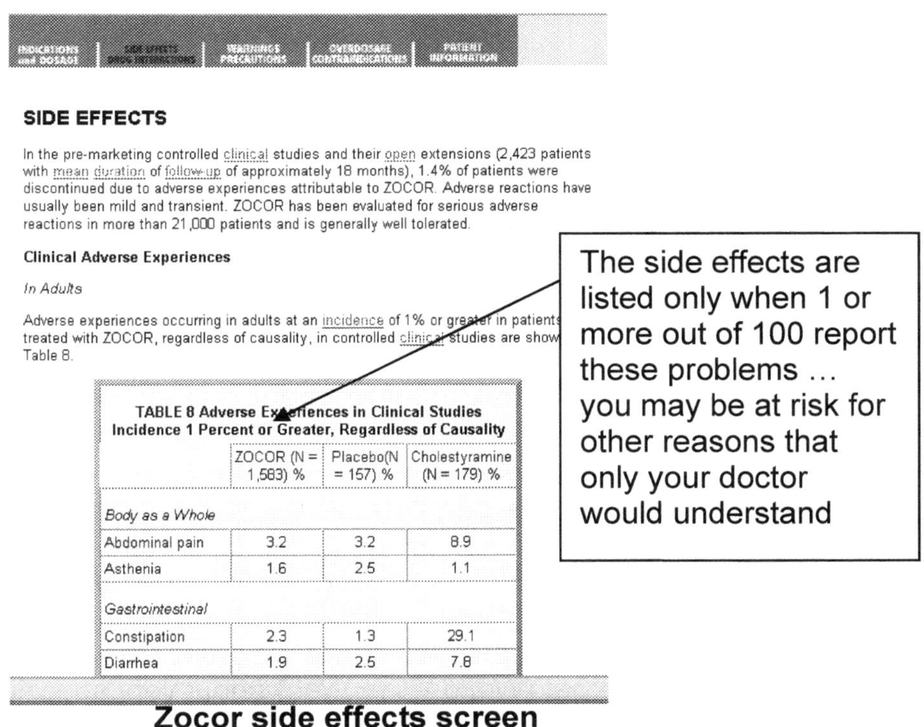

TABLE 8 Adverse Experiences in Clinical Studies Incidence 1 Percent or Greater, Regardless of Causality

	ZOCOR (N = 1,583) %	Placebo(N = 157) %	Cholestyramine (N = 179) %
Body as a Whole			
Abdominal pain	3.2	3.2	8.9
Asthenia	1.6	2.5	1.1
Gastrointestinal			
Constipation	2.3	1.3	29.1
Diarrhea	1.9	2.5	7.8

Zocor side effects screen

Now that you have some idea about the possible side effects, it might be good to look into warnings about using this medicine.

Tab to the **Warnings** tab and **Enter** or click the **Warnings** tab.

Myopathy/Rhabdomyolysis

Simvastatin, like other inhibitors of HMG-CoA reductase, occasionally causes myopath manifested as muscle pain, tenderness or weakness with creatine kinase (CK) above 10X the upper limit of normal (ULN). Myopathy sometimes takes the form of rhabdomyolysis with or without acute renal failure secondary to myoglobinuria, and rare fatalities have occurred. The risk of myopathy is increased by high levels of HMG-CoA reductase inhibitory activity in plasma.

- **The risk of myopathy/rhabdomyolysis is increased by concomitant use of simvastatin with the following:**

Potent inhibitors of CYP3A4 : **Cyclosporine, itraconazole, ketoconazole, erythromycin, clarithromycin, telithromycin, HIV protease inhibitors, nefazodone, or large quantities of grapefruit juice (>1 quart daily), particularly with higher doses of simvastatin** (see below; CLINICAL PHARMACOLOGY, *Pharmacokinetics*; PRECAUTIONS, ***Drug Interactions***, *CYP3A4 Interactions*).

Other drugs : **Gemfibrozil particularly with higher doses of simvastatin** (see below; PRECAUTIONS, ***Drug Interactions***, *Interactions with lipid-lowering drugs that can cause myopathy when given alone*; DOSAGE AND ADMINISTRATION).

Other lipid-lowering drugs (other fibrates or ≥1 g/day of niacin) that can cause myopathy when given alone (see below; PRECAUTIONS, ***Drug Interactions***, *Interactions with lipid-lowering drugs that can cause myopathy when given alone*).

Danazol particularly with higher doses of simvastatin (see below; PRECAUTIONS, ***Drug Interactions***, *Other drug interactions*).

Amiodarone or verapamil with higher doses of simvastatin (see below; PRECAUTIONS, ***Drug Interactions***, *Other drug interactions*). In an ongoing clinical trial, myopathy has been reported in 6% of patients receiving simvastatin 80 mg and amiodarone. In an analysis of clinical trials involving 25,248 patients treated with simvastatin 20 to 80 mg, the incidence of myopathy was higher in patients receiving verapamil and simvastatin (4/635; 0.63%) than in patients taking simvastatin without a calcium channel blocker (13/21,224; 0.061%).

- **The risk of myopathy/rhabdomyolysis is dose related.** The incidence in clinical trials, in which patients were carefully monitored and some interacting drugs were excluded, has been approximately 0.02% at 20 mg, 0.07% at 40 mg and 0.3% at 80 mg.

Consequently

1. Use of simvastatin concomitantly with itraconazole, ketoconazole, erythromycin, clarithromycin, telithromycin, HIV protease inhibitors, nefazodone, or large quantities of grapefruit juice (>1 quart daily) should be avoided. If treatment with itraconazole, ketoconazole, erythromycin, clarithromycin, or telithromycin is unavoidable, therapy with simvastatin should be suspended during the course of treatment. Concomitant use with other medicines labeled as having a potent inhibitory effect on CYP3A4 at therapeutic doses should be avoided unless the benefits of combined therapy outweigh the increased risk.

2. The dose of simvastatin should not exceed 10 mg daily in patients receiving concomitant medication with gemfibrozil. The combined use of simvastatin with gemfibrozil should be avoided, unless the benefits are likely to outweigh the increased risks of this drug combination. Caution should be used when prescribing other lipid-lowering drugs (other fibrates or lipid-lowering doses (≥1 g/day) of niacin) with simvastatin, as these agents can cause myopathy when given alone. **The benefit of further alterations in lipid levels by the combined use of simvastatin with**

Warnings about Zocor

PATIENT INFORMATION

Patients should be advised about substances they should not take concomitantly with simvastatin and be advised to report promptly unexplained muscle pain, tenderness, or weakness (see list below and WARNINGS, *Myopathy/Rhabdomyolysis*). Patients should also be advised to inform other physicians prescribing a new medication that they are taking ZOCOR.

Patient Information about taking Zocor

Now try looking up one of your own medicines.

See if **RxList** tells you something that either your doctor or your pharmacist has not told you about drugs you are taking.

By this time you must be impressed about the great amount of information that is available on the Internet (World Wide Web) about very specific things. But, unless you were adventuresome you probably missed the fact that as you moved your mouse pointer across the text that it would often turn from a pointer to a hand with its index finger pointed upward. If you remember the first lessons about email, you may recall that I mentioned the changes that happened to the mouse pointer as it moves across a place where you can have the computer go to a different page or location. You also may remember that I told you to look particularly at words or groups of words that were blue in color and were underlined. Many times these words or groups could cause the mouse pointer to change its appearance to a hand and that if while the pointer is on such a location and the hand is visible, you may press the left hand mouse button and cause the computer to go to a place that contains information that the "transfer spot" offers.

This reference method was prevalent in an academic paper on Information Retrieval written by C. J. van Rijsbergen (1975). He was trying to put together a book on the progress that the Information Retrieval community was making throughout the world. This "transfer" application was adopted by the people at CERN Laboratory in Switzerland as part of its revolutionary WWW protocol.

Go backward and forward while using your browser.

Before you go on to the next part of this lesson take some time to go back and check out a few of the references that you found in the material about prescription drugs you use. Point to them, click and see what comes up. Then, go back to the page you found the transfer points on and try another. (**Alt/left arrow key** or the **Back button** near the top of the Internet Explorer screen).

The more you use the Internet, the more places you find interesting … sometimes you don't want to forget how to get back there!

If you feel that you might like to check this site again … save it to a place on your computer that creates a list that works just like the Institute's Interesting Places list.

On Internet Explorer, this list is called the "Favorites" list. If you want to get back to the RxList home page, you can save its address in your "Favorites" list. If it is some special bit of information that you wish to refer to again, then you want to save the address for this bit of information. Here is how easy it is to do:

Save the address of a Favorite Internet place

	Keyboard	Mouse
1.	Make sure you are looking at the site you want to get back to and **Ctrl/D**	Make sure you are looking at the site you want to get back to, place the **Mouse pointer** on **Favorites** menu button and click it
2.	**Alt/A** and **Enter**	Click **Add to Favorites…**
3.	**O**	Click **New Folder**

	Keyboard	Mouse
4.	**Alt/C**	Click **Create Folder** button
5.	Type in a name **Ancient Plants** for the new folder to put the **Old Trees** address in	Type in a name **Ancient Plants** for the new folder to put the **Old Trees** address in
6.	**Enter**	Click **OK**
7.	**Up Arrow** to **A World Community of Old Trees**	Click **OK**
8.	**Alt/M**	
9.	**Down Arrow** to **Ancient Plants** folder and **Enter**	

Favorites Menu

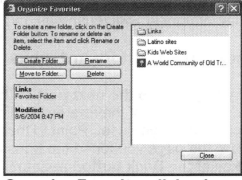

Organize Favorites dialog box

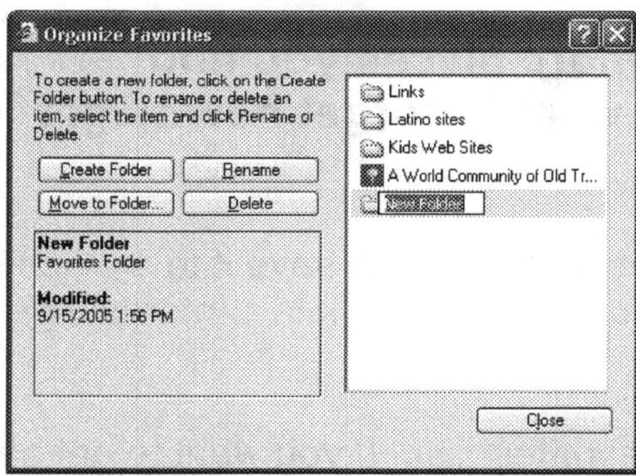

Ready for the Folder Name

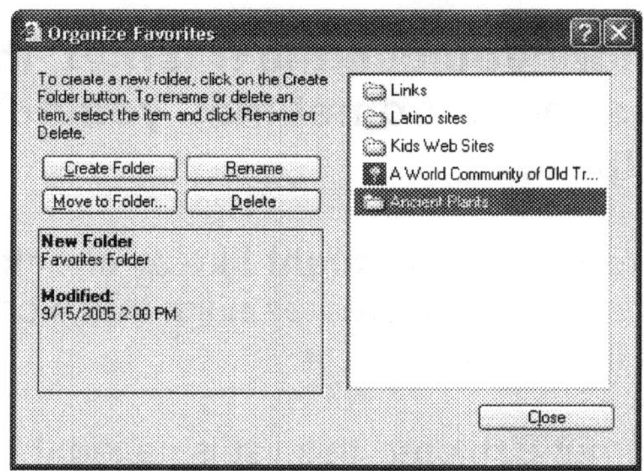

Folder is ready for the new Address

Ancient Plants folder is **Highlighted** now:
Enter or Click **OK**

The Internet is overflowing with famous and interesting exhibits in museums.

Just about every country in the world is proud of its heritage and has interesting artifacts on display. There may be many displays that you would like a picture of for your home. Here is how you can get such pictures.
Mona Lisa is on display at the Louvre in Paris, surely it is so famous that the French want to show it off. I will take you there and help you get a copy for yourself.

Since you are using the Institute's **Interesting Places** as your home page and since you are using this list as a source of addresses to go to, you will need to return to your home page to find the Louvre's Internet address.

Here is a way to give a command to your browser to go to your home page.

Press **Alt/Home** on your keyboard or click the **Home** button in the toolbar.

If you have set Gero-tech's Interesting Places as your homepage, you will find it easy to perform the rest of the exercises in this lesson. If you didn't do this, then you should do it now ... follow the directions given on **pages 87 & 88**.

Now we look for a place where Mona Lisa might be found.
Under the heading of **Libraries and Museums** you will find:
Paris Pages Musée du Louvre

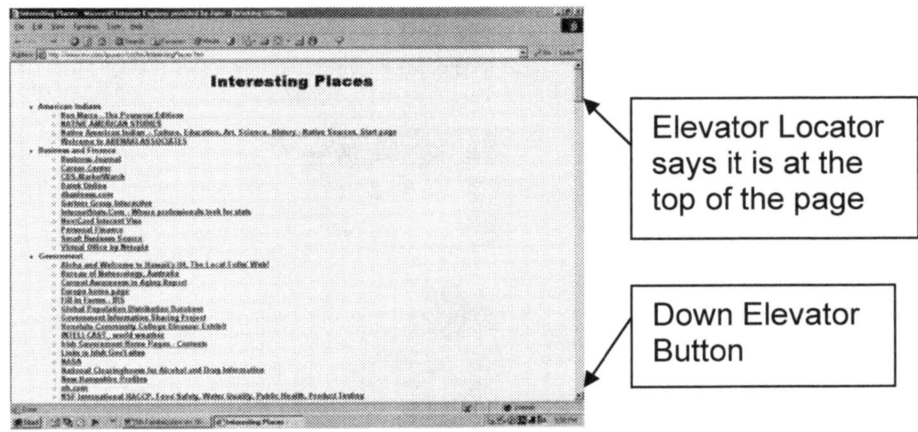

Gero-tech's Interesting Places List

Finding Mona Lisa

	Keyboard	Mouse
1.	**Page Dn** until you come to the **Libraries and Museums** heading	Click the **Elevator Down Button** until **Libraries and Museums** heading, then **Paris Pages Musée du Louvre** appears
2.	Use the **Down Arrow** until you come to **Paris Pages Musée du Louvre**	Click **Paris Pages Musée du Louvre**
3.	**Enter↵**	

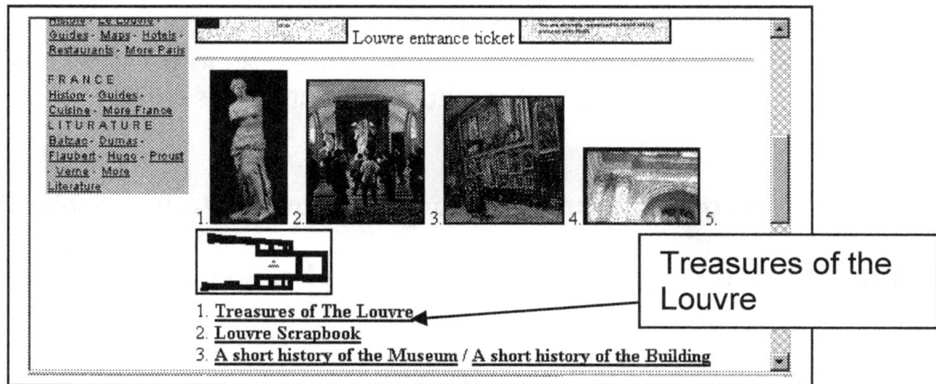

Musée du Louvre home page

These are just the "teaser" lines that give hints about what you can see. We'll have to look farther.

	Keyboard	Mouse
1.	**Tab** several times until <u>**Treasures of the Louvre**</u> is surrounded by dashes	Click <u>**Treasures of the Louvre**</u>
2.	**Enter↵**	

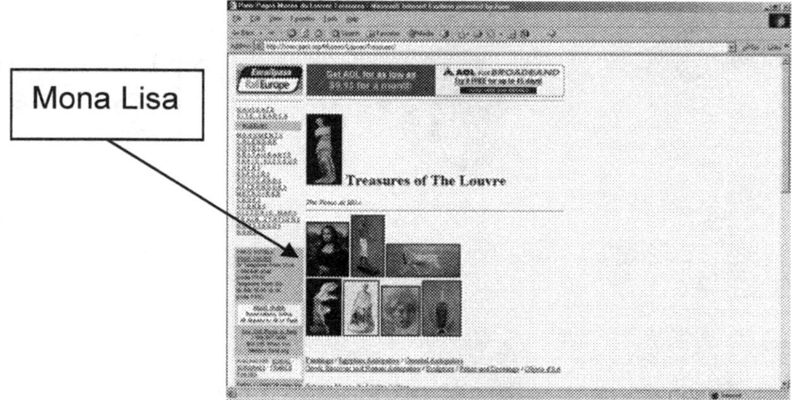

Treasures of the Louvre

Copy the Mona Lisa procedure

	Keyboard	Mouse
1.	**Shift/Tab** to **Pictures/** then press **Enter**	Click the **picture** of **Mona Lisa**
2.	**Shift/Tab** until you see **/Treasures/gifs/Mona_Lisa.html** appear in the bottom left hand corner of your screen … press **Enter**	Click on the larger **picture**
3.	Right click **Mona Lisa**	Right click **Mona Lisa**
4.	**Down Arrow** to **Copy** and **Enter**	Click **Copy Image**

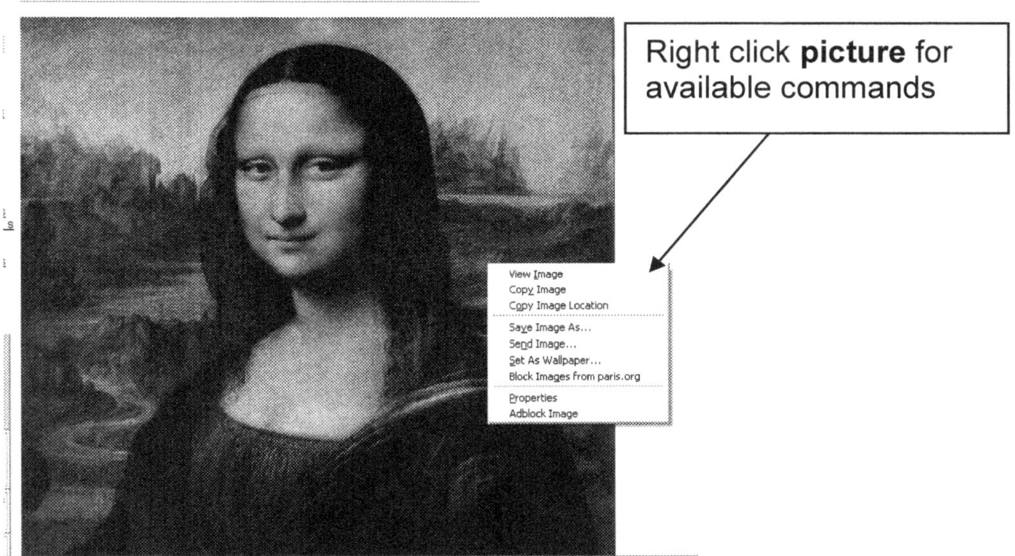

Mona Lisa ready to bring home

We need a place to put it so we can work with it …

- enlarge it or make it smaller
- tell the computer what to call it
- tell the computer where to put it

Get a Word Document to put it on

	Keyboard	Mouse
1.	Start **Microsoft®Word** (not **WordPad**)	Start **Microsoft®Word** (not **WordPad**)
2.	**Ctrl/N**	Click **New Document** button

	Keyboard	Mouse
3.	Name the new document **Mona Lisa picture** and tell the computer where to put it **SaveAs** to your personal file … see page 22	Name the new document **Mona Lisa picture** and tell the computer where to put it **SaveAs** to your personal file … see page 22
4.	**Ctrl/V**	Click **Paste** button

Now you have captured the picture and placed it on a Word document. This will allow you to make some changes to the picture, print it, and save it in your permanent files.

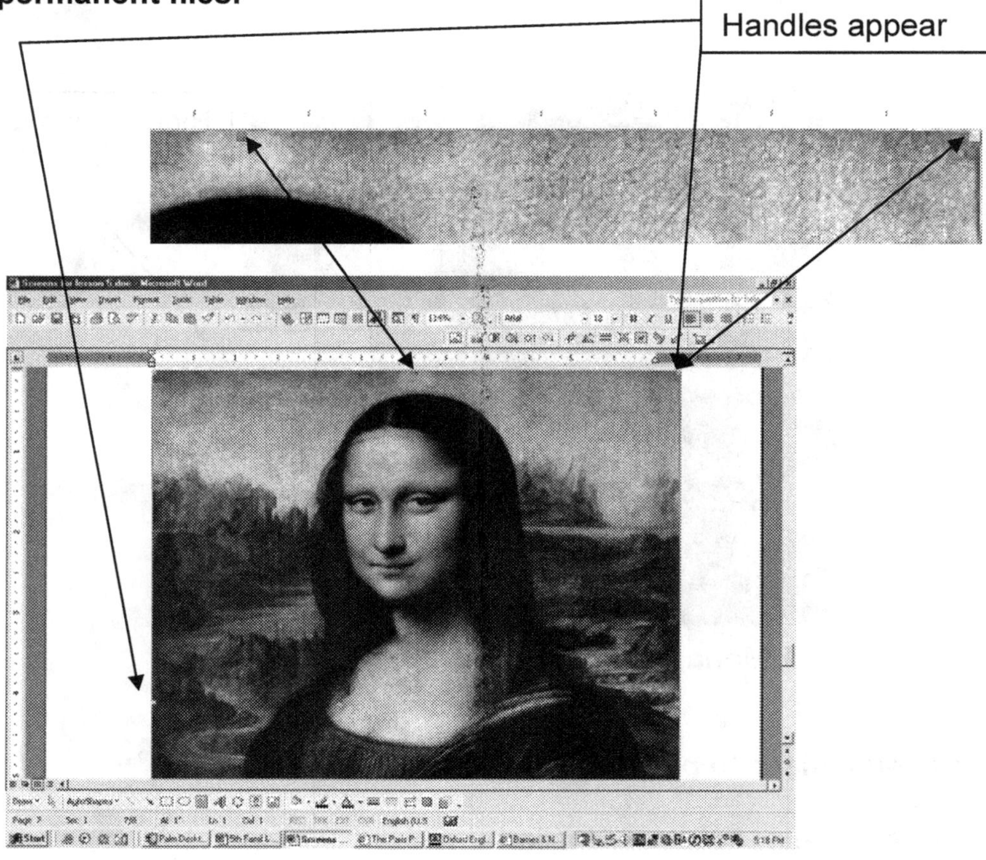

Mona Lisa ready to resize

Make it bigger so it will fill the entire sheet of paper when it is printed.

Change picture size procedure

	Keyboard	Mouse
1.		Put **Mouse Pointer** somewhere in the picture and Click

Keyboard		Mouse
2.		Little square "handles" appear on the edges of the picture. You can use these to change the size of the picture. If you put your pointer on one of the corner handles (it turns to a double headed arrow) and hold the left mouse button down and move the pointer away from the picture it will get larger. If you want it smaller, just move the pointer into the picture.
3.		Once you have the picture the size you want it, you can print it or save it.

Some things for you to find on your own.

- Go to the **Michigan Electronic Library – Internet ...**
  a. **Alt/Home** or Click

  b. Go to **Libraries and Museums** where you will find **Michigan Electronic Library – Internet** either **Tab** to it and **Enter** or Click on it …

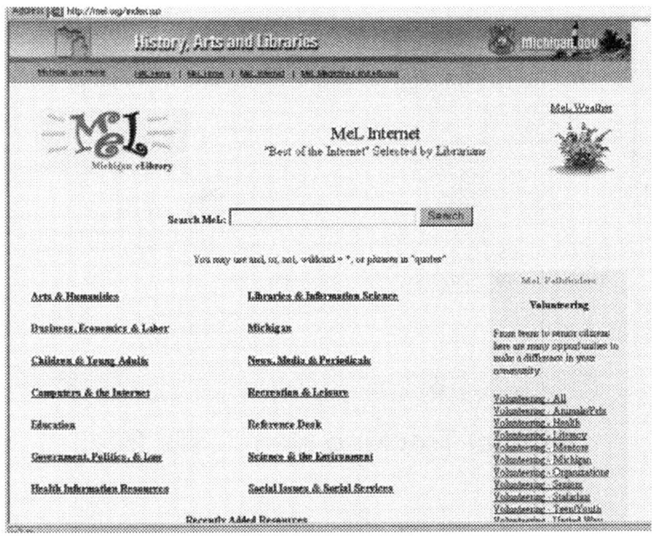

From here on choose a topic
and follow it until you find something that interests you

The page from “**Interesting Places**” … your homepage leads you to an Error page for **MEL**. However, if you click on **MEL Internet** it will take you to a listing that will then take you to **Science & the Environment**. That will lead you to another page which has a destination for **Weather**. From the **Weather** transfer point you get to a large list which in turn gets you to Atlanta Tropical Weather Center .

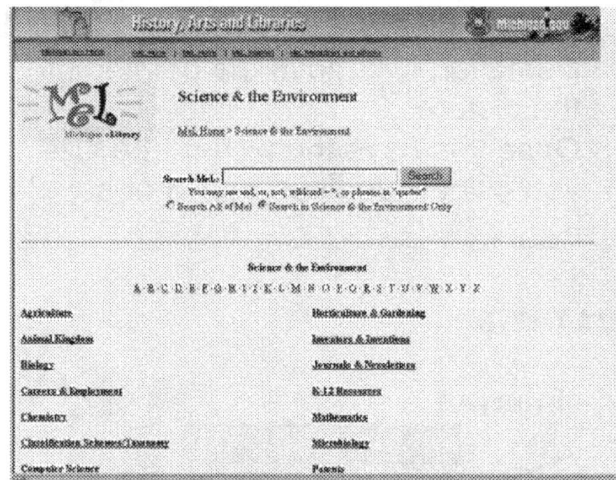

Science & Environment page

Atlanta Tropical Weather Center

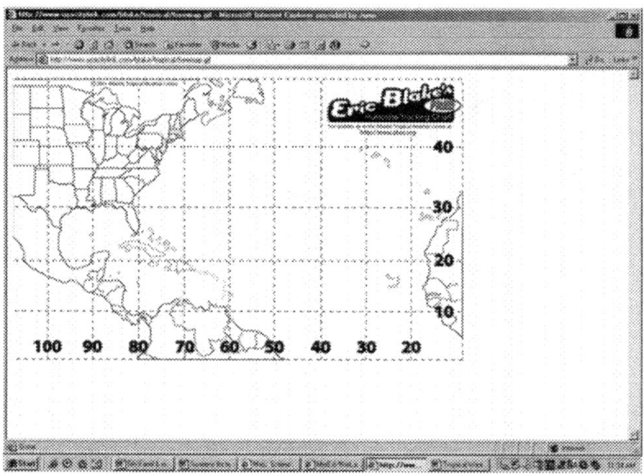

Official Tracking Map … it’s free!

You might want to make your own copy of this one by putting it onto a **Microsoft® Word** document, putting it on a page that is “landscape” oriented, and pulling it out to make it larger to better fit the sheet … you did something like this when you went to the Louvre Museum … see **page 97** for how we worked with the **Mona Lisa**.

Here are some more places to find.

- Find the **Copenhagen to Oslo** train schedule (It's on your home page … Gero-tech Interesting Places under Travel).
    - Can you find a map of Oslo, check the room rates in hotels, and check the entertainment?

Go to **The Ultimate Collection of Winsock Software** (It's on your home page … Gero-tech Interesting Places under Software … **Alt/Home**) and check its software archives.

- Find some email programs … the computer term is *email client.*

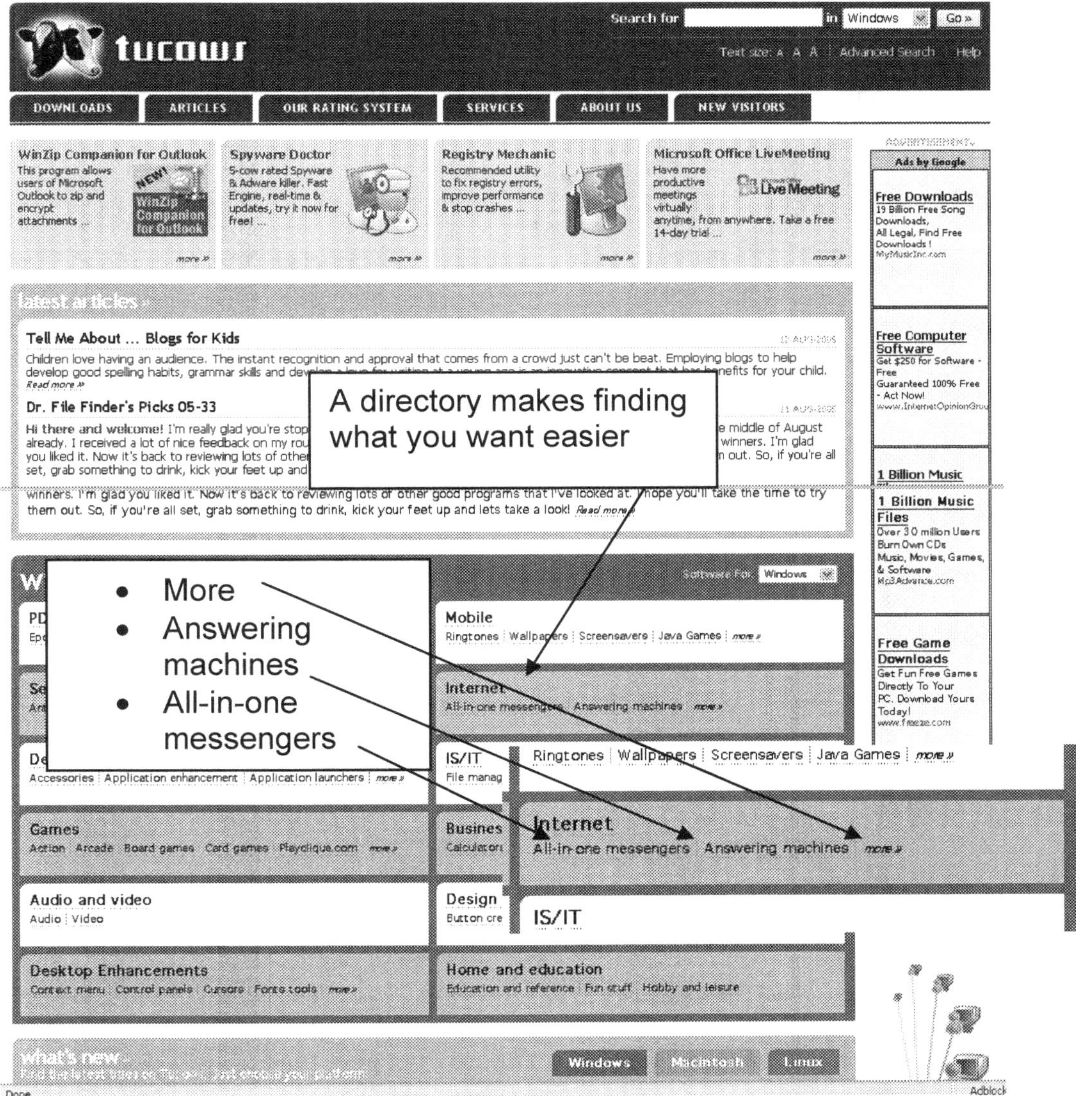

Tucows homepage

Now that you are learning about the Internet perhaps it would be well to look at what **Tucows** considers useful for helping you work with it better. Click in the **Internet** box at a point where your **Mouse pointer** turns into a **hand with its index finger pointing upward**.

Point and click on **More»**

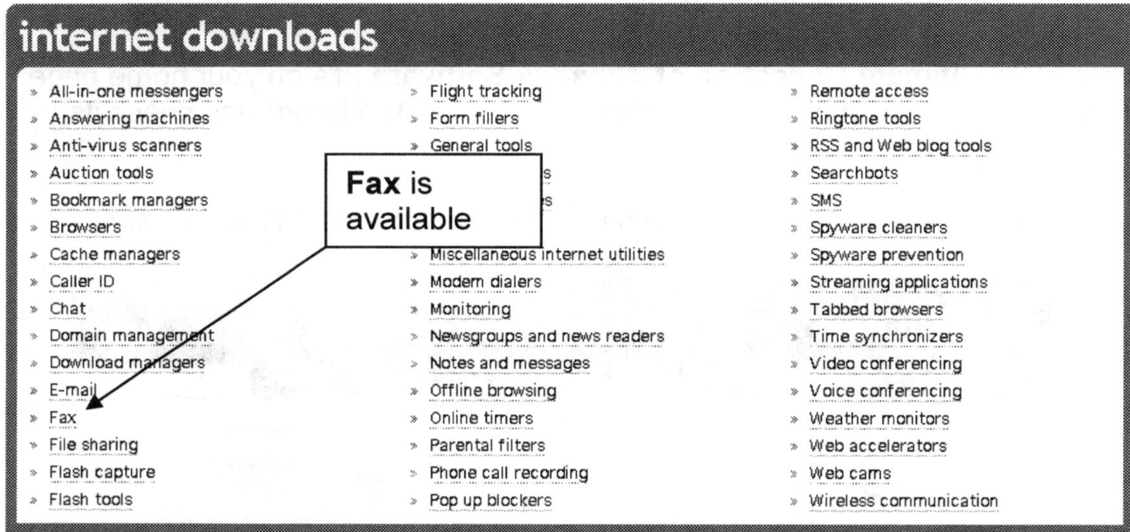

More» display showing choices that are available

It's worth a try if only to see if you like it.

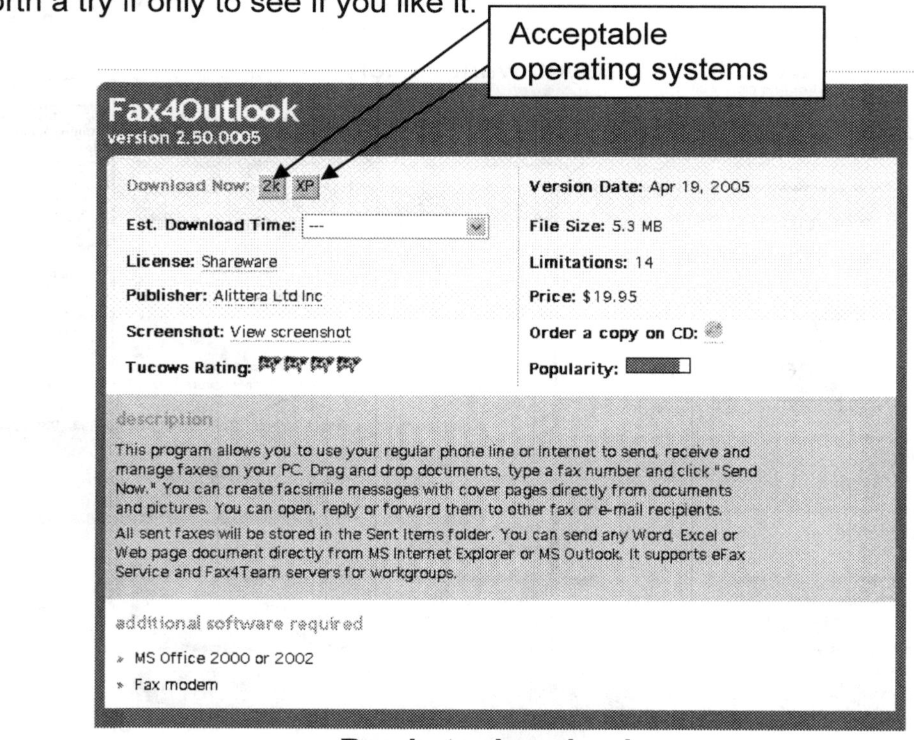

Ready to download

Download procedure for Fax4Outlook

One problem with this program is that it will only work with **Windows 2000** or **Windows XP**. If you have one of the older operating systems, this program will not work. If you have one of the **acceptable operating systems**,

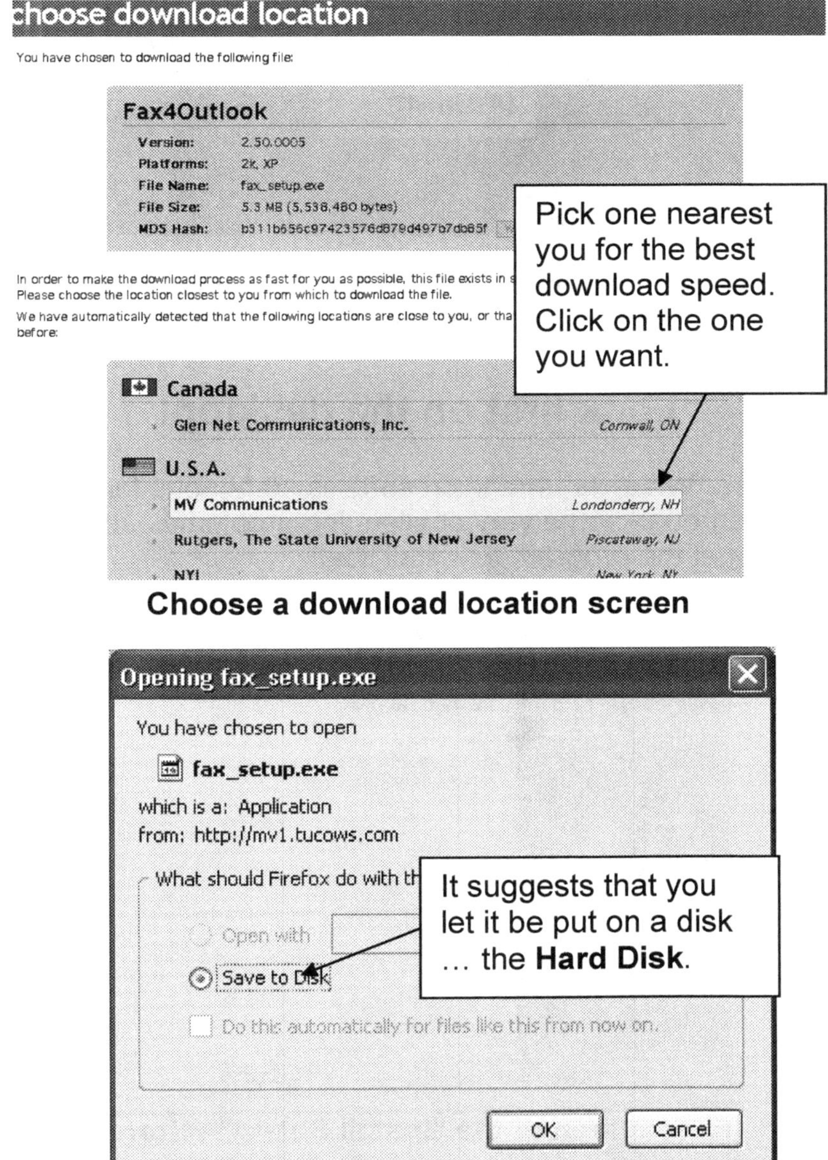

Choose a download location screen

Before the download starts it needs to know what you want to do with the program

Much of the time it is best to take the computer's suggestion so you would just click the **OK** button.

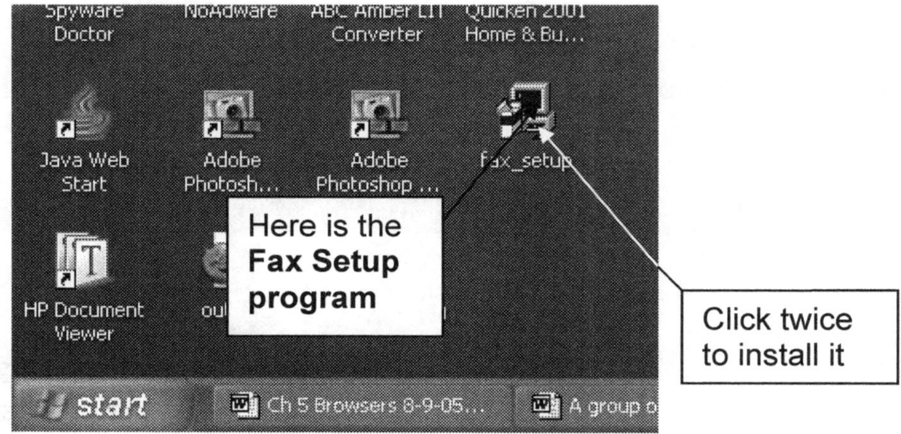

Sometimes you don't get a choice of where it will be put … when that happens,

Look first on the desktop!

This is one of those "**Wizards**" that Microsoft® is so famous for because they are made to help you through some very challenging problems. Just keep clicking or pressing **Enter** to get the program to install itself.

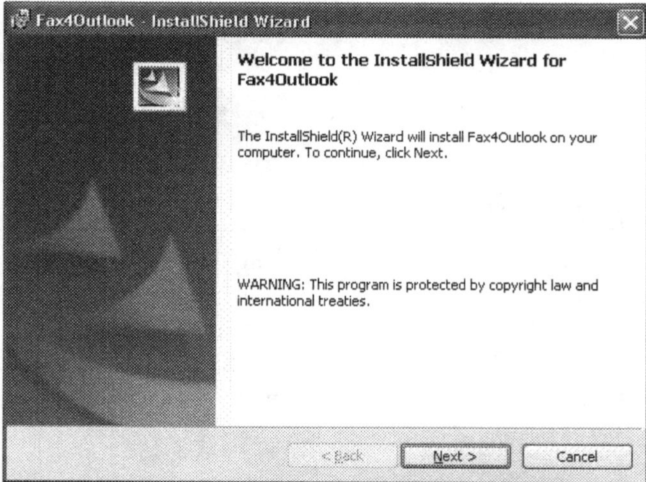

First screen of the "Install Shield" Wizard

One of the tasks the Wizard performs is to check your system/computer to make certain that the new program will perform properly and that it will not cause other programs not to work. This program also makes certain that if you have a program running that would interfere with the successful installation of the program you trying to install … in this case **Fax4Outlook**. I am told by the Wizard that I must close **Microsoft® Word** because the new program must put some switches into the coding for **Microsoft® Word.** Actually, the Wizard does the closing when you give the **OK**.

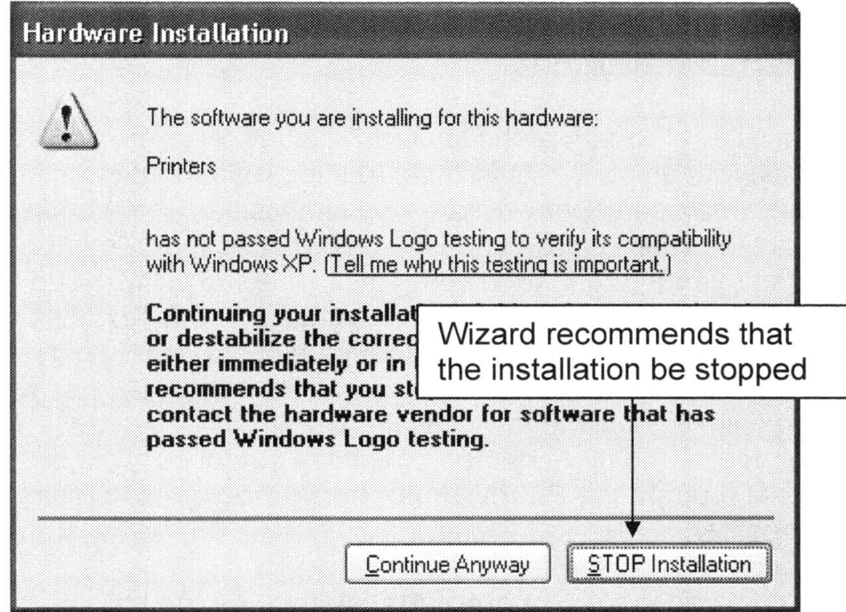

You are warned that Fax4Outlook may impair The way your system operates … it recommends that you STOP Installation

Fax programs are quite intrusive because they imitate printers. In fact they will appear on the **Print dialog box in the box that contains all the printers that your computer can use.**

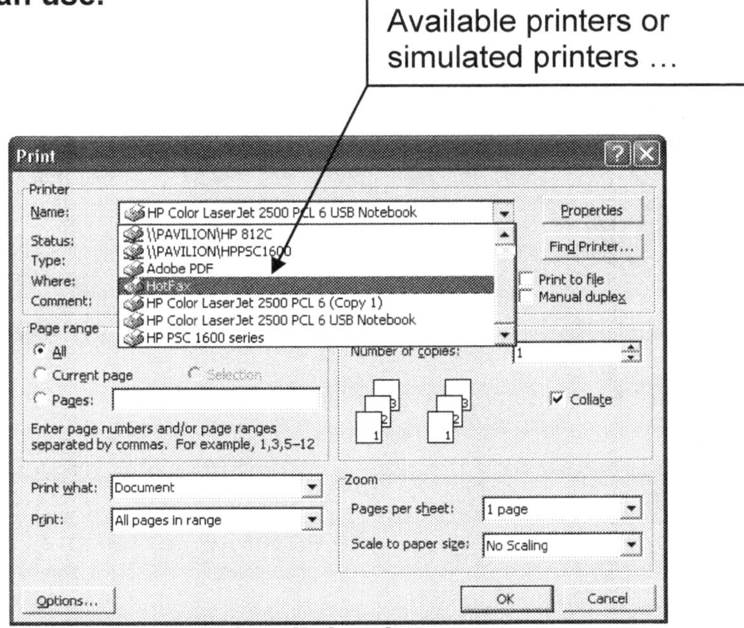

Print dialog box

There are many interesting things to see at our nation's Smithsonian Institution.

Exploring the cultural wealth of the United States is rewarding and fun. Look into things. Satisfy your curiosity. One thing that is great about doing it on the Internet is that it can be spontaneous. You can visit any time of day or night. Nighttime is a time when I need to have some distraction … my medications inhibit sleep so even though I take some mild sleeping pills, I need to look at something that is quieting. The Smithsonian has so many exhibits on line that it seems they never run out of places to go and things to see.

Another almost limitless place to visit is the Library of Congress with its vast collections of books and documents. I will have you check that one out on your own. For now I thought the **Smithsonian Institution** would be a good place to whet your appetite.

You can locate it under the **Government** category on the Interesting Places listing. Click it or tab down to it and press Enter.

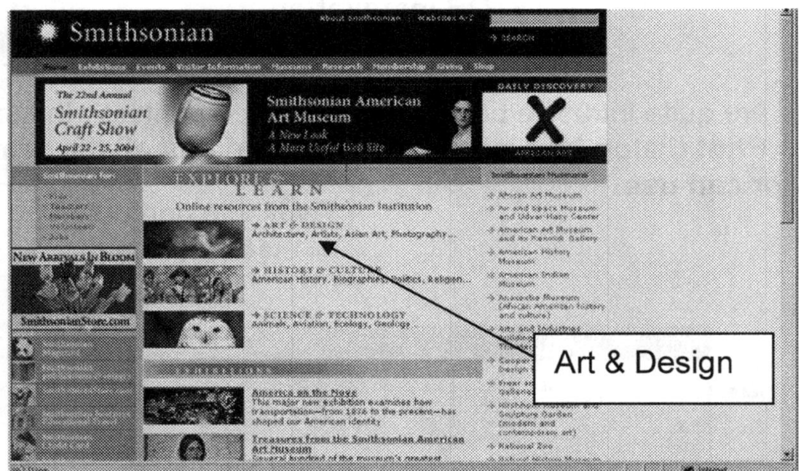

Smithsonian American Art Museum home page

Choosing the first category is not a bad idea.

It presents many ways to tour its site. On the left of the page is a list of topics to explore that are listed by category. If you are just browsing and you enjoy special topics, one of these might make an interesting area of interest to check out.

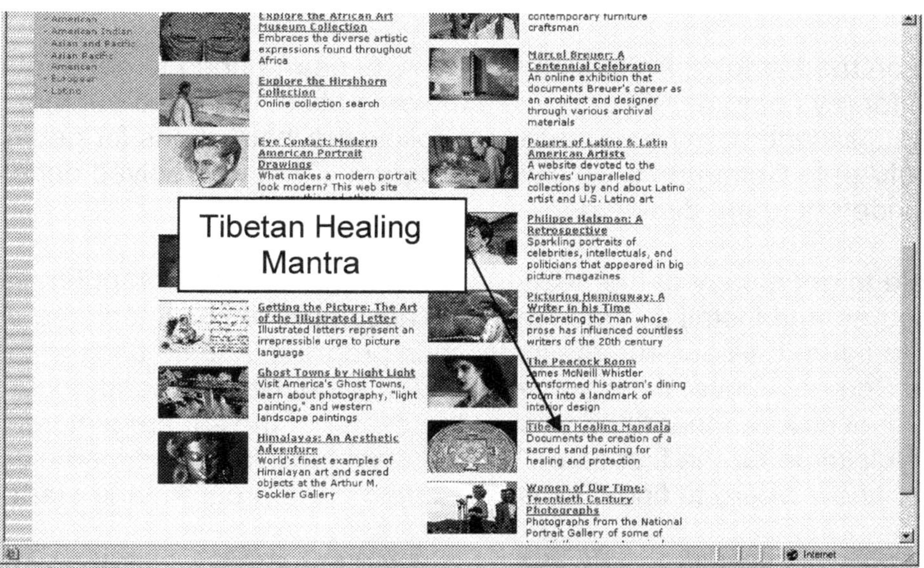

Art and Design page

I thought it might be fun to look at one of the special exhibits that are featured on the Art and Design page. After looking at the descriptions of each of the twenty-four items, I thought it would be fun to check out the Tibetan Healing Mandala. The monks offered to prepare it to seek healing for the United States following the September 11 tragedy. Pictures of this healing ritual were recorded and are available.

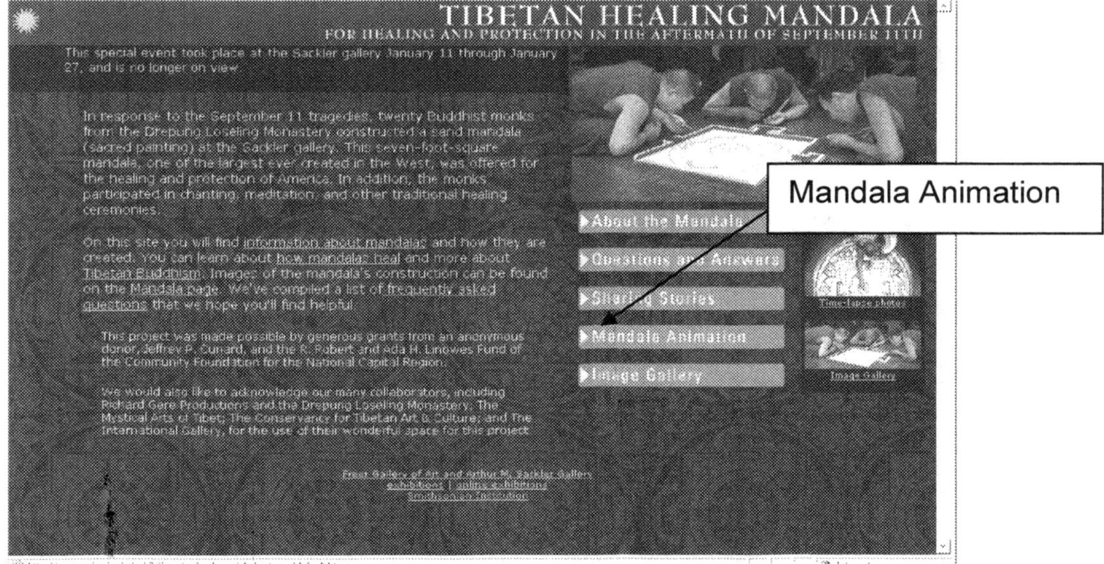

How it is done and more

I clicked on the Mandala Animation button. Oh, dear, I need to get another program for my computer if I am to see the animation. It turned out that it was no problem … except for my own inability to follow the instructions for getting a free version of Apple Computer's Quicktime program. That was solved once I was able to understand the directions.

I was able to get a copy of the needed program from Apple Computer, store it in my computer, and install it. Once that was accomplished … it took me about half an hour to figure it all out, run the installation program, and go back to the Mandala Screen. Once at the screen I kind of scratched my head about what to do next. I discovered that I had to click the center of the square picture location to start Quicktime for the first time. When I went back later and tried it again, my computer knew where to find Quicktime. It found the program and started it.

After getting the Quicktime slide show to work, I thought it might do to check into what the other buttons on the first screen for the Mandala had to offer. They turned out to be quite fascinating as well. One of the buttons brought out a story about Mandalas. Its content was most enlightening because it gave the background for what it was, how it was constructed, and what it could do for those who built it and for those who view it.

The Image Gallery is comprised of many pictures that were taken during the Mandala process. Thumbnails of these images appear on the left of the page. Each can be clicked at which point an enlarged image emerges in the vacant space to the right. In all there are more than 50 pictures about the happening.

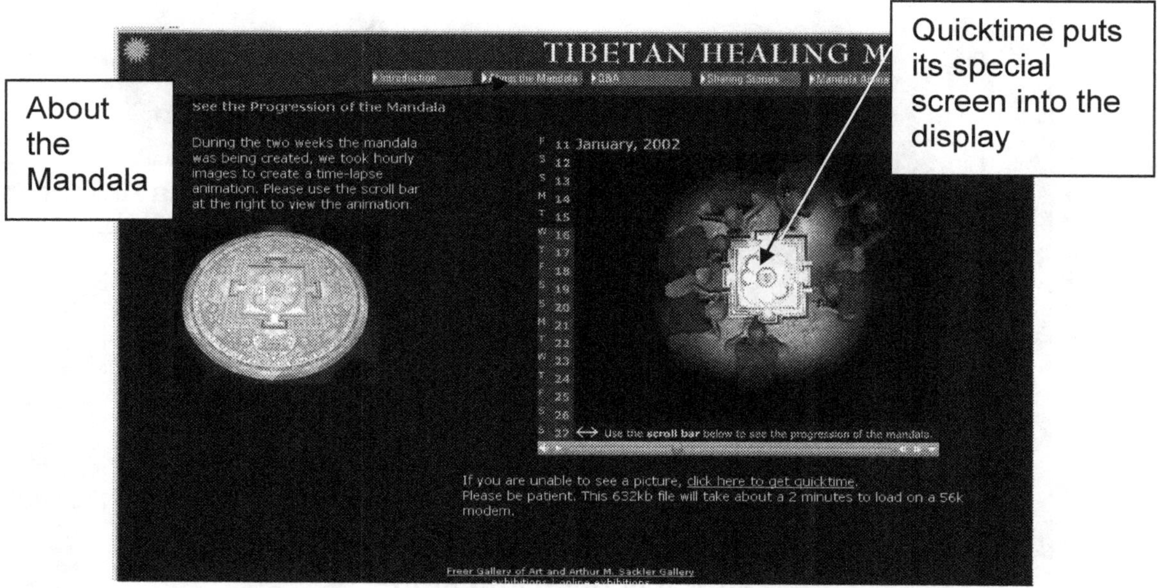

A Quicktime movie is available to show the progress

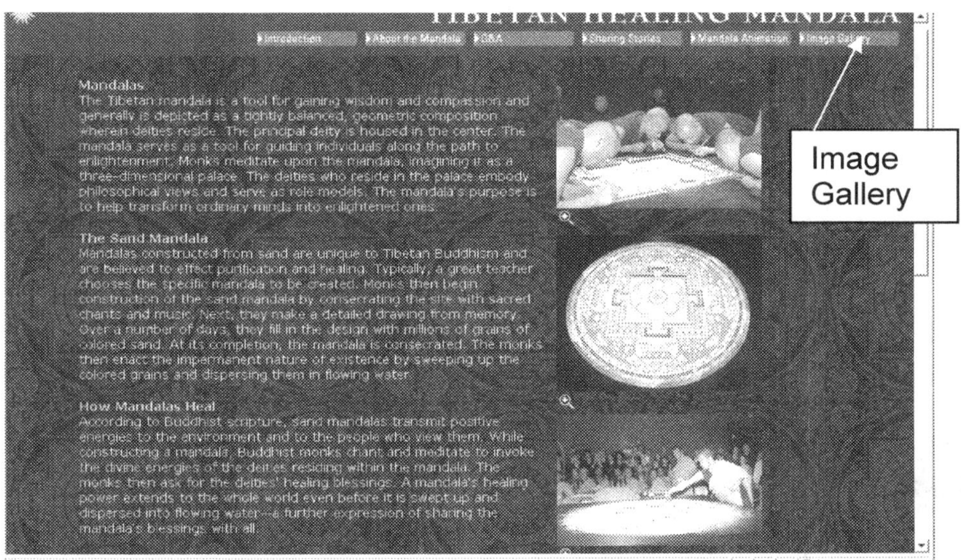

The story of the Mandala is a fascinating one

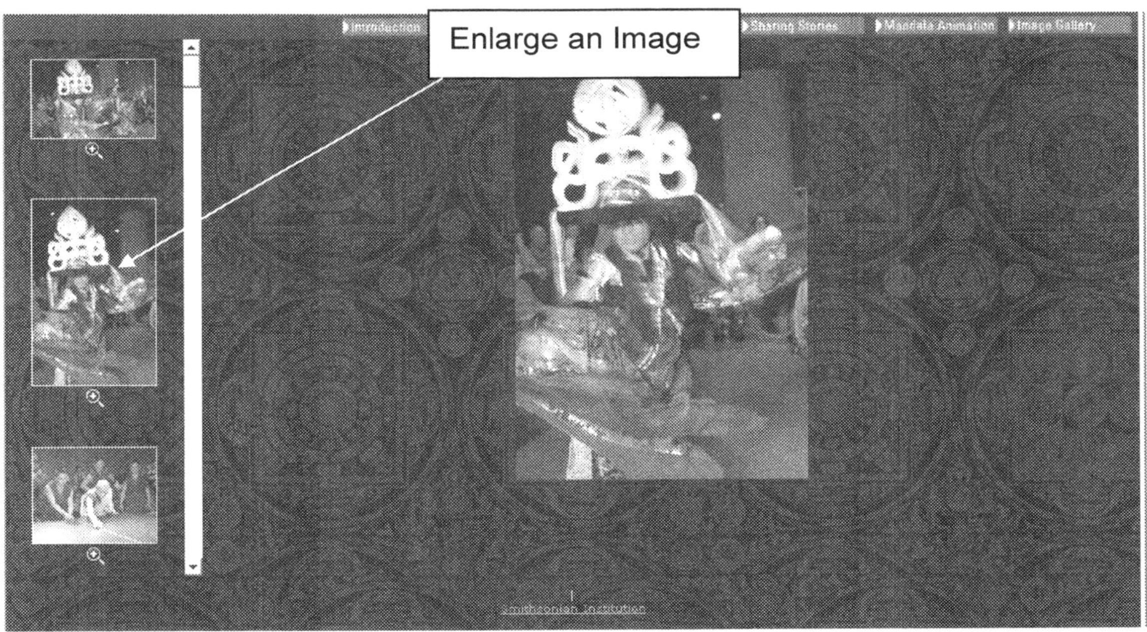

The Image Gallery contains many pictures that can be clicked on and enlarged

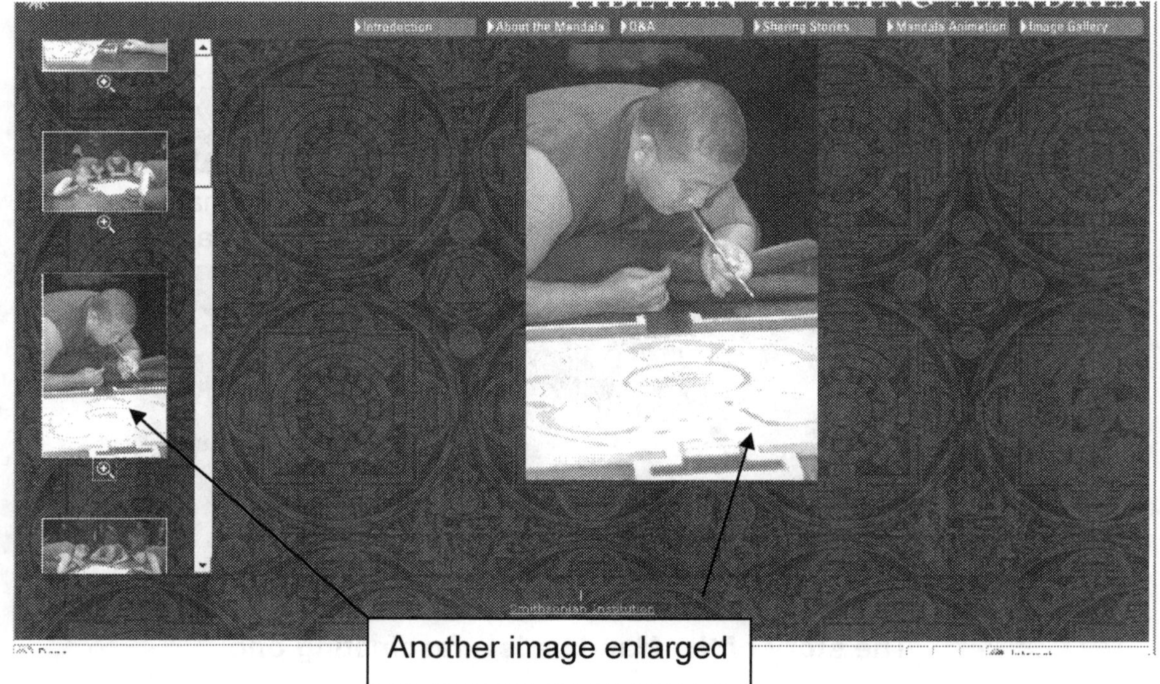
Introduction
About the Mandala
Q&A
Sharing Stories
Mandala Animation
Image Gallery
Smithsonian Institution
Another image enlarged

Using Search Engines
Lesson 6

Search engines, what are they?

We have come a long way since the time when the Internet first gave us the chance to look about and see if there was anything out there that might be of interest. Internet gave people a chance to find out what was happening around the world. People at colleges and universities were the first to be able to take advantage of the "Electronic Super-highway" because educational researchers were used to design and develop it.

It was slow going at first because there were no lists of addresses available so one's success in locating something depended upon one's ingenuity and ability to guess the name that was given to a destination. Once dependable and quick connections became available, people began collecting code names of places that they visited and saving them electronically on master computers all around the "highway." These lists were put together and programs to search them were written.

Then came the development of Hyper-Text Markup Language (HTML) by Tim Berners-Lee and Robert Cailliau of CERN Laboratories in Switzerland. This development made it possible to hide the usually complicated addresses and replace them with names that could be more easily understood. While HTML was meant to make checking references in a scientific paper simpler, the Internet community used it to shape the World Wide Web.

The **search engine** was developed to speed up our searching of these now seemingly endless lists to find where to go for the information we are looking for. While there are hundreds of **search engines** available for the asking, There are just a few that receive the greatest use.

Major search engines

Search engines of the past have survived in peculiar ways. With the exception of major engines like **Google, Yahoo!**, and **Ask Jeeves**, most of the better, new search engines have been absorbed by the major ones or have been set up as very specialized search engines for such things as legal or medical searches. For instance, the search engine for literary references, **Northern light** is now serving the legal community. It charges for its service. Shortly after **All the Web** made its appearance on the Internet, it was bought by a company whose name was **Lycos**. Its name was changed to **Fast Find**. **Fast Find** is no longer a general search engine. It is now used to find mortgage money, educational loans, credit card purveyors, and automobile loans. **All the Web**'s original search engine is still running and doing a very good search job. **Deja News,**

specializing in news groups along with its archives is now owned by **Google**. **Deja News** contained a collection of e-mail interest groups that were very much like today's **blogs**. The news media are finding these **blogs** to be an excellent source of news material. One last search engine, **HotBot**, interestingly enough, now uses both **Google** and **Ask Jeeves** as well as its own engine whose name is **Inktomie** to handle its searches. Information about artificial intelligence programs available web can be found on **HotBot**.

How do you use them

It used to be that search engines were much more difficult to use because to find anything you had to use things called "keywords" because this is the way the **search engine** would know where to go to locate information. Now, the more information you put in concerning what it is you're looking for the the closer the results will be to the information you seek. And, interestingly and often, the **search engine** suggests spellings of words which overcome a questioner's bad spelling.

Unless you use a **search engine** such as, **Northern Light** that charges for its searches, you may be hampered by addresses that will send you to web sites that are selling things. Sometimes, certain locations will be suggested at the very beginning of the list, not because they don't qualify, but because they are paid advertiser. Google, Yahoo!, and Ask Jeeves are all supported by advertising. Many times, these advertisers are referred to as "sponsors." These are the people who keep so many of the free services going on the Internet.

First let's look at Yahoo!

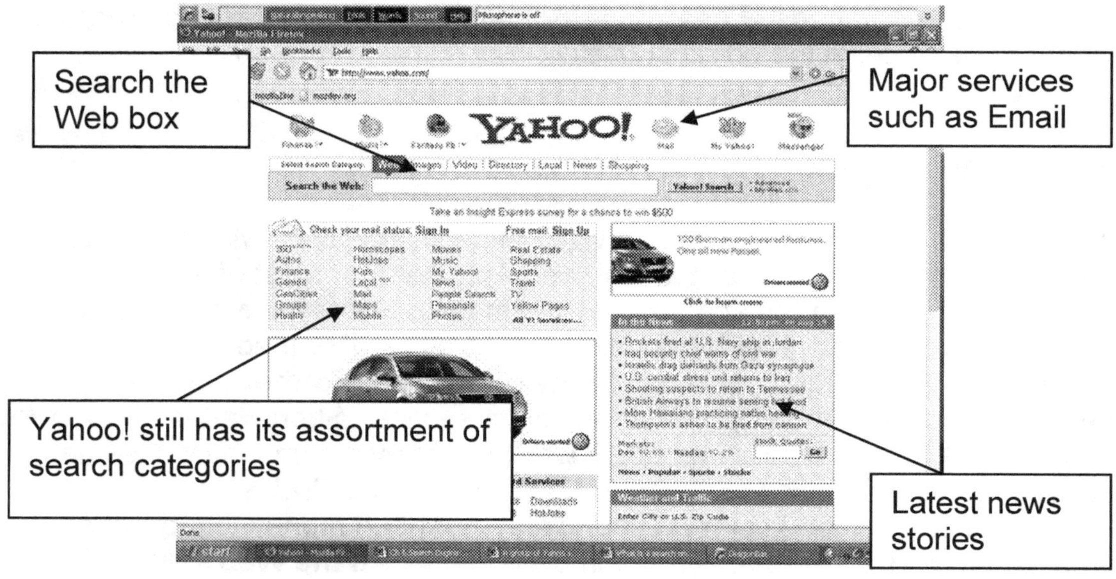

Yahoo's Home Page

Yahoo! features many interesting listings:

Email	Street maps	Today's News	Personals
Email Pager	Classifieds	Weather	Chat
Phone numbers	Online shopping	Sports	Message Boards
Yellow pages			People

Now I'm going to show you what the results of a Yahoo search look like.

We will be getting a chance to compare the information coming out from each one of the **search engines** after each answers the same search request. I will be looking for information on an archbishop of the Church of Ireland whose name was Miler McGrath. Miler was born in the year 1521. He died in the year 1621 before the birthday that would have given him a full hundred years of life on Earth. Information about Miler McGrath is contained in many church records and several books. The most famous book about Miler was written by Robert Wise Jackson a bishop of the Anglican Church. The book's title is Archbishop McGrath: *the Scoundrel of Cashel.*

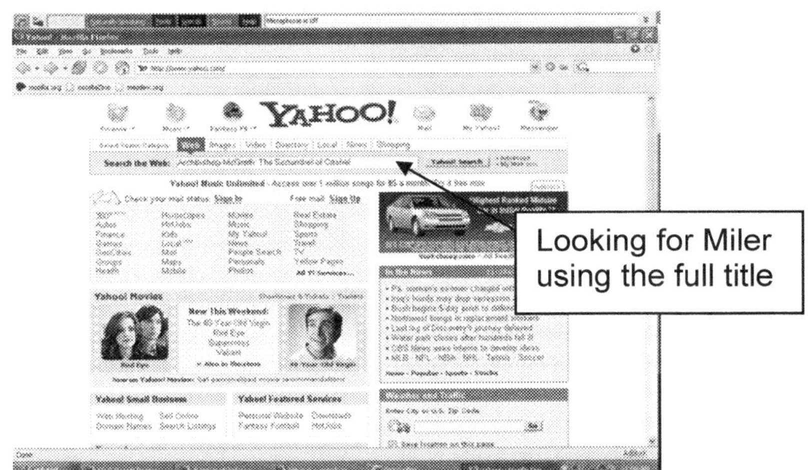

"Archbishop McGrath: The Scoundrel of Cashel"

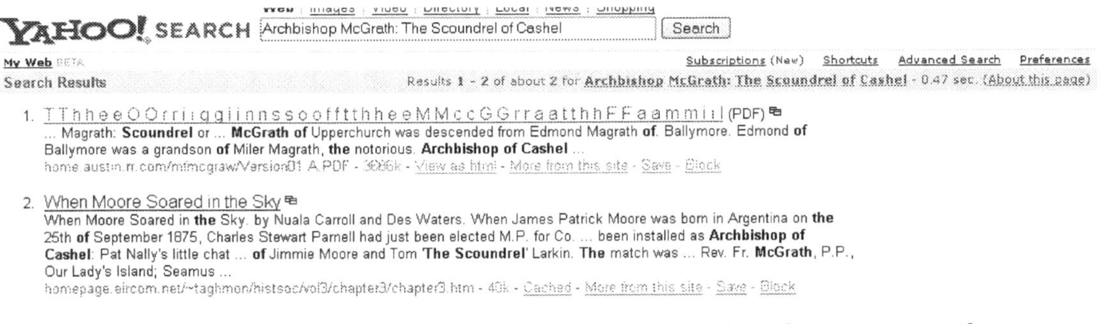

Only two references are found ... neither is what we want!

Web | Images | Video | Directory | Local | News | Shopping

YAHOO! SEARCH Archbishop Magrath The scoundrel of cashel [Search]

My Web BETA — Subscriptions (New) Shortcuts Advanced Search Preferences

Search Results — Results 1 - 10 of about 13 for Archbishop Magrath The scoundrel of cashel - 0.75 sec. (About this page)

1. Jackson (1974) **Archbishop Magrath: The scoundrel of Cashel**
   An academic directory and search engine ... Add to Bookstack | Show Bookstack | Change Bookstack. **Archbishop Magrath: The scoundrel of Cashel** ... SUBJECT(S): **Magrath**, Miller. DISCIPLINE: No discipline assigned ...
   www.getcited.org/?PUB=101723768&showStat=Ratings - 26k - Cached - More from this site - Save - Block

2. **Archbishop Magrath: the scoundrel of Cashel** / - Book at Yahoo! Shopping
   Yahoo! Shopping is **the** best place to comparison shop for **Archbishop Magrath: the scoundrel of Cashel** / - Book. Compare products, compare prices, read reviews and merchant ratings.
   shopping.yahoo.com/p:**Archbishop Magrath: the scoundrel** of **Cashel** /... - More from this site - Save - Block

3. Book : **Archbishop Magrath: The scoundrel of Cashel**
   Shop for **Archbishop Magrath: The scoundrel of Cashel** Books in **the** Model Railroads.Net model railroad book store. Read book reviews and item reviews from other shoppers.
   modelrailroads.net/cgi-modelrailroads/shop-item_id-0853424012-searc... - 11k - Cached - More from this site - Save - Block

4. Used : **Archbishop Magrath: The scoundrel of Cashel**
   Shop for **Archbishop Magrath: The scoundrel of Cashel** Books in **the** Model Railroads.Net model railroad book store. Read book reviews and item reviews from other shoppers.
   modelrailroads.net/cgi-modelrailroads/shop-item_id-0853424012-searc... - 14k - Cached - More from this site - Save - Block

5. Robert Wyse Jackson Books: Search Results from Alibris
   Author: Robert Wyse Jackson - 3 matching titles including '**Archbishop Magrath : the scoundrel of Cashel**' Used, New and Out **of** Print. Buy Robert Wyse Jackson books at Alibris and Save!
   www.alibris.com/search/books/author/Robert_Wyse_Jackson - More from this site - Save - Block

6. Day 16
   General Tom poses at **the** final resting place **of** his hero, **Archbishop Magrath, the Scoundrel of Cashel**. Apparently, **the**

Spelling the Archbishop's name Magrath instead of McGrath brings better results

Now another major search engine … All the Web (Fast Find last time I looked at it)

I will ask it to find: **Archbishop Magrath: The Scoundrel of Cashel** and see what it says about it.

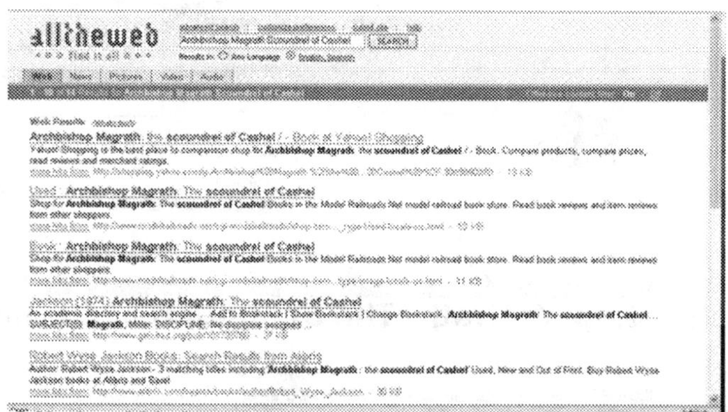

All the Web and Yahoo! results are identical
could they both be using the same search engine?

Ask Jeeves is another that says they are a general search engine. I will ask it the same (almost) question … of **Ask Jeeves** you must seek an answer to a <u>question</u>.

Ask Jeeves home page

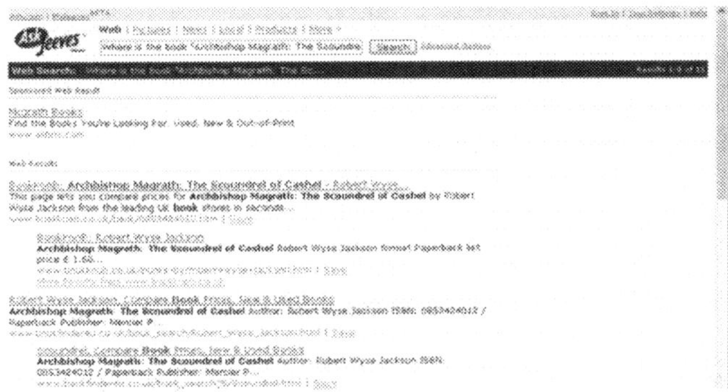

Jeeves comes up with a respectable list

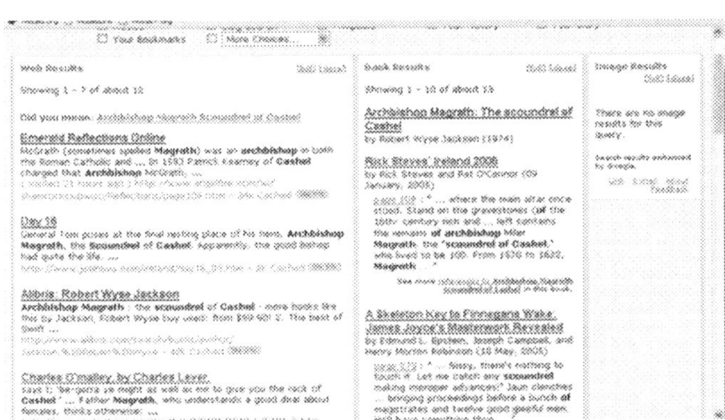

Amazon's A9 search engine doesn't give the result in its main listing

but a tab on the right called "Book Results" gives the name of the very thing we were searching for!

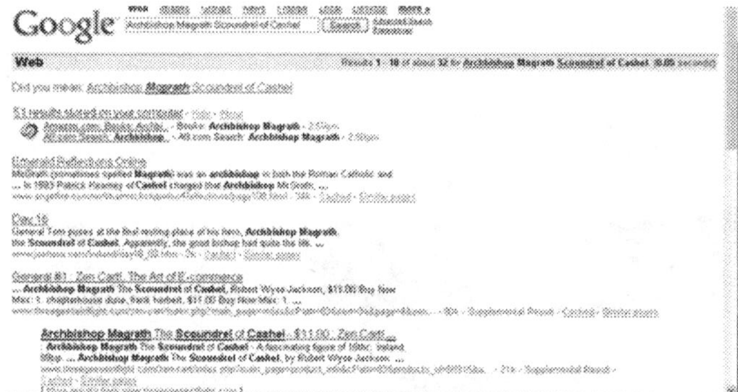

Google comes up with a place that says it has a copy of the book!

It's interesting that **Yahoo!** and **All the Web** seemed to choose exactly the same documents … perhaps Yahoo! Uses the **All the Web** search engine. Amazon, probably because it is primarily a book dealer, came up with a sidebar reference to the exact document I was looking to find.

Ask Jeeves format is different from the others.

I separated it from the others because its presentation of the question was different and its answers many times lead to other places to seek the information that I want. These additional questions also as me to become more precise like the treatment we get when ordering things in a restaurant … large or small and the like. These questions will many times make me reconsider what I have asked for. Sometimes, I will take a very different approach to my problem and be able to understand my problem better.

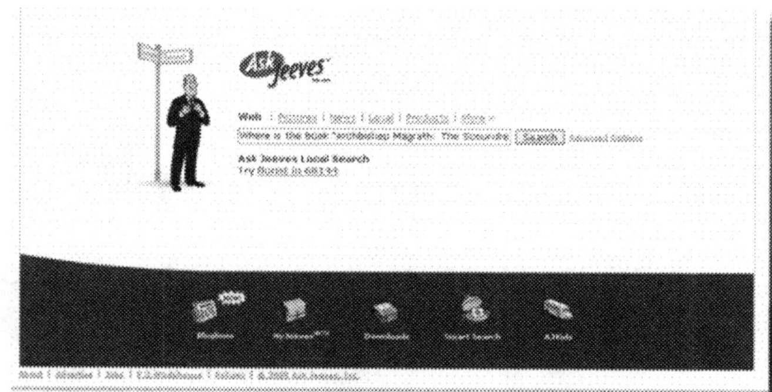

Ask Jeeves homepage

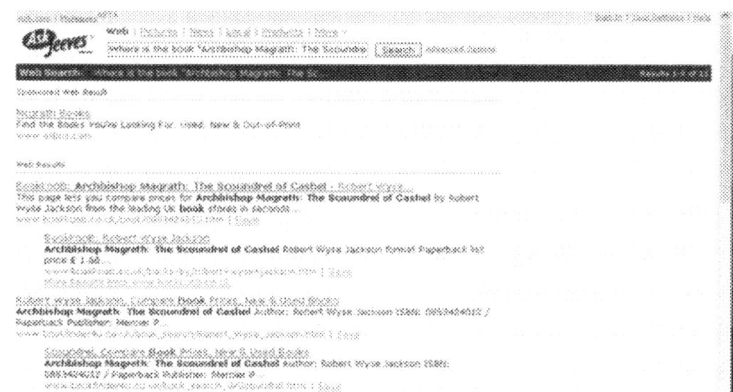

Ask Jeeves answers are many and very appropriate

There are other places to look if you really want to read a book. Try some libraries. I did this and found a couple of copies in Ireland, one in Scotland, a copy at Harvard … I stopped there. For some reason I began searching for book sellers in Ireland to see if they had such an article. I found a copy at Green's Bookstore in Dublin. I bought the book for a very reasonable price and am quite satisfied. This long story tells you that locating some things will be difficult. These are the things that I hope to help you find through strategies that you will find in this book.

At one time I became very despondent about not being able to locate a copy of the book about Miler Magrath so I decided to see if I could locate one in a nearby library from which I might borrow the book. After many hours (days actually) I found a copy of *Archbishop Magrath* in the **Hollis** catalog. If worst came to worst, I would be able to either read the book at Harvard, borrow it from Harvard, or find a nearby academic library that could get Harvard to loan it to them so it would be less of a journey for me to get there to read it.

In my searches to put this information in this book I became acquainted with bookstores in Ireland and England (United Kingdom, I guess) that said they had the book on hand. Well, when I tried to complete the purchase, all but one bookstore … Green's in Dublin … said they didn't have a copy on hand but would notify me if they located one. Green's sold me their last copy for about $6.00. It was in good shape and was exactly what I needed.

Exploring Irish libraries did bring success but I found that I must search for the author. Once I looked for Robert Wyse Jackson, the National Library of Ireland shows that it has 13 books by that particular author. One of these is about our

Archbishop ... Milar Magrath. We look further and find that it is available. The catalog tells us where we can find it and that it is available to check out.

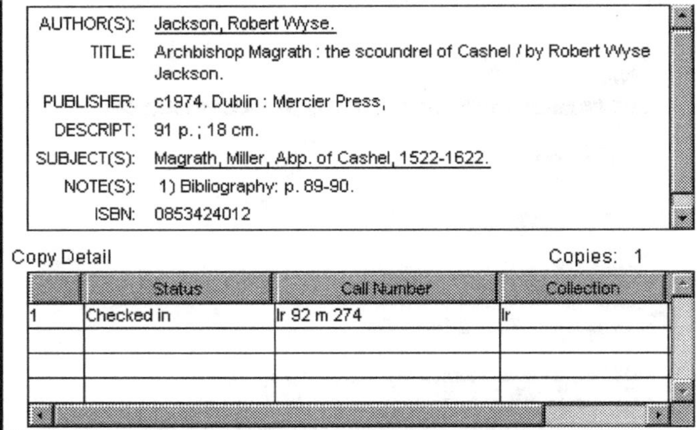

AUTHOR(S): Jackson, Robert Wyse.
TITLE: Archbishop Magrath : the scoundrel of Cashel / by Robert Wyse Jackson.
PUBLISHER: c1974. Dublin : Mercier Press,
DESCRIPT: 91 p. ; 18 cm.
SUBJECT(S): Magrath, Miller, Abp. of Cashel, 1522-1622.
NOTE(S): 1) Bibliography: p. 89-90.
ISBN: 0853424012

Copy Detail Copies: 1

	Status	Call Number	Collection
1	Checked in	Ir 92 m 274	Ir

A Library catalog record

What I have tried to demonstrate is that most anything can be located on the web but that one must develop a strategy for finding it.

Finding something to buy is probably the easiest of the searches because the search engines are all tuned to commerce. Engines like Google, Ask Jeeves, Yahoo, and All the Web charge companies for advertising. As a result they must guarantee that they and their products will be moved to the top of any result list (or to some other prominent place). Trying to locate intellectual items is a difficult process though Google and Ask Jeeves have attempted to work in the academic area as well. You must develop a strategy that includes places to look and ways to describe what it is that you wish to find.

Some lessons we learned by just changing our "Search" terms.

None of the search engines were able to find the book we wanted when we misspelled Miler Magrath's name.

Sometimes alternate spellings of people's names bring results. Many last names and first names as well were given strange spellings by the clerks who recorded their entry into a country. Polish last names in the United States are notorious for such treatment. So we can't rely on very spellings that we know. All spoken languages change quite frequently do the people using words in many ways that were unexpected. When you are doing a name that you're going to be putting in search, try to think of all the way somebody could spell that is based upon the way the name sounds. In the case of Miler Magrath, we found that spelled Magrath, McGrath, McGraw, or Magraw. In fact the further back in history to go, the more variation you will find in the spelling of everything.

The words "Scoundrel of Cashel" brought many results from all the search engines … perhaps they are all setting up groups of words that seem in be special to some target.
Sometimes we can look for something different, such as a book repository … a library … that is located in a part of the world where such a group of words would mean something, such as, local history.

The next part of this lesson will demonstrate how easy it is to miss finding something when the words are arranged differently from the way are given in a web site

The art museum in Dallas, Texas has many interesting exhibits and many interesting activities going on every day.

Here is how to find it with a search engine … it is possible to guess the way to put its address in the browser's **address box** search engines can make it easier to find places.

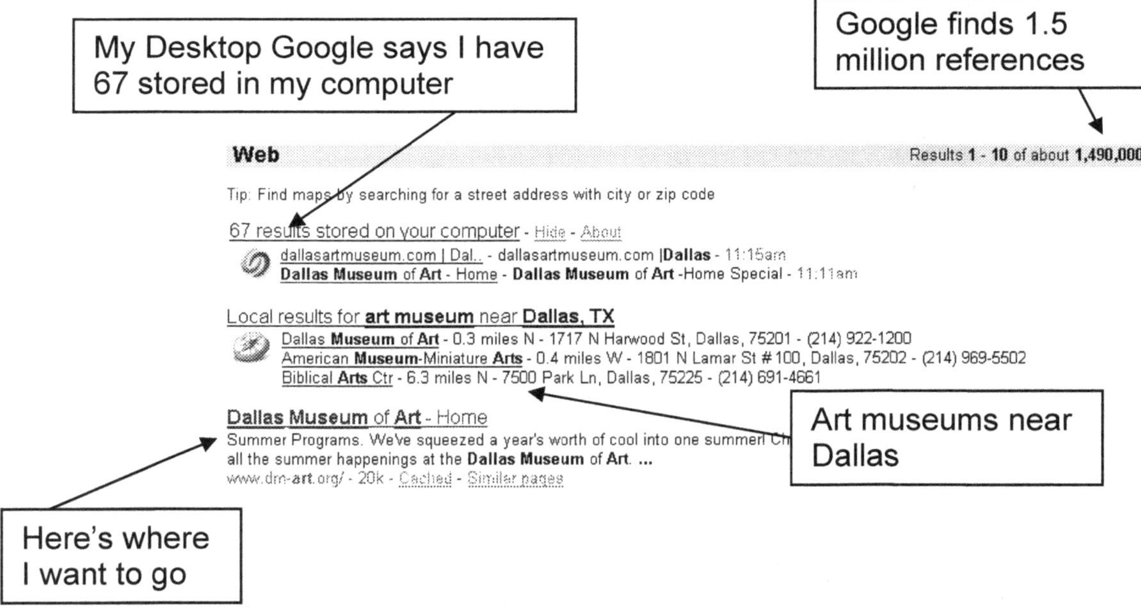

	Internet Explorer	Mozilla/Firefox	Opera
1.	**Alt/D**	**Alt/D**	**F2**
2.	Type **google.com**	Type **google.com**	Type **google.com**
3.	**Enter↵**	**Enter↵**	**Enter↵**

Type in "Dallas Texas Art Museum" & click Google Search

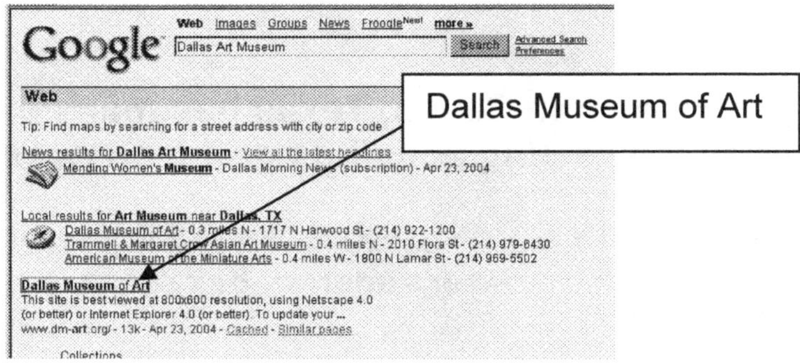

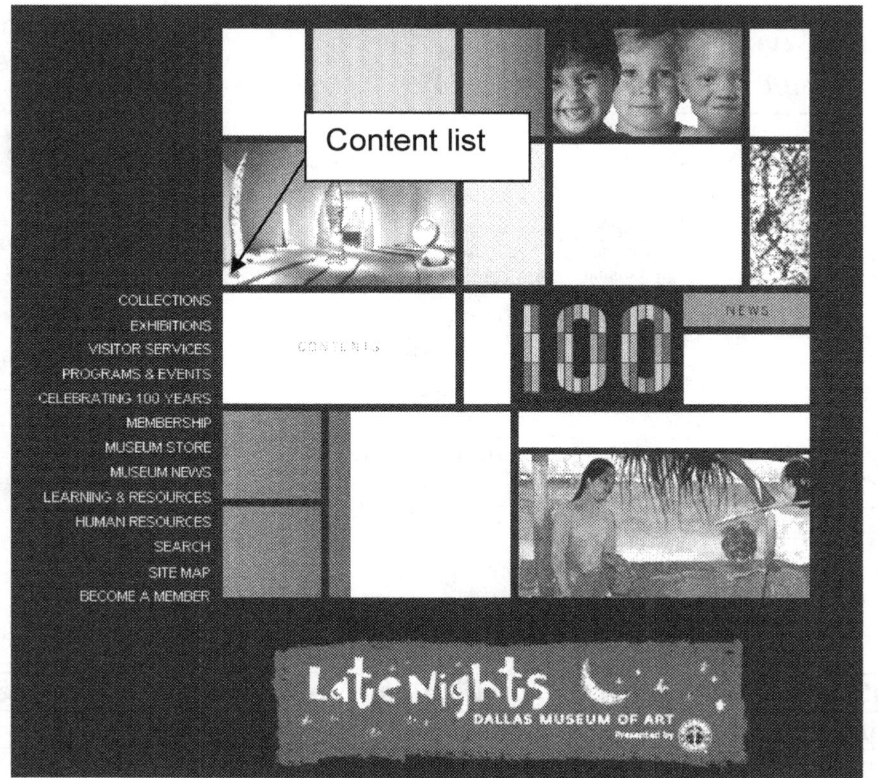

Put your mouse pointer on the **CONTENTS list**, move it to **PROGRAMS & EVENTS** and click

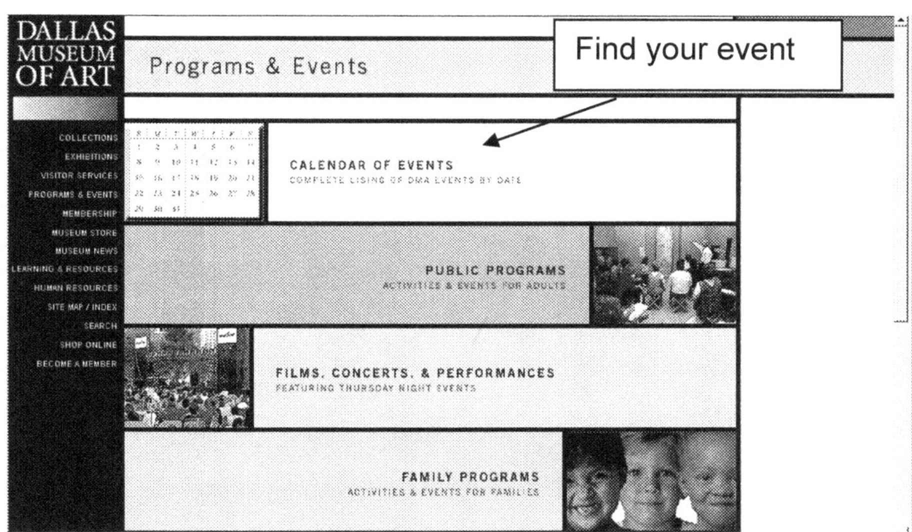

You have just begun to find out what today's search engines have to offer.

When you work on your own, check out what some of the features are that your chosen search engine offers. It may surprise you to find out how easy it is to locate exactly what you want. This is because today's search engines are competing with each other to attract more people. It means that the more successful engines will attract greater advertising revenues. It also means that you, the searcher, will receive ever improving service that is free if you don't mind a little advertising.

Take time to try some of the features that the search engine offers. While writing this lesson, I spent a little time looking at Google, Yahoo, and Ask Jeeves. All three of these search engines offered me a chance to narrow my search by giving me classifications that once I said I was looking within a particular group of items the results were much more accurate and they came to me much quicker.

Here are a few problems to work out on your own.

Start with one of the search engines ... **Google, All the Web, Ask Jeeves, or Yahoo.** Move around using the suggestions available at each site. Be creative ... you will get ever closer to what you are looking for. The more specific your goal is the more difficult it is to reach but only by defining and redefining your target will you be able to succeed.

Search exercises:

Exercise 1. Find online games ...

Step 1. **Alt/D** or click the **Address** box

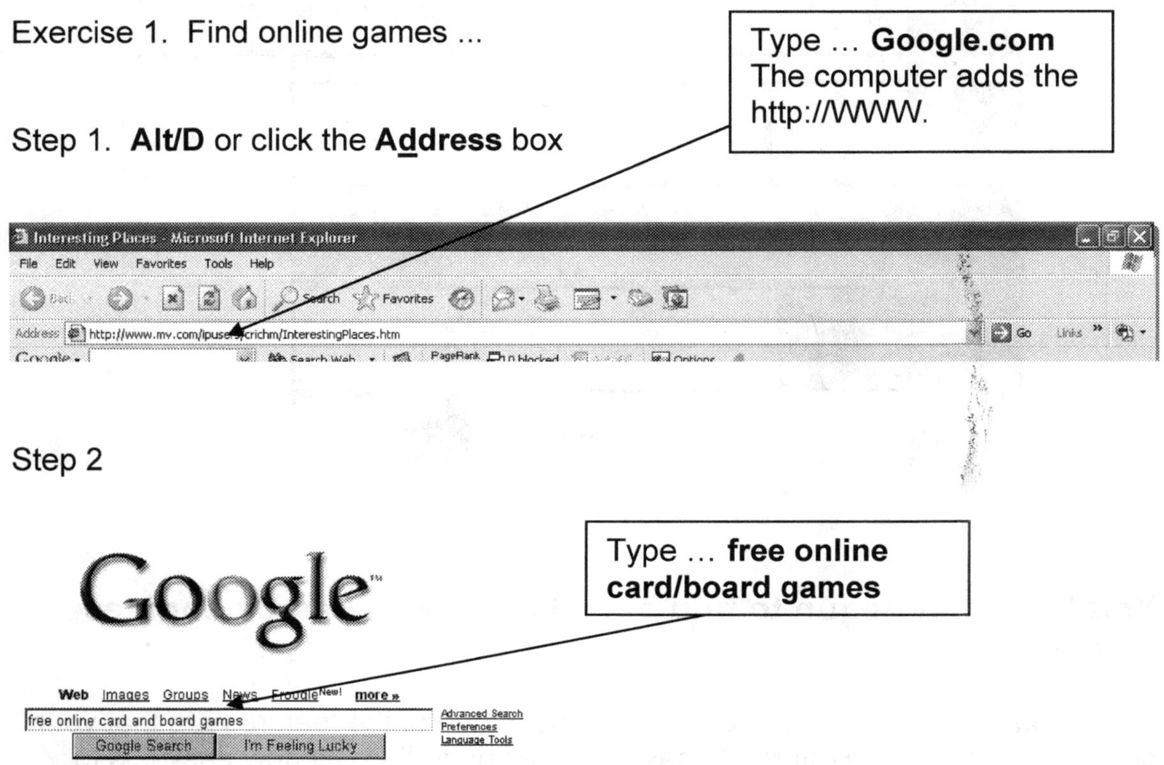

Step 2

Step 3

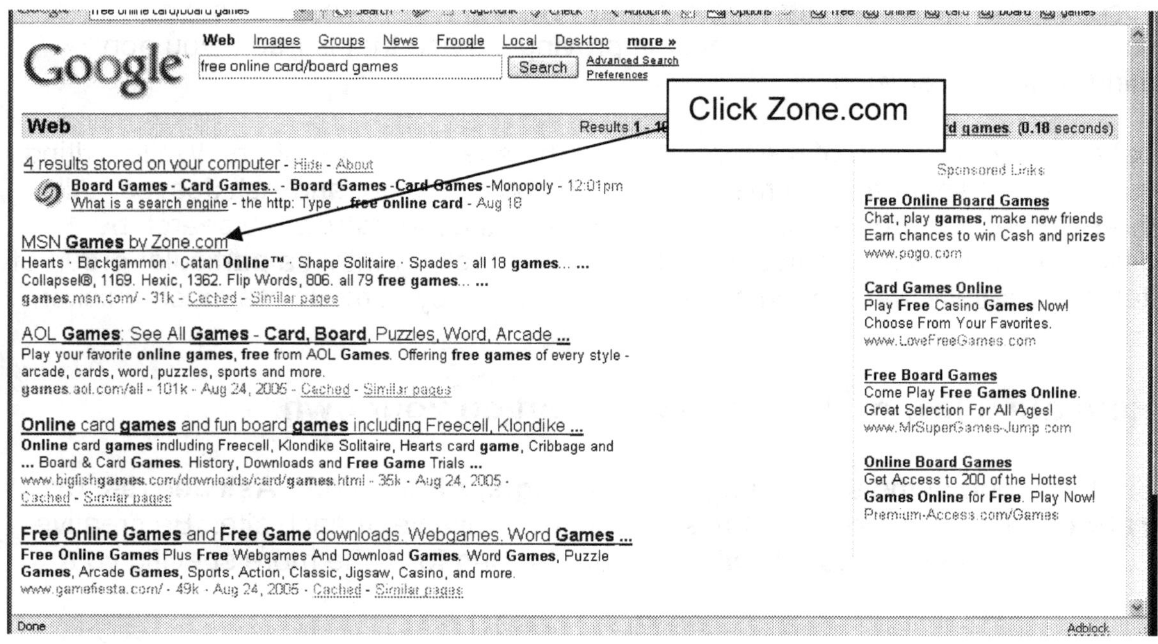

Step 4

The latest "Home Page" for Zone (now Microsoft®)

Microsoft has changed Zone.com's home page into a very glitzy one that is closely akin to what you will find at gambling sites. The simulated folder tabs across the top of the display are easy to find with the mouse. You must move your mouse pointer over the tabs until the tab name is shown underlined … your pointer becomes a hand. Each of the advertising squares below contains a "hot point" where the mouse pointer becomes a hand. You can have your browser go to the site you choose by pressing the left hand mouse button.

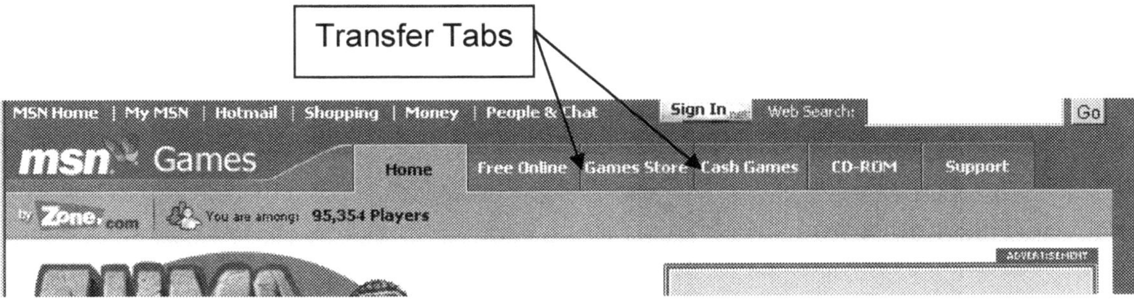

If you are persistent, you can also work this page using the keyboard. The trick is to press the **Tab** key and watch the changes at the bottom of the screen … left hand side just above the **Start** button … what shows up here will be the web address of the "hot spot" that is being surrounded by dashes. If you press the **Enter** key, the browser will try to go to that address and display its information.

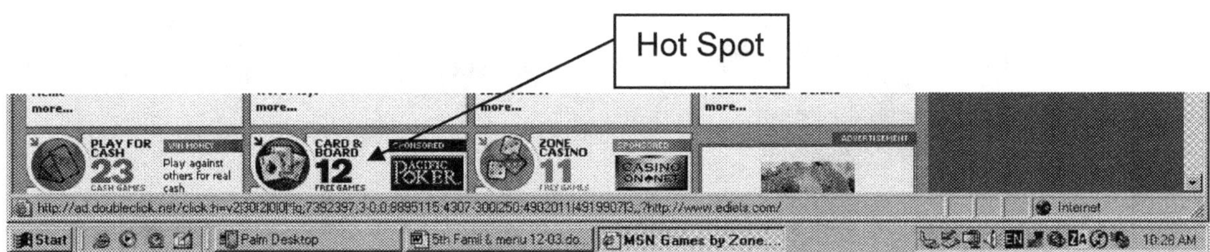

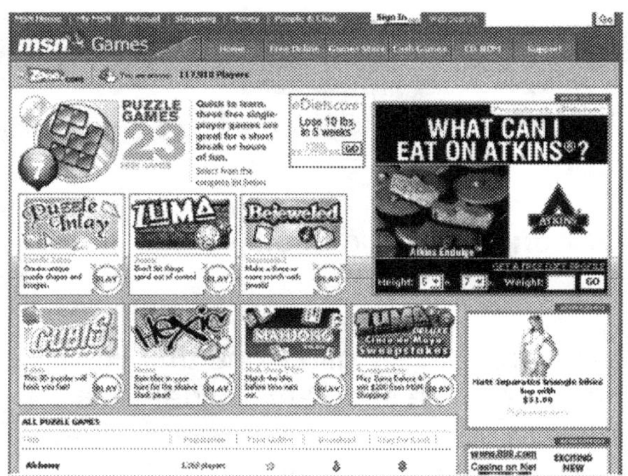

Challenge yourself

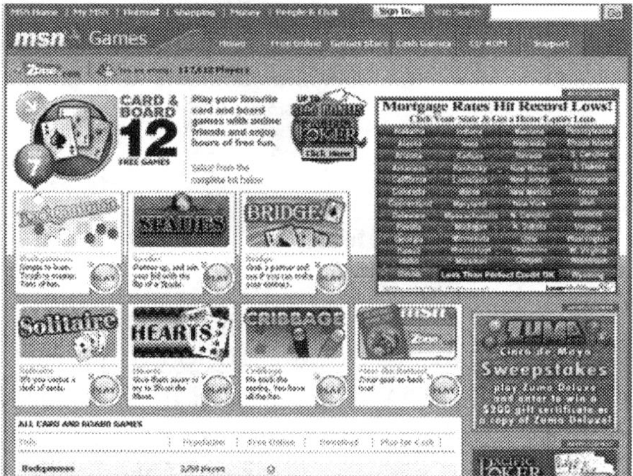

Challenge yourself

Play with others anywhere in the world, any time of day

Be careful when you check out the games and other things that are displayed on the screen. Even in a single square you can be fooled into going to something that is going to cost you money.

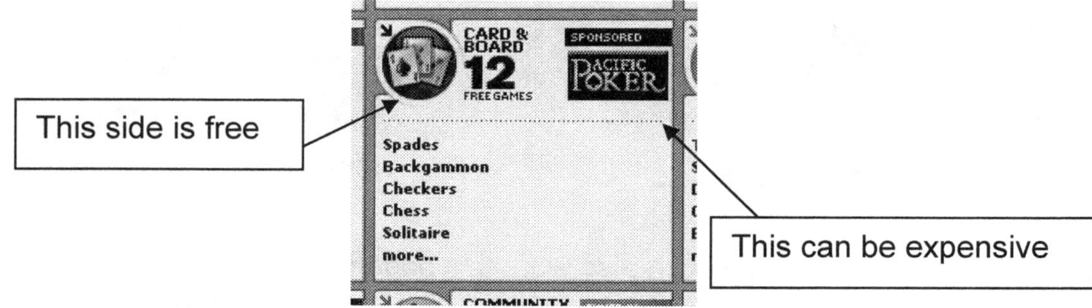

There are two sides (left & right) to this area make sure you click the correct one

Exercise 2. See if you can find **your own telephone number** … use **Yahoo** and its telephone search, or look for **telephone numbers** using **Google**

Exercise 3. Check the yellow pages for one of your **local stores** … **Yahoo** has a good **Yellow Page** section.

Exercise 4. Look for some classic poetry on the Web … there are universities out there that have excellent collections that can be found on the Web. Try putting in part of a line of a poem you would like to find … "**and greasy Joan doth keel the pot**" from Shakespeare. See what the **search engine** comes up with.

Exercise 5. Find the web address for the **New York Times** newspaper. ... make sure to: have the word "newspaper" in your set of key words. Sometimes unexpected results appear in answer to perfectly innocent requests.

Exercise 6. Check out the weather in **Melbourne, Australia**. ... you can put this one in search term.

Exercise 7. Where can you charter a yacht in the Caribbean?

Search for something more difficult.

Exercise 8. Find **Roget's Thesaurus** in Project Gutenberg..

I think Google can find what I want if you put in a detailed description.

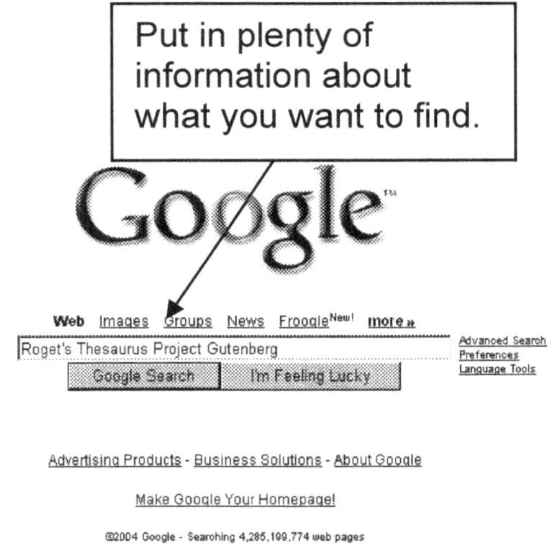

I will try the first one to see if its ranking is deserved … click it or get there using the **Tab** key then press **Enter**

The answers are quite reasonable. I will explore some of the possible choices with you so you can understand how to sort through the material to find what you want.

asadz.com
eBuilders

Rogets Thesaurus

As distributed by Project Gutenberg

This is an interface onto the Project Gutenberg Etext of Roget's Thesaurus No. Two, which is derived from the version of Roget's Thesaurus published in 1911.

Before using this thesaurus, you should read the small print for Project Gutenberg.

Enter word or phrase:
Submit

This thesaurus has been prepared by MICRA, Inc. (May 1991).

asadz.com home page

This is a service which lets you search the thesaurus without your having to store it on your computer. For those with limited hard disk storage space that will be fine but you should set a "Favorite" or "Bookmark" for your browser to use when you want to check more words. See page 93.

This site gives you're the choice of reading it online or of downloading it to your computer

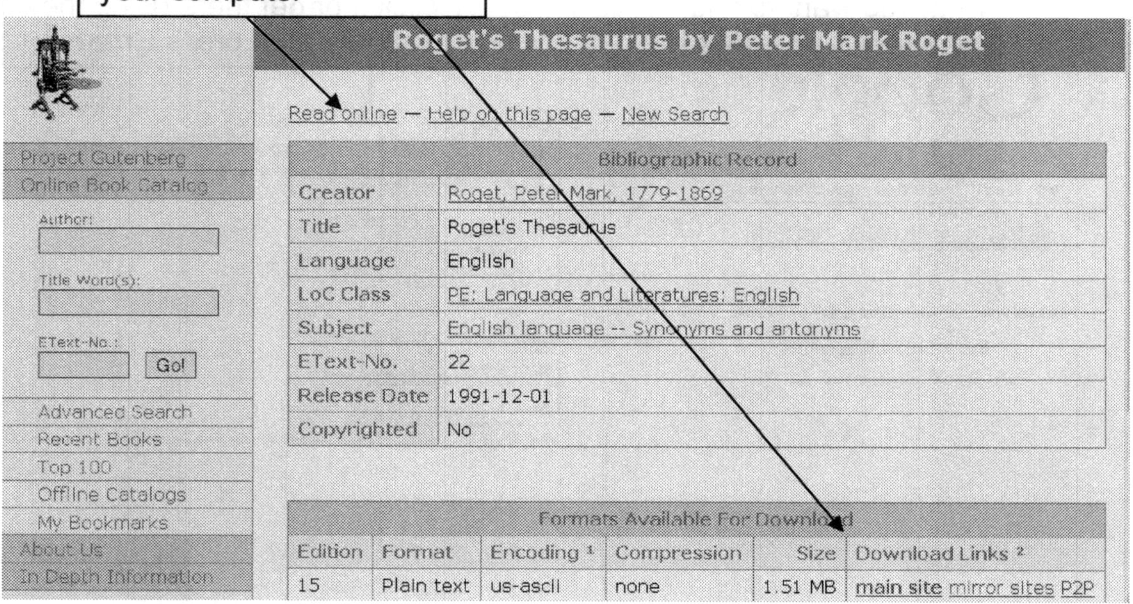
Roget's Thesaurus by Peter Mark Roget

Read online — Help on this page — New Search

Project Gutenberg
Online Book Catalog
Author:
Title Word(s):
EText-No.:
Go!
Advanced Search
Recent Books
Top 100
Offline Catalogs
My Bookmarks
About Us
In Depth Information

Bibliographic Record	
Creator	Roget, Peter Mark, 1779-1869
Title	Roget's Thesaurus
Language	English
LoC Class	PE: Language and Literatures: English
Subject	English language -- Synonyms and antonyms
EText-No.	22
Release Date	1991-12-01
Copyrighted	No

Formats Available For Download

Edition	Format	Encoding [1]	Compression	Size	Download Links [2]
15	Plain text	us-ascii	none	1.51 MB	main site mirror sites P2P

One Project Gutenberg site's home page

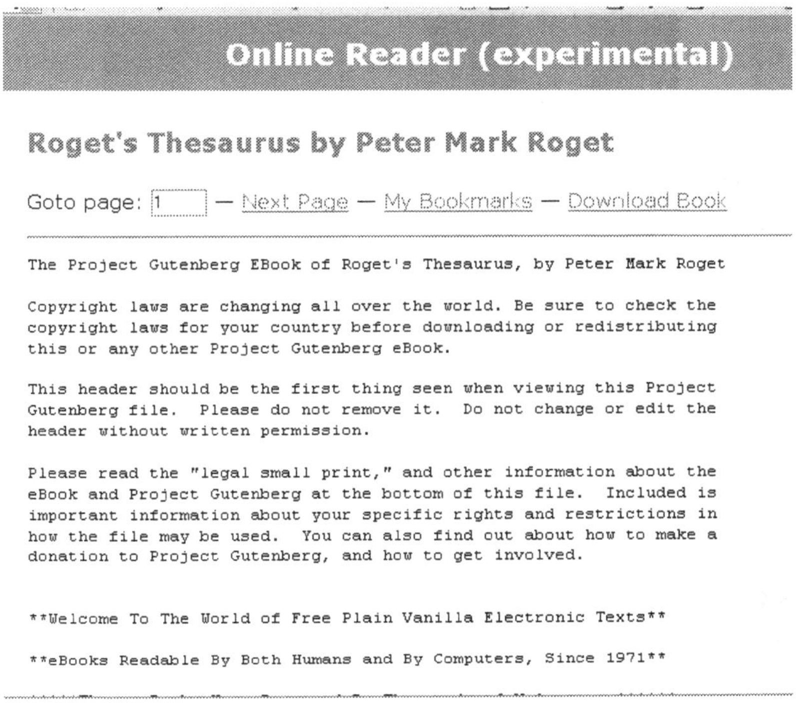

Online Reader (experimental)

Roget's Thesaurus by Peter Mark Roget

Goto page: 1 — Next Page — My Bookmarks — Download Book

The Project Gutenberg EBook of Roget's Thesaurus, by Peter Mark Roget

Copyright laws are changing all over the world. Be sure to check the copyright laws for your country before downloading or redistributing this or any other Project Gutenberg eBook.

This header should be the first thing seen when viewing this Project Gutenberg file. Please do not remove it. Do not change or edit the header without written permission.

Please read the "legal small print," and other information about the eBook and Project Gutenberg at the bottom of this file. Included is important information about your specific rights and restrictions in how the file may be used. You can also find out about how to make a donation to Project Gutenberg, and how to get involved.

Welcome To The World of Free Plain Vanilla Electronic Texts

eBooks Readable By Both Humans and By Computers, Since 1971

Here is the first page ... there is no way to search this one

There are other versions of this famous thesaurus that are available in electronic form. You might want to get a copy of this material for yourself ... Google tells you were you can find them. As long as you have come this far, check any out that may seem interesting. You know how to do it now.

Don't forget, it you just want to keep a record of where you can find a certain version, just set a "Favorites" entry. Go back to page 93 in Lesson 5 to find out how to do it.

Exercise 9 Find the **Dinosaur Exhibit** at Honolulu Community College, HI.

Exercise 10 Find the **Whitehouse** in Washington, DC.

Let's look at some products of the Artificial Intelligence Community using BotSpot. The locations that show them have specialized lists similar to Gero-tech's Interesting Places.

The Home Page shown below has indexes that refer to what are called "Bots" which is short for robot. These programs perform searches of the Internet in much the same fashion that Veronica did for the Gopher client by going out on the Internet and checking all the places that were connected to it. Then there are the AI (Artificial Intelligence) bots that can carry on a conversation with you if you are so inclined.

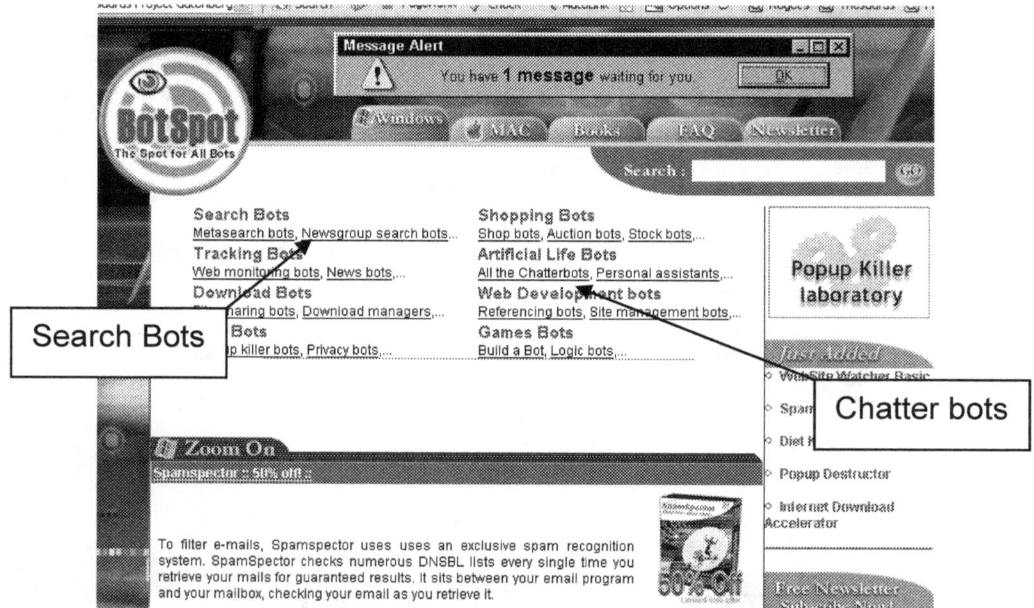

The BotSpot

Finding Bots and Bot spotters

You get to the **BotSpot** page by doing the following:

Press **Alt/D**, type in **www.botspot.com**, press **Enter** to find the **BotSpot** list.
The following are found using the **Bot Spot** page

Some things to search for.

1. **Eliza** one of the older "chatter" bots

2. **Alice** (Artificial Linguistic Internet Computer Entity)

3. Find out what at “Tracking Bot” is.

4. Find some **bots** that help you suppress advertising.

5. Check the type of book you can find on the **BotSpot** site.

*** Some very specialized search engines ... put these addresses into the Address box (Alt/D) of Internet Explorer, Location box (Alt/O) of Mozilla/Firefox, or Remote (F2) of Opera**

1. Ask-An-Expert Page ... http://njnie.dl.stevens-tech.edu/askanexpert.html
2. More ... http://www.cln.org/int_expert.html
3. Learn to treat a toothache, etc. ... http://www.howstuffworks.com
4. Another Ask an Expert ... http://www.askanexpert.com

* These two items were published in **TOURBUS**, an electronic magazine that is **FREE.** It is easy to subscribe to ... just go to WWW.Tourbus.com and fill in the form!

Appendix

Keyboard & Mouse Commands

Appendix A

For more Keyboard Commands check MS Word Help ... "keyboard shortcuts"

Command	Keyboard	Mouse
Word Processing Menus		
File Menu	**Alt/F**	Click File
Edit Menu	**Alt/E**	Click Edit
View Menu	**Alt/V**	Click View
Insert Menu	**Alt/I**	Click Insert
Format Menu	**Alt/O**	Click Format
Tools Menu	**Alt/T**	Click Tools
Table Menu	**Alt/A**	Click Table
Window Menu	**Alt/W**	Click Window
Help Menu	**Alt/H**	Click Help
Help search engine	**F1**	Click "?" button
Internet Explorer		
File Menu	**Alt/F**	Click File
Edit Menu	**Alt/E**	Click Edit
View Menu	**Alt/V**	Click View
Favorites Menu	**Alt/A**	Click Favorites
Tools Menu	**Alt/T**	Click Tools
Help Menu	**Alt/H**	Click Help
Help Search engine	**F1**	Click Help Contents and Index
Return to Home Page	**Alt/Home**	Click Home Page button
Document control commands		
New document	**Ctrl/N**	Click New document button
Bring in (Open) an old document	**Ctrl/O**	Click Open folder button
Save As ... name a document	**F12**	Click File menu then Click SaveAs…
Save document	**Ctrl/S**	Click Floppy disk button
Close (erase from screen)	**Ctrl/W**	Click the lower "X" button

Command	Keyboard	Mouse
Print document	**Ctrl/P**	Click Printer button
Print preview	**Alt/Ctrl/I**	Click Preview button
Text editing commands		
Spell check	**F7**	Click √abc button
Select (highlight) all	**Ctrl/A**	Put Mouse pointer to the left of the 1st line, hold down the left Mouse button, move the pointer to the end of the document, and release the Mouse button
Thesaurus	**Shift/F7**	Click Tools then Click Language then Click Thesaurus
Select some text	**shift/ arrow key**	Put the Mouse pointer at either end of the text you want to "select," press the left Mouse button, move the pointer over the text, and release the Mouse button.
Unselect	Any **arrow key**	Click anywhere below the selected area
Cut text	**Ctrl/X**	Click Scissors button
Copy text	**Ctrl/C**	Click 2 pieces of paper button
Paste text	**Ctrl/V**	Click Clipbord & paper button
Undo typing	**Ctrl/Z**	Click Left turning arrow button
Redo typing	**Ctrl/Y**	Click Right turning arrow button
Character formatting		
Font	**Ctrl/shift/F** then name font	Click **Font** button then click **name**
Type size	**Ctrl/shift/>** or **<**	Click Size button then click size

Command	Keyboard	Mouse
Bold face	**Ctrl/B**	Click **B** button
Italicize	**Ctrl/I**	Click *I* button
Underline	**Ctrl/U**	Click U button
Superscript	**Ctrl/Shift/+**	
Subscript	**Ctrl/=**	
Margin alignment		
Left align	**Ctrl/L**	Click **Straight left margin** button
Center align	**Ctrl/E**	Click **Uneven margin** button
Right align	**Ctrl/R**	Click **Straight right margin** button
Justify	**Ctrl/J**	Click **Straight both margin** button
Temporary indent	**Tab**	
Permanent left indent	**Ctrl/M**	Drag **Left indent** button Indent
Reduce perm. left indent	**Ctrl/shift/M**	Drag **Left indent** button
Hanging indent each paragraph	**Ctrl/T**	Drag **Hanging indent** button to the right
Reduce hanging indent	**Ctrl/shift/T**	Drag **Hanging indent** button to the left Hanging indent
Special characters	**Using the keypad** (numlock on)	
é	**Alt/130**	
è	**Alt/138**	
ô	**Alt/147**	
ç	**Alt/135**	
ñ	**Alt/164**	

For more accented letters and special symbols ... go to the next page

Accent marks using the numeric pad

Making accented letters: Hold **Alt** down while entering the **three numbers**

a	e	i	o	u	c n y ¡
à 133	**é 130**	**ï 139**	**ô 147**	**ü 129**	**ç 135**
â 131	**ê 136**	**î 140**	**ö 148**	**û 150**	**Ç 128**
ä 132	**ë 137**	**ì 141**	**ò 149**	**ù 151**	
å 134	**è 138**	**í 161**	**ó 162**	**ú 163**	**ñ 164**
á 160	**É 144**		**Ö 153**	**Ü 154**	**Ñ 165**
Ä 142					
Å 143					**ÿ 152**
					¿ 168
					¡ 173
					« 174
					» 175

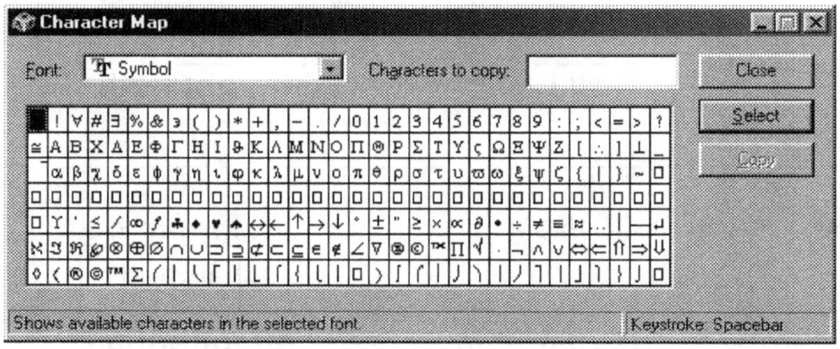

Keyboard		Mouse
1.	**Ctrl/Esc** (cursor is where you want to put the special character)	Click **Start** button (cursor is where you want to put the special character)
2.	**P**	Click **Programs**
3.	**Right Arrow**	Click **Accessories**
4.	**S**	Click **System Tools**
5.	**Right Arrow**	
6.	**C**	Click **Character Map**
7.	**Enter**	
8.	**Tab** twice	
9.	**Arrow key** to the symbol you want	Click the character you want
10.	**Alt/S**	Click **Select**
11.	**Alt/C**	Click **Copy**
12.	**Alt/Tab**	Click **Microsoft® Word** button at the bottom of your screen
13.	**Ctrl/V**	Click **Paste** 

Starting the Word Processor

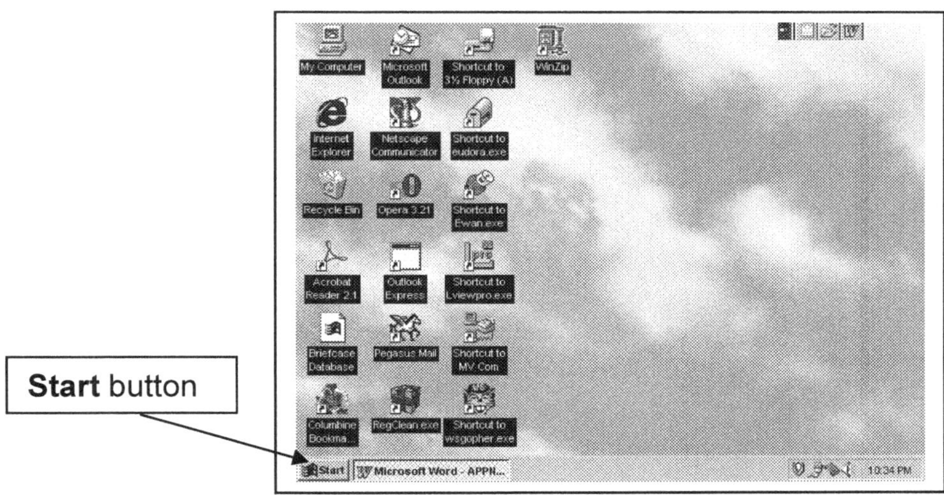

The "Desktop" showing "Shortcut" Icons

Starting a program

	Keyboard	Mouse
1.	**Ctrl/Esc** or **Start Menu** button	Click **Start** button
2.	**P** until **All Programs** or **Programs** is **highlighted**	Click **All Programs** or **Programs**
3.	Use the **arrow keys** to move the selection highlight over the wanted program and press **Enter**↵.	Click once or twice on the wanted program

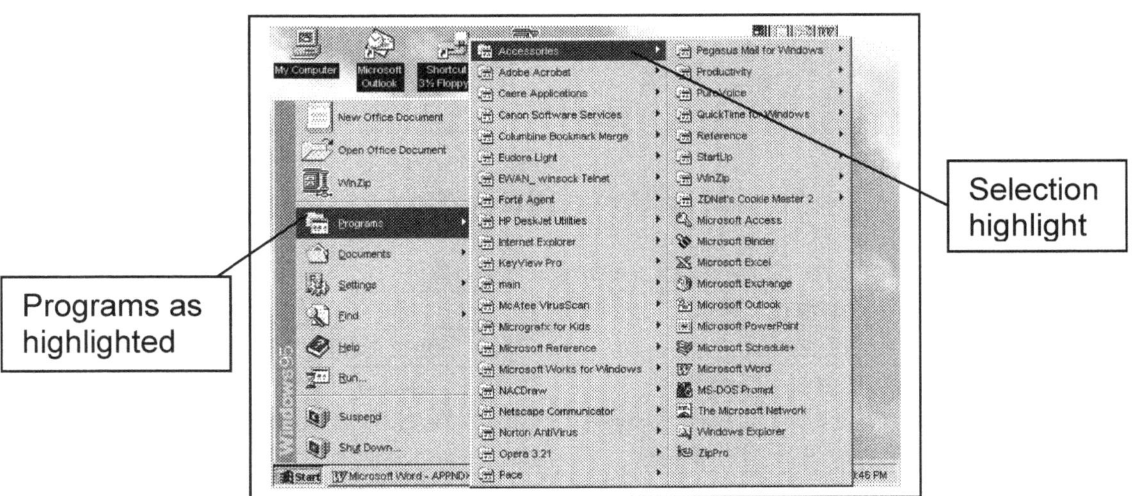

Programs Menu Classic presentation

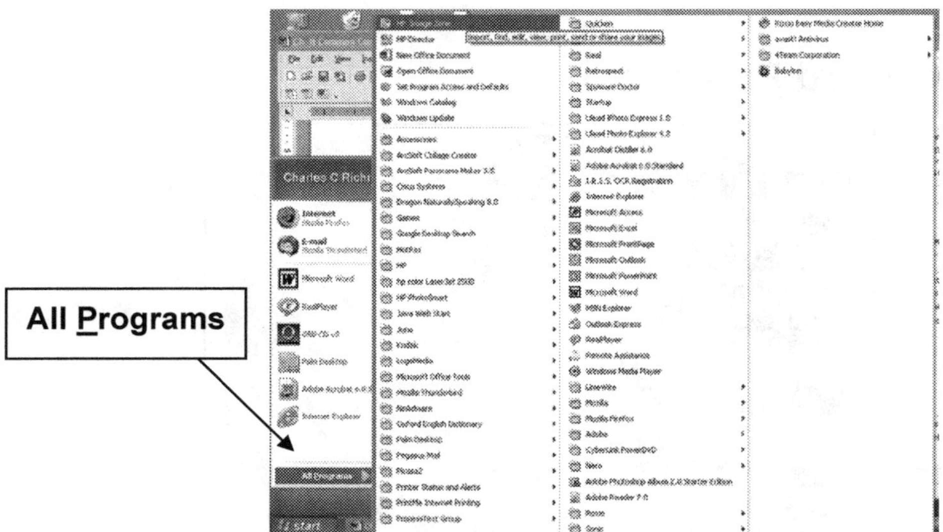

Programs Menu XP view

Turning a program off.

Keyboard		Mouse
1.	**Alt/F4**	Click the topmost right hand **"x" box**

Turn the computer off

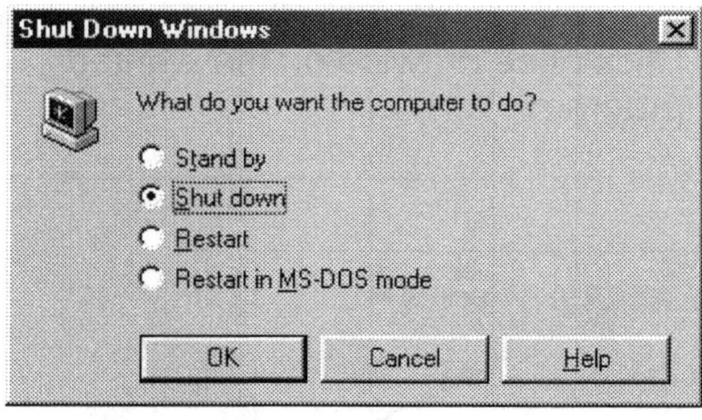

Classic

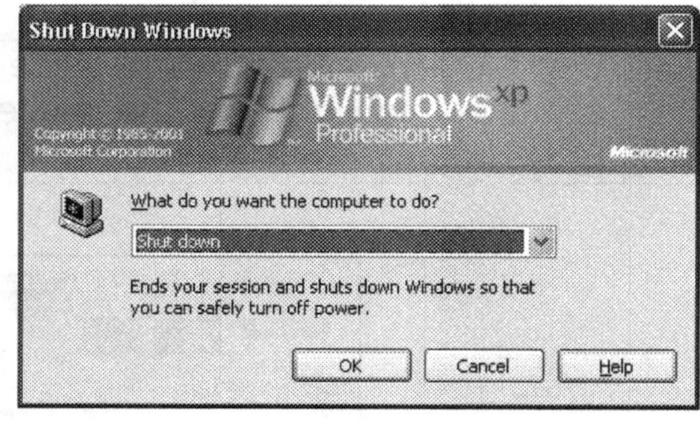

XP

Shut Down Dialog Box

Shut Down procedure … turn the computer off.

Keyboard		Mouse
1.	**Ctrl/Esc** or **Start Menu** key	Click **Start** button
2.	If **Shut Down** is not identified, **Alt/S** or **Arrow** either **Up** or **Down** until **Shut Down** is highlighted	If **Shut Down** is not identified, click the **Down Triangle** button or in the "instruction" box
3.	**Enter↵**	Click the **Shut Down** instruction location and click **OK**

Make the "Toolbar" button bigger for Internet Explorer

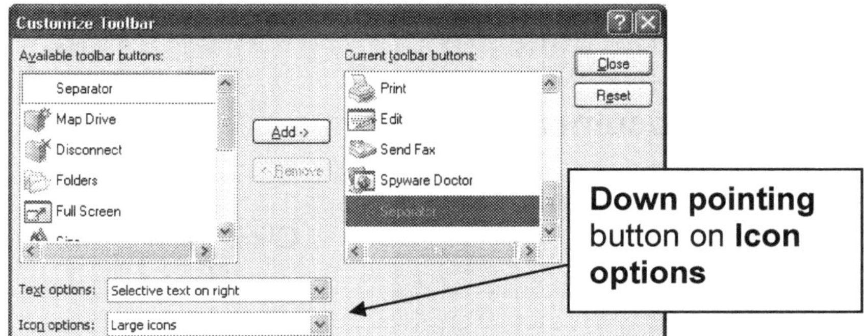

Customize Toolbar dialog box

Keyboard		Mouse
1.	**Alt/V**	Click **View**
2.	**T**	Click **Toolbars**
3.	**C**	Click **Customize**
4.	**Alt/N**	Click **Down pointing** button on **Icon options**
5.	**Down Arrow** to **Large icons**	Click **Large icons**
6.	**Enter**↵	Click **Close**

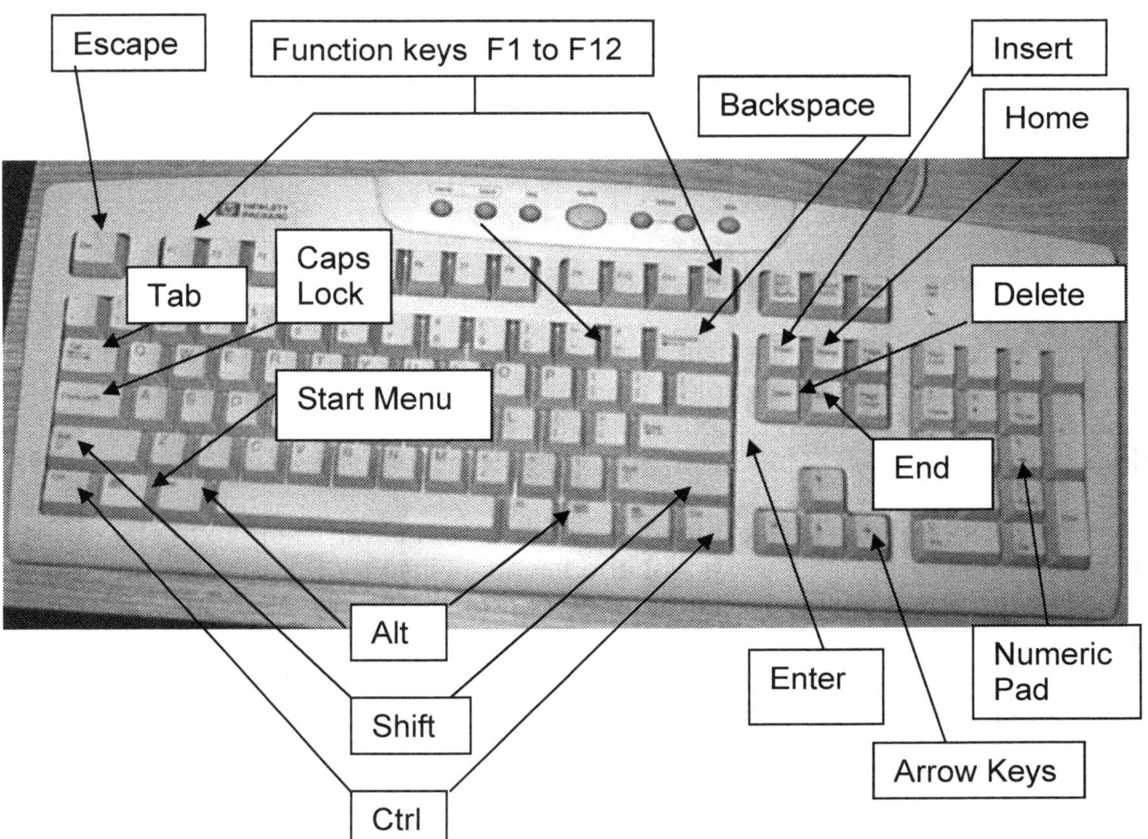

Standard Operations using WordPad ... Step by Step

Start a new document

	Keyboard	Mouse
1.	**Ctrl/N**	Click **New Document** button

Set up a new Folder to put your document in and give your document a name when using WordPad ... SaveAs

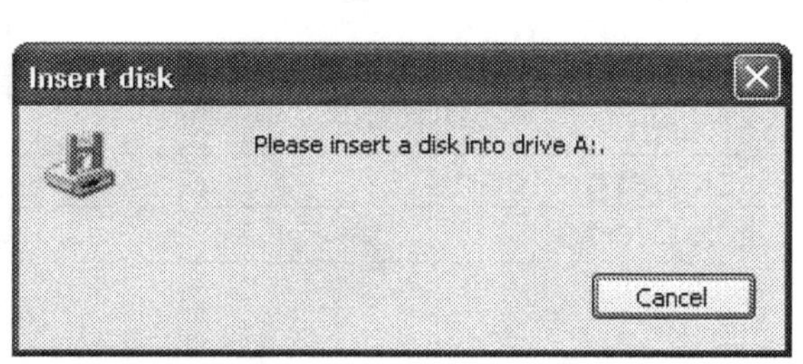

Insert disk dialog box

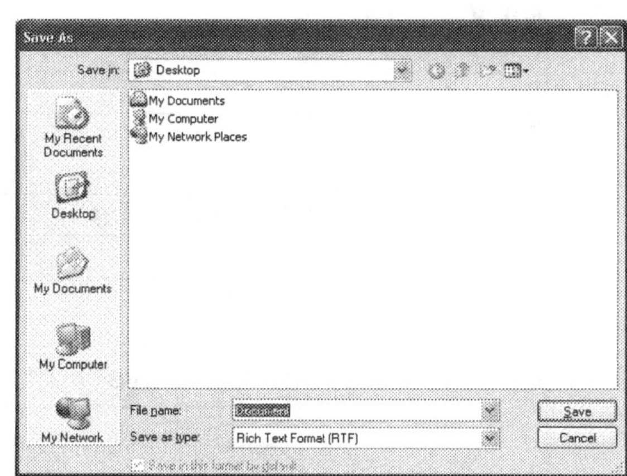

SaveAs… dialog box

Figure out where to put your new folder…

The computer is not very creative about where your new document should be saved. It has set up a place (folder) called **My Documents** which should be easy to remember but can become cluttered which would make a particular document difficult to find. It doesn't take long to accumulate 40 or 50 documents.

I find that it is better to set up a few folders that mean something to me by giving them a name that would giver a hint about what is inside. Some topics that I usually write about such as: different members of my family, clubs or club members, the bank or Internal Revenue, my town government, just so many things are all things that separating my documents by these topics would make documents easier to locate.

A folder named **My Family** might be a good one to begin with. It is easy to set up under **My Documents**.

New Folder procedure.

You must have a **Document – WordPad** showing in **WordPad**'s window … a document that has not yet received a name and has not yet been filed.

Keyboard		Mouse
1.	**Ctrl/S**	Click on the **Save** button
2.	**Alt/I**	
3.	**Tab**	
4.	**Right Arrow** one or more times to the **New Folder** button	Click the **New Folder** button
5.	**Space**	
6.	Type in the name you want for your new folder *	Type in the name you want for your new folder *
7.	**Enter** and **Esc** or **Alt/O**	Click **Open** and **SaveAs…** "**X**" box

* You can use letters and numbers but no special marks like "*" or "/" or ", (comma)" or ". (period)."

Put your document away.

Keyboard		Mouse
1.	**Ctrl/ S**	Click on **Save** button

Open … Bring back something that you have put away.

Keyboard		Mouse
1.	**Ctrl/O**	Click on **Open** button
3.	**Shift/Tab**	Click twice on the name of the document you want
4.	Use the arrow keys to move the move the **highlight** to the document you want and **Enter**↵	

Change type face, size, shape, underline, indent ... you must highlight whatever you wish to change before you tell the computer what to do!

If you wish to change as much as a line or a paragraph, move the cursor (|) to the beginning (left hand end) of the line or top left hand corner of the paragraph. Hold down the **Shift** key and use your **arrow** key to move the cursor down or across ... the text will be surrounded by black. Now you can go to the **Format** menu (hold down **Alt** and press **O** or click on **Format)** and choose the command you want to use.

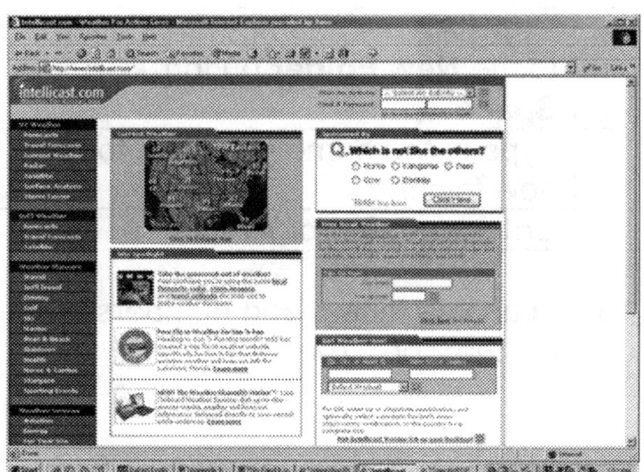

Save a "Favorites" Internet address.

With the page on the screen that you want to make a "Favorites," press **Ctrl/D**

If you want it in a particular "Folder," press **Alt/A** then press **O**. Follow the directions in the **Organize Favorites** dialog box

Glossary

A

Address Book ... a feature made available by a good **email client** which enables you to collect email addresses of those whom you wish to communicate with. It provides a foolproof way of preserving correct email addresses.

Archie ... is the first of what today we call a **Search Engine**. When it was first introduced, it was called an **agent** that could look around all the known FTP sites for things that were available for the taking. Archie could lead you to programs, books, or pictures that could be moved from where they were to your computer using **File Transfer Protocol**.

B

Blog ... short for Web log. A personal web page that is used as a journal by its author and is available for viewing by the general public. A private news source that is similar in intent to a **newsgroup**.

Bookmark ... a tagged item or location that can be moved to quickly for reference. It is frequently used for marking a Help topic or later viewing.

Browse ... is a term used to describe a casual checking out of information available on the web. It indicates that the person is doing much like he/she would do when searching for an interesting book in a bookstore.

Browser ... is the name that Internet people have given to **programs** that are able to go from one place to another on the World Wide Web and display their contents on a "page by page" basis.

C

CD ROM ... this storage medium was originally designed to produce music. The name *CD ROM* is an acronym made by taking the first letter of each of the several words which make up its definition ... **Compact Disk Read Only Memory** (read only memory in this case is the recorded digital marks which cannot be erased or rewritten). It worked so well because discrete digital marks were used to generate sound that the computer industry investigate the technique and found that computer characters and pictures could be placed on them.

Cell ... one rectangle of a table. This unit can accept data. Data in it can be manipulated and mathematical formulas can be used to determine its contents.

Chat Room ... is a place where on can go to communicate with many people throughout the world simultaneously. it is made possible by a **program** that is known as **Internet Relay Chat** that works much the same as a Citizen's Band radio. These communications, unlike email that goes out as a package, appear in the **chat room** at the same time that you enter them from your keyboard. In **chat rooms** you use a fictitious name to protect yourself from unwanted intrusions on your safety or privacy.

Clipboard ... an area set up in memory to hold materials sent to it by programs running on the Windows operating system. The clipboard may be used to send text or pictures from one application program to another. i.e. **Copy** text or pictures to the clipboard and **Paste** them to a document in another program ... text moved from **Word** to an **Email Program.**

Close ... stop using a document or file ... erase it from the screen.

Command ... an instruction that the computer program understands that tells it to perform a specific task.

Cursor ... a vertical line that appears in a document that blinks to show the point at which the next keyboard character, pasted material, or activity will take place.

D

Data base ... very similar to the **spreadsheet** except that only a single record (line of a spread sheet) is usually kept in memory at one time. **Data bases** usually contain too many records to permit it.

Default ... settings that are automatically turned on when an activity is chosen for which more than one condition is available. For instance: if you have more than one printer on your system, the one most likely to be chosen will be set as the default printer. You can change default setting temporarily or permanently.

Dialog Box ... a collection of commands you can issue to have your program perform some complicated tasks. i.e. the **SaveAs** dialog box that you use to give your document an unique name, tell the computer where to store the document, tell the computer how to **format** it, and many other options.

DOS ... another acronym -- **Disk Operating System** ... in rather cryptic terms it means what it says. It is the **program** that permits the computer to send and record information on a disk or read the recorded information from the disk and bring it into the computer's memory. It works with **hard disks, floppy disks,** or **CD ROM**s. In fact, the **CD ROM** must be recorded in a way that **DOS** can understand.

Download ... the act of bringing something from the Internet to your computer. This term usually applies to things fetched using **File Transfer Protocol** or otherwise referred to as **FTP**.

DVD ... Digital Video Disk but lately, Digital Versatile Disk basically the same as a **CD-ROM** but the manner in which the material is recorded on the disk is different.

Drag ... Placing the **Mouse pointer** on something, holding down the left **Mouse button** while you move the pointer from one place to another ... to move a picture or some highlighted text.

E

Elevator ... a group of three buttons ... an Up button, a Down button, and an elevator position pointer.

Email ... is the term used to describe messages that have been composed in one location and are transmitted electronically over the Internet to a recipient or to multiple recipients. These messages were the earliest practical, public use for the Internet.

Email Attachment ... something that you send along with an email message that is not a part of the message itself. For instance: any word processing document that you would like to send, any picture, or even a recorded voice message (even music or moving pictures).

Email Client ... is a **program** that prepares, sends, and receives email. Present day clients are also capable of performing most of the functions of current word processing programs. They also have many automated features like the ability to sign the message, to go to any other email account you may have and check for new messages, and to send the same message of a large group of people.

F

File ... a group of related records (information about one particular topic).

Flexible, diskette, or floppy disk ... a portable apparatus which is small enough to be transported and stored easily. It is used in much the same way as the **hard disk** for storing computer information ... either character or picture forms. Today's *floppy* disks are most often about 3-1/2" square with a metal slide on one side which protects the flexible magnetic medium inside.

FTP ... is a protocol or detailed procedure used for the electronic transmission of information from one computer to another over a network.

G

Gopher ... one of the earliest of the **programs** that made moving around the internet simple. It uses a text based menu system to transfer from one site to another.

H

Hard disk ... a device which is usually permanently mounted in side a computer which is capable of recording, storing, and retrieving information or pictures. These devices have extremely large capacities. Storage capacities of several billion characters of information are quite common these days. There are hard disk units available now which can be inserted and removed which improves data security and portability.

Hardware ... the electronic machine which performs assigned tasks. This is the part which has a chord that plugs into an electric outlet, can be turned on and off, and physically delivers the expected results.

Highlight ... to show letters, words, pictures, etc. in reverse (white on black) so the computer will understand what it is that you wish it to perform a task on.

Homepage ... an initial or beginning page of a group of related pages that is used to route a person to other information about the owner of a site or information that the site owner makes available through the Internet.

Hyperlink ... a special word or location in text that will send the reader to another location where specially related information can be found. This link is operated by placing the mouse pointer over it and "clicked".

Hypertext ... Hypertext was developed in Cern Switzerland as a method for writing academic and scientific papers with their numerous references in such a way that these references could be called up by someone reading the paper just by pointing a mouse pointer at a transfer point and clicking. The source material could be brought in for the reader to examine.

I

Icon ... a picture that is used to represent a command of some sort that when pointed to and clicked on with the mouse will execute.

Internet ... is a service that is available 24 hours a day, world wide. It is controlled by a large number of super computers. It was designed as an uninterruptible electronic communications system for use by United States armed forces. Originally, it was a "wired" network. Now optical cables, satellites, and other "wireless" media are included as transmission sources.

ISP ... short for Internet Service Provider.

J

Jughead ... a program that is a limited agent or search engine used by Gopher clients. It is confined to searching only data that is a part of its own client system. It cannot, like Veronica, search Gopherspace.

K

Kermit ... a **program** that uses **FTP** protocols to move electronic information from a remote place to your computer (**download)** or from your computer to a remote storage area (**upload**).

Keyboard ... a device which is used to put information into the computer one character at a time. Computer keyboards are similar to those used by mechanical or electric typewriters even to the extent that the letter arrangements designed to slow typists down to keep from jamming the original, slow, mechanical devices are used.

Keyword ... a word that is descriptive of the contents of a site that you are searching for. These words may be used in combination with each other to tell the search engine more about what you want to find.

AOL and other Internet providers define certain sites by assigning them a specific *keyword*. This is a technique which gives a faster lookup for favored locations ... those sites that pay for this privilege.

L

List Processor ... a **program** that can send a single message (regardless of message size) to groups of people or to places that collect messages that are made available for public viewing (bulletin board). The size of these recipient lists can reach into the thousands and as a result will require a powerful program to distribute information to so many people or locations.

Load(ing) ... bringing in the information.

Login ... a name you give to web sites that will identify you each time you use their service. These services want to know how frequently you use them and for what purpose.

M

Mailing group ... a group of email addresses that will direct a single email message to each of the group's members.

Mailing List ... a list of people or groups that comprise the bunch of people or entities that will receive the **mailings** of a specific type from a **List Processor**.

Memory ... an area inside the computer hardware that can hold information which the computer can use as long as a program that uses it is running and the computer is turned on.

Message packet ... a group of characters that are being sent from one location to another on the Internet. These packets are coded in such a way that the sending and receiving computers can assure that all parts of the message are sent and received completely and accurately. These packets may not go from the sending computer to the receiving computer on exactly the same route so some packets may get lost. The receiving computer that detects a packet as being missing will request the sending computer to resend any such missing packet and the sending computer will comply with this request.

Monitor or Video ... a device which is used to display characters and/or pictures in black and white or in color. These are so-called *digital* devices are the forerunners of the newest television technology.

Mosaic ... is the earliest of today's browsers. It utilized pictures (now termed **icons**) to act as transfer points when pointed to and "clicked on" by a mouse attachment.

N

Newsgroup ... is an interest group which is part of **Usenet**. It provides a way to communicate with many people throughout the world who are interested in the same topic you are writing about using **email**.

O

On-line ... the **Browser** or **Email Client** are connected to the **Internet** now.

On-line ... information which is available on the **Internet**.

Open ... find and make available information from a permanent storage device ... floppy disk, hard disk, optical disk, or CD-ROM.

P

Paragraph ... text that is ended by using the **Enter↵** key. As you know, the computer figures how long lines are and "word-wraps" or "wraps around" when it runs out of space on a line so between the time a paragraph is started until it is ended with an **Enter↵**, that group of text is considered to be a single paragraph. A single line or an empty line are both considered to be paragraph by the program.

Password ... a special combination of letter, numbers and symbols that you use to verify that you are the person "logging in" to a service. You will find passwords used wherever security is a factor. (It is always a good idea to change your passwords frequently).

Program ... a group of instructions which the computer can understand and which when followed will perform tasks.

Q, R

Record ... a collection of related information about a single topic.

S

Save ... send information to a permanent storage device ... floppy disk, hard disk, or optical disk. You must already have told it how and where to do the saving through a **SaveAs** command dialog box.

SaveAs... name the document (when you tell the program to start a **New Document** it gives it a general name like **DOCUMENT1.DOC)**. To make sure that you don't store something else in the same place on your disk, you need to give the new document a special name. It also lets you tell the computer what disk to put your new document on and the way you want it written.

Search Engine ... is a **program** that gathers information from the Internet, analyzes its content, arranges it for searching, and responds to queries by displaying Internet addresses for places that it, the **program**, believes matches what someone has asked it to find. Sometimes it finds nothing, sometimes it finds millions of items that seem to be what it was asked to locate.

Select ... to show letters, words, pictures, etc. in reverse (white on black) so the computer will understand what it is that you wish it to perform a task on.

Shortcut Button ... a square or oblong area that appears in what have been termed "toolbars" which contain pictures or icons that hint at what activity will take place if the mouse pointer is placed over them and "clicked".

Software ... the instructions which control the machine's performance. It is the group of instructions which tell the device how to complete a required task.

Spreadsheet ... the name given to programs which create displays that are similar to an accountant's *spreadsheet* which was used for "what if" and other types of financial analysis.

Subscriber ... a person who asks to be included in a **mailing list**, **bulletin board**, or other service that requires one to either **login** or receive periodic **mailings** of specific information.

T

Telnet ... one of the earliest methods for linking computer systems. It is still being used by libraries around the world so people can check their catalogs remotely.

Text Box ... a rectangle that is generated in some area of your document at your direction that can hold text or a picture. This box may be moved about and placed where you wish it to be. You can also say whether text from your document that is outside this box can be "wrapped around" the box or if the box will stand alone surrounded by blank space.

Toolbar ... a group of **Buttons** that are assigned to certain tasks. These are displayed above and below the area used for typing the document. To give the commands that the buttons represent, one moves the mouse pointer over a button and one clicks the left mouse button.

U

Unix ... software that is used to run a computer system that primarily links several computers and handles the processing of messages among them.

Upload ... is the act of sending material from your computer to another computer or remote storage area.

Usenet ... is the predecessor to the **Chat Room**. It provides a way to communicate with many people throughout the world who are interested in the same topic you are writing about using **email**.

V

Veronica ... is a **program** (a search engine or agent) that can find things anywhere in **Gopherspace**. Veronica is not limited to sites as specific as those used by Archie.

W

Windows 3.x, 95, 98, NT, 2000 ... this is the name of a **program** (the numbers that follow the name "Windows" merely indicate "version number") which controls how and when other **programs** can run. This **program** makes it possible for the computer to be using several programs at the same time. ***Windows*** is the name given by its manufacturer, Microsoft, it permits opening "*windows*" to view what is happening in one or more programs that may be running at the moment of viewing.

Word Processing ... the name given to programs that accept instructions from input devices {keyboards or microphones) and record them as show them as letters, numbers or drawings which can become letters, brochures, posters or other items. These are the easiest of programs to use. They produce results similar to that which one can get from a typewriter. Names for such programs are: **Microsoft Write, Microsoft Works, Microsoft Word, Microsoft Word Pad, Word Perfect,** and **Claris Works.**

Word-wrap ... means that the computer can figure out where to end a line and where to begin a new line.

X, Y, Z

Other sources for word definition and acronym information.

Acronym Finder	www.acronymfinder.com
Country Codes	www.radio101.de/radio101/codes.htm
Medical Terms	www.medterms.com/main/alphaidx.asp?p=a_dict
Webopedia	www.webopedia.com

Index

General

WordPad

Email

Internet

About the Author

Charles Clark Richmond's 8 decades of life have been filled with learning, assimilating, presenting and teaching fresh ideas. He began his long association with electronic computers in 1956 at which time he recognized a future need for teaching non-technical people how to use these powerful machines. He and Carl Perry Worthy Ellsworth began exploring ways to explain technical things and complex concepts in ways that non-technical people might understand them. It wasn't until he received his doctorate in Instructional Technology from the University of Massachusetts Amherst in 2000 that he commenced work on bringing computer literacy to those who had never worked with computers in school.

This text was assembled after almost a decade of teaching computer skills to students whose ages ranged from 21 to 94. He used his doctoral research to assemble and test his concepts about how best to present this information to people who had been denied the chance to work with these machines during their developmental years. He has continued to assemble, present, and analyze new ideas about bringing these skills to those who need it most… Those who need it to keep or get jobs, those who need it to keep in touch with their loved ones, and those who need it to keep their minds active.

This book is just the beginning, the starting place for the uninitiated.

Email: ccr@crichm.mv.com

Web: www.computersforklutzes.com

www.ingramcontent.com/pod-product-compliance
Lightning Source LLC
Chambersburg PA
CBHW082110070326
40689CB00052B/4278
9781420827132